MILITANT COSMOPOLITICS

MILITANT COSMOPOLITICS

Another World Horizon

Tamara Caraus

EDINBURGH
University Press

Edinburgh University Press is one of the leading university presses in the UK. We publish academic books and journals in our selected subject areas across the humanities and social sciences, combining cutting-edge scholarship with high editorial and production values to produce academic works of lasting importance. For more information visit our website: edinburghuniversitypress.com

Edinburgh University Press Ltd
The Tun – Holyrood Road
12(2f) Jackson's Entry
Edinburgh EH8 8PJ

First published in hardback by Edinburgh University Press 2022

This work is part of the project *Cosmopolitanism: Justice, Democracy and Citizenship without Borders* (PTDC/FER-FIL/ 30686/2017) financed by FCT – Fundação para a Ciência e a Tecnologia, IP, Portugal

Typeset in 11/13 Adobe Sabon by
IDSUK (DataConnection) Ltd, and
printed and bound by CPI Group (UK) Ltd,
Croydon, CR0 4YY

A CIP record for this book is available from the British Library

ISBN 978-1-3995-0790-5 (hardback)
ISBN 978-1-3995-0791-2 (paperback)
ISBN 978-1-3995-0792-9 (webready PDF)
ISBN 978-1-3995-0793-6 (epub)

CONTENTS

═══════

INTRODUCTION
'YOU HAVE TO HAVE A POSITION!'

═══════

Who wants to be illegal? Who wants that by moving on this Earth, at a certain point, to be punished for his movement? 'As human beings, we all inhabit the planet Earth as a shared space'[1] and we all should have equal entitlements with everyone else, everywhere in the world. This idea is simple and immediately appealing to everyone, everywhere, yet the very fact of saying it invites scorn and ridicule, and those who affirm it are declared naive. A person may indulge for some moments in a vision of a world without borders, of himself being a citizen of the world, yet, in the next moment, to shake his head to 'remove' the idea, laughing that it is naive. Or a person may start thinking how it would be like to be a citizen of the world, but he may realise that he alone cannot rethink the current world order and, without laughing, he clings to the existing ways of living, in a world with nation-states with their exclusionary and discriminatory borders, which do not exist for those from the 'first world' countries and for those with high purchasing power, no matter from which country. The person has a glimpse that 'things' in this world could have been different, but how exactly? He does not know. If this person will turn to political philosophers – those who according to the current division of labour must think and imagine the world in a just way – he will discover that political philosophers laugh themselves at the idea of a citizen of the world. They scorn the idea and refuse to think about it, affirming that it is utopic, or that it will lead to a 'global despotism'. Political philosophers want to be 'realistic' and they build theories without examining the 'given' building blocks: nation-states and their borders. In doing so, political philosophy legitimises the nation-state and its exclusionary borders, and thus it ends up making people illegal. The building blocks of political philosophy are the first trap for thinking a just world, and this book starts by examining a fall into this trap.

1

'THEORETICAL TRAUMA'

After defending my PhD on ethics of deconstruction, I fell into the trap of studying national identity 'set' by a grant-giving body for a certain fellowship which gave preference to the topics of the alleged immediate relevance of philosophy for society. Without doubt, the main factor responsible for building the trap and falling into it was my intention to clarify whether national identity is necessary or not (Caraus 2011). In the years that followed the 'fall', I tried to identify the initial moment when I decided to clarify what national identity is, and to see what was so inescapable in my decision. I visualise vividly the process of writing two research projects concomitantly: one on ethics of deconstruction, in continuation of the PhD thesis, and the other with a title 'National Identity: Necessity or Invention?' based on a case study. After several days of indecision, only one project remains in the application file, and I'm left with the regret of not choosing the alternative. In making this choice, I probably tried to see the projects through the eyes of the 'funding bodies': they were (still) looking for an explanation for the revival of nationalism in post-Soviet states and in the Balkans, but who was looking for an ethics of deconstruction? I am not sure if this was an opportunistic choice, but I am sure that the projects were not so radically different in the method since I intended to deconstruct national identity. The attention to this topic intended to be brief, followed by a prompt return to properly philosophical topics and approaches.

Anyone who has opened any academic work that aimed to analyse nationalism came across the distinction between primordialists and modernists, decoded briefly as follows: primordialists believe that nation is natural, it exists from primordial or at least immemorial times, and modernists claim that nation is a recent invention and a product of social engineering. These theories were largely sociological theories, not normative, that is, they were not saying that nation ought to exist in one way or another, but only described how the so-called national phenomena take place. I looked very carefully at the primordial theories promising to explain many aspects vehiculated by nationalist discourses, such as blood, emotions, passions and so on, but the modernist theories were those enabling my deconstructive method. These theories included Ernest Gellner's theory of nation and nationalism as resulting from the needs of industrial society (Gellner 1983), Benedict Anderson's theory of the nation as an imagined community, Elie Kedourie's approach of nationalism as a political religion of modernity produced by the Western modernity, and other different authors who argued that nations were created by the economic and military activities of modern states, especially in the

West, by the design of diplomats and politicians through international treaties at the end of wars waged by kings for their own amusement and glory. The nations' character of invention and discourse placed the study of nationalism in the post-structuralist sphere, making national phenomena and discourses of national identity a very plausible object of deconstruction and critique.

Deconstruction was both my method and the envisaged outcome of studying this 'acute', at that time, topic. As a method 'invented' and practiced by Jacques Derrida, deconstruction involves a close reading of two layers of a text: the dominant interpretation of that text, that is, a consensus concerning its intelligibility, and the text itself. The deconstructive reading arrives at a confrontation between the dominant meaning established by the dominant interpretation, and the text itself. Usually, the dominant meaning was constituted by ignoring or suppressing other meanings. The wanting-to-say of the text undermine the dominant meaning or, in other words, in a deconstructive reading, the text undermines its own meaning, coherence and stability. Deconstruction destabilises meanings and puts them into an aporia. As a figure central to Derrida's thinking, 'aporia' means non-path, difficulty of passing, an impasse of some sort. The purpose of deconstruction is to identify the aporia and to show how the way out of the aporia is never accomplished without an act of violence. Aporia, paradox, double bind, undecidability, contradiction, although not absolute synonyms, point to the same logic exposed by Derrida's reading of different texts. The experience of undecidability reached by deconstruction does not intend to reject meanings, to enhance nihilist attitudes, but to make us see how a meaning is established through the inaugural violence of excluding other meanings. Thus, equipped with the insights of deconstruction, I engaged in reading national identity discourses, showing their contradictions and exclusions, assuming that these revelations would be illuminating and liberating for those in need of a national identity. Instead of liberating others, I, myself, fell into a trap.

The project entitled 'National Identity: Necessity or Invention?' brought me unexpectedly to a top university, at a top college, at a top department. I had a supervisor, colleagues, the chance to take part in research seminars, and the unexpected opportunity to receive high-profile feedback on several presentations of 'my work'. In every attempt at a paper, I was invariably applying my only method: a deconstruction of every aspect of the idea of nation and national identity, showing how these are socially constructed and how they work, leaving them exposed and disassembled and, to my understanding, already irrelevant and useless. The discussions of my papers kept reaching the same point, when the supervisor had to say, again: it is a good work of clarification. Now you have to have a position. After having dissected all mechanisms of national identification and showing how these produce falsities, you have to start a normative approach by advancing norms according to which a national identity should function in order to avoid these falsities. You have to start building an argument or several arguments, which must be mutually coherent, and this construction of arguments could be your contribution to the discussion on this particular topic or, if you argue sufficiently convincing, it could be your position within political theory . . . But when I had the next chance to present 'my work', I came again with a paper full of endless questioning, tearing the veil of 'false consciousness' from what was supposed to be a national identity. I preferred endless questions to a theoretical construction with norms, recommendations and solutions. One day, after the repeated advice, 'Now you have to have a position', I heard myself whispering: 'A position would not be an ideology?' I hoped that no one heard my whispered question, but the answer followed: 'Every political philosopher has a position; do you consider them ideologists?' Another whisper, 'No' . . . Probably, that was the moment when I decided to look for *a* position.

At that point in time and in that place, political philosophy seemed a temple dedicated mainly to one political philosopher – John Rawls. A newcomer had to have a position by situating himself within the Rawlsian framework, which contained two contradictory theories, so it had a rich enough spectrum for others to position themselves. The two theories were *A Theory of Justice* (1971), considered a ground-breaking book that revived academic interest in political philosophy in the normative style, and which Rawls declared to be elaborated for the liberal state only, and a theory for the world as whole presented in *The Law of Peoples* (1999), published twenty-eight years later. At that time the question, 'How do Rawls's two theories fit together?' was somehow urgent. Thus, everyone seemed in the 'Rawls temple': some contesting the theses of the master, others justifying them. However, to read the few books of the canonical philosopher was not enough – it was necessary to know what others said about Rawls and to refer to them constantly. Although I tried, I could not enter the 'Rawls temple'. Perhaps I did not work sufficiently hard to qualify, but there was another reason for staying outside the 'temple': the trap which I was trying to escape, that of the national identity, was there, since Rawls did not reject it. On the contrary, he affirmed it expressly in his second theory on the 'law of the people'.

Looking outside Rawls's temple, I 'discovered' and attended a weekly seminar on 'Ideology and Discourse Analysis', convened by a political theorist writing on ideologies (Freeden 1996). Unlike most political

theorists who consider their (normative) theories beyond or above ideology, Michael Freeden asserted that political philosophies and ideologies
produce the same thing – rearrangements of political concepts, such as
freedom, justice, power, rights and so on, which are deeply debatable or
contested concepts with a plurality of meanings. Political concepts have
also non-eliminable components, for example, despite the various meanings, the notion of freedom still seems plausible, just as we identify a
table as a table although the shape of the table may vary substantially
depending on the designer's vision. Further, as a room could be furnished
in different ways, so are political concepts rearranged differently in different ideologies. Each ideology rejects other rival definitions of a concept
and tries to 'cement' a meaning: 'Here is what freedom, justice, authority mean!', and so ideologies inject certainties into a world of plural and
contestable meanings. Ideology and political philosophy are both forms
of political thinking and are not mutually exclusive. The final product
of political philosophy may not differ from that of an ideology, but the
alignment of concepts will certainly be different: the philosopher will try
to justify rationally and morally all the components included in his construction, while the ideologist will also accept emotional justifications.
Those engaged in an ideological discourse seek to legitimise actions, while
political philosophy requires continuous reflection. Political philosophy
is for a narrow circle of specialists and individuals, while ideologies are
formulated for the masses. The major difference is that ideologies are the
expression of the inability to live with uncertainty and insist on establishing a certainty, even an illusory one, necessary for political decision and
action in general, while philosophers ought to live with a certain level of
uncertainty. However, despite uncertainty, they also have a position. 'You
should have a position and you cannot avoid having one', was the advice
that the theorist of ideologies gave to me.

But was not I having a position already? As Derrida repeatedly said,
engaging in a work of deconstruction means not leaving things the way
they are. Deconstruction 'is not neutral. It intervenes' (Derrida 1981:
93). Although taking a position in philosophy has been considered 'scandalous', a force of rupture with the norms of traditional philosophical
discourse is implicit in all attempts to think, argued Derrida, so 'there is
no effective and efficient position, no veritable force of rupture, without
a minute, rigorous, extended analysis, an analysis that is as differentiated and as scientific as possible' (Derrida 1981: 94). Positioning is
questioning the given: 'the greatest number of possible givens, and of the
most diverse givens' (Derrida 1981: 94) and it is inherent to thinking.

Thus, I was already positioning myself in relation to an obscure idea
of nation and nationality by contesting them as 'given'. However, for

the audience to whom I presented my work, this positioning was only a work of clarification: 'It is a good work of clarification, now you have to start building an argument or several arguments that could be your position within political theory.' But what kind of argument could 'construct' the position that, apparently, I was already having?

In my total contestation of nation and nationality, there was one implicit position – a world without nations, only with human beings. Such a position – and I was aware of it – was called 'cosmopolitanism'. I considered my deconstruction of national identity already cosmopolitan, and I was invariably stopping there. There was a serious obstacle in building an argument and affirming a cosmopolitan position: I shared a postmodern sensibility called the fear of *grand narratives* (Lyotard 1984). I made an inventory of approaches of cosmopolitanism existing in the academic year 2002–3, and I came across criticisms claiming that given the universality of cosmopolitan principles, a shadow of totalitarianism is present in every cosmopolitan theory, that a theory for the entire world cannot be otherwise than totalising, that each new proposal of a cosmopolitan approach risks formulating a new grand narrative. When I embraced deconstruction as a method, I had exactly the intention to dismantle the 'totalising' grand narratives of modernity (Caraus 2003). To affirm cosmopolitanism – my only possible position – would mean to complete a full circle from rejecting grand narratives to embracing a new grand narrative, and thus a totalising position. My potentially 'constructed' position sounded to me a theoretical crime! Thus, I remained stuck in destruction mode, without any chance of advancing an argument that would have been 'my position'.

And so, deconstructing national identity again and again, the academic year 2002–3 ended. I returned to the place where, according to the conditions of fellowship, I had to contribute to changing society and strengthening democracy. I came back with an invisible 'theoretical trauma' that had a visible effect on determining my further academic trajectory or lack of it. My 'theoretical trauma' was provoked by the fact that during one academic year I had to study national identity from the perspective of normative political theory at the University of Oxford. This was not forced research, of course, and no one in particular produced the 'trauma'. The trauma appeared from my horizon of expectation. I did not expect to go to the University of Oxford and to elaborate theoretical and normative constructions of an 'ideal national identity' – it sounded like a joke. The horizon of expectation was that at an institution where the cutting-edge research in all fields is conducted, one does not affirm normatively national identity, but only criticises and 'destroys' it. But I affirmed it, even deconstructing it, since to talk about national identity, even critically, means to reaffirm it. The vigour of the debate on national identity is not a sign of decay and of lack of significance, but of rebirth and renewal (Smith 1999). Although theorists use a language and perspective different from everyday identity discourse, they do not escape this trap. And theorists, like any other person who talks about identity, reconfigure it, renew it and reaffirm it. It has been noticed that in the nineteenth century, students from all over Eastern Europe who attended courses by Fichte, Herder, Schiller and Michelet went to their homelands and started to awaken the people, to liberate them through movements of 'national rebirth', which ended with the creation of new nation-states. Similarly, in the 1960s, students at the London School of Economics returned to their countries, particularly in Asia and Africa, and did social engineering according to the theory of nations and nationalism advanced by Gellner (Smith 1999: 2–3).

My research on national identity happened in the last wave of an academic fashion – an attempt by academia to explain the ethnic and national conflicts that had erupted in the Balkans and the former Soviet space after the Cold War – then the rapid devaluation of these studies started. Fortunately, the institutionalisation of the study of nations and nationalism was sporadic as there is no proper study to institutionalise. Benedict Anderson asserted that 'unlike most other isms, nationalism has never produced its own grand thinkers: no Hobbeses, Tocquevilles, Marxes, or Webers' (Anderson 1991: 5). So, I was captive in this minor field of study, and the minor status intensified my 'theoretical trauma'. I left the 'top place' of political philosophy without having my own argument and, for several years, silenced by my own gesture of affirming, even indirectly, the idea of national identity from the perspective of philosophy, through the simple fact of making it my temporary topic of research.

DISCOVERING THE EASTERN EUROPEAN DISSIDENCE

The imperative 'You have to have a position' was doubled by another one: 'You have to undo the effect of affirming, even if indirectly, national identity.' There was only one way to undo this effect: affirming a cosmopolitan position, but the dark shadows of a grand narrative were still threatening. Attempting to go back to deconstruction and the continental style of doing political philosophy, I ended up with a project, 'Derrida and Europe's Double Duties', which aimed to map Derrida's idea of a deconstructed Europe in order to overcome Eurocentrism from the inside of (thinking) the very idea of Europe. The main feature of Derrida's approach to everything, and Europe is not an exception, is a close-reading of some chosen texts. Since one always has to read what Derrida reads, I read a text by a Czech philosopher and dissident, Jan Patočka, that Derrida was reading in his reflections on European responsibility. Soon, I have chosen to inherit the legacy of the Eastern European dissidence, some forty years after it happened, since in this legacy I found a way of advancing a position and affirming cosmopolitanism. I identified in the concepts of 'permanent questioning', 'living in problematicity' and 'shaken solidarities' advanced by Patočka, the theoretical resource to confront the fear of a new grand narrative. Nevertheless, I was somehow 'permanently questioning' everything in my previous deconstructive attempts. So why only now was questioning a way of properly positioning and constructing an argument for cosmopolitanism? The 'secret' is that these three elements came already embodied in a practice – the dissident movement of *Charta 77*. My first published paper on cosmopolitanism (Caraus 2013) identified in Patočka's philosophy a potential cosmopolitan theory and in *Charta 77* a cosmopolitan practice. The shadow of a new and threatening grand narrative dissipated.

Thus, under the auspices of Patočka's philosophy and Eastern European dissidence, I embarked on a journey of researching and affirming cosmopolitanism as permanent questioning and a life in problematicity. I started my approach by advancing the notion of cosmopolitanism of dissent as a practice and action from below (Chapter 1). Cosmopolitanism of the Eastern European dissidence as a contestatory action from below was further 'tested', in teamwork, in dissent cases around the world. Thus, the volume, *Cosmopolitanism and the Legacies of Dissent* (Caraus 2014a, 2014b; Caraus and Parvu 2014), examined paradigmatic historical cases of dissidence (Gandhi, Luther King, Mandela, Sakharov, Havel, Aung San Suu Kyi, Liu Xiaobo and others) and their legacy for cosmopolitanism. The cosmopolitanism of dissent was explored further in 'Cosmopolitanism and Global Protests' (Caraus 2017; Caraus and Parvu 2017a, 2017b), which examined the cosmopolitan dimension of global protests from Zapatista to Occupy and beyond. The volume *Migration, Protest Movements and the Politics of Resistance: A Radical Political Philosophy of Cosmopolitanism* (Caraus 2018a, 2018b; Caraus and Paris 2018) tested the findings in the cases of migrants' protest movements such as *Sans Papiers*, No One Is Illegal, No Borders, protests related to Lampedusa or Calais camps, and others migrant protests from the last decade. The further theoretical implications of these contestatory forms of cosmopolitanism have been developed in *Re-Grounding Cosmopolitanism: Towards a Post-Foundational Cosmopolitanism* (Caraus 2015a, 2015b, 2016a, 2016b; Caraus and Paris 2016), which advances the notion of post-foundational cosmopolitanism as a non-totalising theory of cosmopolitanism, compatible with the plurality of social, cultural and political interpretative standpoints in the contemporary world.

The journey from the fear of grand narrative towards affirming and 'constructing' a position is the very structure of this book, which advances chronologically through doing and undoing a theory of cosmopolitanism, from one cluster of cases studies to another, from doubts to enthusiasm, new doubts and new discoveries. The doubts and the predicaments were unexpected and challenging. Thus, while I was arguing that cosmopolitanism of dissent was contestatory and radical, I also realised that radicalism disappears into the nation-state (see Chapters 1 and 3) and that my concept of cosmopolitanism of dissent was still captive in methodological nationalism since it did not envisage going behind the imaginary confinements of the nation-state. This 'discovery' showed that a cosmopolitan practice from below has to be completed by an affirmative action from above, that a theory of cosmopolitanism has to endorse the idea of a World Republic otherwise it undermines itself (Chapter 4). Once the idea of a World Republic is reaffirmed, the fears of a world institution cannot be ignored (Chapter 5), as well as the other apparently insurmountable criticisms, such as those which see in cosmopolitanism a privilege of the elite with their glamorous lifestyle and consumption (Chapter 6) and those who see in cosmopolitanism a naive and impossible 'love of humanity' (Chapter 7). However, the breakthrough 'discovery' was that my novel concept of cosmopolitanism of dissent was not new at all – it was reiterating the birth of cosmopolitanism and the first cosmopolitical stance: that of the Ancient Cynics.

BACK TO THE FIRST CITIZENS OF THE WORLD: THE ANCIENT CYNICS

A crucial part of the methodology of this book is a reading of the cosmopolitan stance of the Ancient Cynics, showing that cosmopolitanism was born radical, and it could not be born otherwise than in the Cynics' milieu. Cosmopolitanism was born radical, through a sustained critique of the given meanings, habits and customs, through *parrhesia* and a life in truth, all performed by the Ancient Cynics who, guided by the principle 'Alter the currency!' and performing a dog-life philosophical experiment, unveiled the roots of every convention of life in the Greek antiquity, and of the polis itself as the ultimate convention, and declared themselves 'citizens of the universe' (*kosmopolitês*). As well, cosmopolitanism was born as a political stance coming from the experience of statelessness and exile, through a practice 'from below' and a militant action, through a self-transformation and transformation of the world according to the

Cynic principle 'Alter the currency!', the care for the others/*philanthropia*, and the idea of the 'true commonwealth in the cosmos', as the first expression of the idea of a World Republic.

There has been a recent revival of interest in the Ancient Cynics, starting with Peter Sloterdijk's *Critique of Cynical Reason* published in 1983 in German (and in English in 1987), which celebrates Ancient Cynicism as the solution to the ills of modernity, contrasting it to a generalised cynicism (with a small 'c'), and Michel Foucault's *The Courage of Thought*, his last lecture course at the Collège de France, delivered in 1983–4. Both Foucault and Sloterdijk sought to recapture the moral strength of the Cynic ethos as a needed corrective to contemporary critique which loses its transformative power philosophy and as the last hope for keeping the spirit of the Enlightenment alive. Both authors reclaim the Ancient Cynics for similar purposes but in different ways. Thus, Sloterdijk emphasises two characteristics of the Ancient Cynics: Diogenes' satirical rhetoric with its attendant shocking gestures, and his decision to live in harmony with the doctrines he preached. Cynicism is for him the catalyst of a 'most communal world' where authentic life is experienced 'in love and sexual intoxication, in irony and laughter, creativity and responsibility, meditation and ecstasy' (Sloterdijk 1987: 207). By reviving Cynicism, Sloterdijk intends to give philosophy the power of laughter, of the breaking of taboos and of hierarchical reversals, in order to make critique effective in a cynical society (Shea 2010: 150–3). But in this way Sloterdijk reduces Cynicism to 'authenticity' and makes the Cynic's aggressivity benign (Shea 2010: 163–4), overlooking their 'remarkable passion for virtue and moral freedom' (Navia 1996: 6). Foucault's account of the Cynics rehabilitates their radicalism, presenting the Ancient Cynics' life as 'true life' and the courage for truth or *parrhesia*.

Sloterdijk and Foucault do not explore the Cynics' radical cosmopolitics. They barely give attention to the fact that the Ancient Cynics coined the word 'cosmopolitan' and expressed a cosmopolitan world view. Unlike Foucault who never mentions this fact, Sloterdijk at least reserved half of a page for clarifying the meaning of two famous expressions, 'I am a citizen of the world', the answer from Diogenes the Cynic when he was asked where he came from, and that 'The only true commonwealth' is 'as wide as the universe' (Laertius 1925: 6.63, 6.72; henceforth DL). Thus, he sees the concept of the citizen of the world as a 'grandiose' concept, which nevertheless is subversive of the local confines:

> In the concept of citizen of the world, ancient Kynicism passes on its most valuable gift to world culture. 'The only true order of state I find is in the cosmos.' Cosmopolitan sages as bearers of living reason will accordingly

only be able to integrate themselves unreservedly into a society when it has become a worldpolis. Until then, their role is inevitably that of subversives; they remain the biting conscience of every dominating self-satisfaction and the affliction of every local narrowing. (Sloterdijk 1987: 164)

Foucault's account of the Cynics ignores their cosmopolitanism. However, the ignored cosmopolitanism comes back unexpectedly in the final picture of the Cynics' true life: the Cynic establishes 'an intense bond with the whole of humankind' (Foucault 2011: 300), cares 'for all mankind' and for the whole world as a 'functionary of humanity' (2011: 303) and, as 'the scout of humanity' (2011: 300), he prefigures the future and exercises 'the government of the universe' (2011: 303). Foucault's account of the Cynics rediscovered the very logic of becoming cosmopolitan through living another life and aiming at another world.

After Sloterdijk and Foucault, the studies of the Ancient Cynics flourished (Allen 2020). However, with few exceptions, the histories of the idea of cosmopolitanism 'forget' that it was advanced by the Cynics, attributing it to Stoics (see Chapter 2), although, as this book argues, cosmopolitanism cannot be born otherwise than in the Cynics' milieu and through implementation of the Cynics' principle 'Alter the currency!' Thus, the hypothesis of this book is that a theory of cosmopolitanism has to be advanced by assuming cosmopolitanism's radical core, which is not a moral or cultural disposition but a contestatory political action from below that challenges the constituted forms of authority, legitimacy and belonging. The discovery that cosmopolitanism was born radical shapes the entire approach of the book, and the Cynics' radical cosmopolitics serves as a framework for integrating a cluster of concepts – cosmopolitanism of dissent, post-foundational cosmopolitanism, cosmopolitan ontology, the institution of critique, critique of 'cosmopolitan' desire, radical cosmopolitical love – into a coherent theoretical approach: a radical and militant cosmopolitics

COSMOPOLITICS: THE STATE-OF-THE-ART

The convergence of the cosmopolitanism of dissent and of the first cosmopolitan stance of the Ancient Cynics is called in this book radical and militant cosmopolitics. The term *cosmopolitics* has been advanced by several authors but with different meanings. The collective volume *Cosmopolitics: Thinking and Feeling Beyond the Nation* (1998), edited by Bruce Robbins and Pheng Cheah, was built on the premise that cosmopolitanism could no longer rely on Enlightenment notions of freedom, reason, autonomy, individual interest and unquestioned human rights. The editors critiqued these Kantian and humanist traditions of cosmopolitanism, and advanced the term 'cosmopolitics', which as Robbins explains in 'Introduction Part I', 'represents one effort to describe, from within multiculturalism, a name for the genuine striving toward common norms and mutual translatability that is also part of multiculturalism' (Robbins 1998: 12). In 'Introduction Part II', Cheah points out that Kant's initial formulation of cosmopolitanism preceded the formation of the modem nation-state and thus cannot be cast as a concept that seeks to erode nationalism (Cheah 1998: 22–4), thus 'cosmopolitanism need not be postnationalist' (1998: 36). Although the volume's editors and contributors admit that existing transnational movements may 'translate into actually existing popular cosmopolitanisms understood as pluralized forms of popular global political consciousness comparable to the national imagining of political community' (1998: 36), the main question for them was 'whether this claim is premature' (1998: 36). The *Cosmopolitics* volume included contributions from a variety of fields, such as political theory, cultural anthropology, sociology, critical theory, cultural studies, comparative literature and so on, without any unifying idea. The volume celebrated the discrepancies between its contributors as if to claim that effective resistance to the new global order must be disorganised. Since then, for more than two decades, both the discrepant plurality of voices and the ambiguous affirmation of cosmopolitanism as a good but a premature idea became de rigueur in approaching cosmopolitanism. Another volume that marked the allegedly 'critical' approach to cosmopolitanism in the 1990s, Timothy Brennan's *At Home in the World: Cosmopolitanism Now* (1997), was written in similar terms. It suspected cosmopolitanism of complicity with US-centredness and with transnational capitalism and showed its insensitivity to indigenous issues and dismissiveness towards post-colonial nationalism. Although these critiques sounded at that time ground-breaking, the solutions provided were not. For Brennan, the nation-state remains the linchpin of any attempt to counter the workings of transnational capitalism, since 'any meaningful politics is still about the control of states' (1997: 317). Acknowledging that the world is global and that the innumerable authors from a diversity of fields that he reviews or analyses, mainly in the areas of cultural studies and comparative literature, do feel 'at home in the world', the book ends with the statement that 'Nationalism is not dead. And it is good that it is not' (Brennan 1997: 317). These books appeared ground-breaking at the moment of publishing, as they provided a critique of humanist, Enlightenment cosmopolitanisms, as well as a critique of the human right-based approaches of cosmopolitanism. But these approaches inaugurated and consecrated a trend of affirming cosmopolitanism with one hand only, while another hand was writing in the defence of the nation-state.

The exercise of writing about cosmopolitanism, declaring it premature and marrying it continually with nationalism and nation-state, is a self-cancelling stance, and theories of cosmopolitanism have to go beyond this trap.

The concept of cosmopolitics has been elaborated without exploring its full potential. For example, Archibugi considers that 'cosmopolitics already exists, but it is still confined to narrow groups of institutions' (Archibugi 2003: ix) and the purpose of the political theorist is to make it to serve justice in the global condition. Other uses of 'cosmopolitics' refer to notions such as untranslatability or 'border of Europe'. For example, Balibar's work was read as a cosmopolitics of translation which is a medium of linguistic exchange (Apter 2020). Engaging with the problem of translation is beyond the aim of this book; however, languages and translation cannot but lead to a moderate, conciliatory cosmopolitanism. The world's wealth of languages must be protected, as well as the real language learning; however, this is not – and should not be – an impediment for thinking and imagining a world where No One Is Illegal. The other motive identified in the work of Balibar as cosmopolitics is the theme of Europe and the borders of Europe (Apter 2020). For Balibar 'Europe' is the name for a border that misrecognises itself, and the stakes of this misrecognition are high: either Europe will remake itself by revolutionising its territorial nomos or Europe will destroy itself by denying reality and staying fixated on fetishes of the past, while, in fact, Europe is a complex of overlapping borderlands and disparate modes of governance. This book does not engage with the topic of Europe or its borders as a cosmopolitan motive. In a radical cosmopolitics that contests all existing arrangements, Europe is part of the current world order, and it has to be contested together will the entire world order.

Another shift from cosmopolitanism to cosmopolitics was proposed by James D. Ingram in *Radical Cosmopolitics: The Ethics and Politics of Democratic Universalism* (2013), who advances a different account of cosmopolitics – radical cosmopolitics – as a bottom-up practice of universalisation or 'a critical politics of universalization, a practice that asserts universal values against what denies them here and now' (Ingram 2013: 8). The newness of Ingram's approach lies in an account of negative universality, an argument that democracy as political action has a cosmopolitan potential, and in detecting a logic of cosmopolitanism, mapped by the author through different affirmations of cosmopolitanism. The book explores some authors and theoretical resources that until recently have been ignored by theorists of cosmopolitanism: Claude Lefort, Sheldon Wolin, Miguel Abensour, Jacques Rancière, Étienne Balibar and other thinkers of radical democracy, and it is still unique in the current approaches of cosmopolitanism. *Militant Cosmopolitics* inscribes itself in this hopefully inaugural tradition of radical cosmopolitics – radicalising it further by reclaiming the Cynics' legacy.

Isabelle Stengers used the word 'cosmopolitics' in her books *Cosmopolitics I* and *II* published in 1997 in French (and published in English in 2010 and 2011), and since then in different other texts. Analysing politics of science, Stengers arrives at the conclusion that the whole way of doing science should be changed and that 'Another Science Is Possible' (Stengers 2018), and this 'another science' should be possible through 'cosmopolitics'. Her 'cosmopolitical proposal' is a proposal 'to "slow down" reasoning and create an opportunity to arouse a slightly different awareness of the problems and situations mobilizing us' (Stengers 2005: 994). The 'slowing down' of science is done by the conceptual figure of the idiot from Deleuze's *What is Philosophy?* For Stengers, the idiot is 'the one who always slows the others down, who resists the consensual way in which the situation is presented and in which emergencies mobilize thought or action' (2005: 994). The idiot is a presence that produces an interstice, a space for hesitation regarding what it means to say 'good for all'. Stengers appropriates for her use of the term 'cosmopolitics' another figure – Bartleby, the character from the famous short story by Herman Melville, who confronts his boss with disturbing formula, 'I would prefer not to.' While the enigmatic formula was the object of interpretation by most of the contemporary continental philosophers (Deleuze, Agamben, Badiou, Žižek and others), Stengers's points to the Bartelby's boss's reaction to this enigma. The boss struggles with the formula, is profoundly disturbed and unable not to feel guilty; he is prepared to do anything to have Bartleby accept some return to normalcy, to return to the common world. But Bartleby disrupts this world exactly by making it possible to think that it can be different – that something is perpetually excluded and, further, that someone will prefer not to be included. There is an insistent question, a disturbance and an indeterminacy entrancing Bartelby and his boss: 'Giving this insistence a name, *cosmos*, inventing the way in which "politics," our signature, could proceed, construct its legitimate reasons "in the presence of" that which remains deaf to this legitimacy: That is the cosmopolitical proposal' (2005: 996). The idiot and Bartleby generate 'the power to activate thinking, a thinking that belongs to no one, in which no one is right' (2005: 1001). For Stengers, *cosmos* is an operator of 'putting into equality', but equality does not mean that they all have the same say in the matter but that 'they all have to be present in the mode that makes the decision as difficult as possible, that precludes any shortcut or simplification, any differentiation a priori between that which counts and that which does not' (2005: 1003). Thus,

Stengers's cosmopolitics is a call to activate the possibility of resisting/ contesting the given, a call for generating imaginative, scientific and political resources that may enable us to think about other peoples and natures, or to think about 'another science' and 'another world'.

Stengers's account of cosmopolitics becomes a cornerstone in rehabilitating, although involuntarily, the Cynics' tamed and forgotten radical cosmopolitics. Curiously enough, as Stengers herself admits, the term 'cosmopolitics' was proposed without being aware of the tradition of thinking cosmopolitanism, not even of the most famous – the Kantian one: 'I have to plead guilty. I was unaware of Kantian usage while working on the first volume of what was to become a series of seven *Cosmopolitiques* in 1996; this term imposed itself on me' (2005: 994). However, what Stengers's account of cosmopolitics confirms is not mainly the Kantian cosmopolitanisms. This arrival by accident at the notion of 'cosmopolitics' is intriguing since it displays the very logic of the birth of cosmopolitanism in the first cosmopolitan stance of the Ancient Cynics 'altering the currency'. Stengers's account of cosmopolitics confirms the logic of cosmopolitanism as it was born in the Ancient Cynics milieu, since her cosmopolitics is expressed through the alteration of the currency of science. The alteration of currency is done not by the dog-like style of life of the Cynics, but by the conceptual figure of the idiot and by the figure of Bartelby, but with the same effect – creating a disturbance. Also it precedes and 'illustrates' the logic of cosmopolitanism as described by Ingram (who does not reference Stengers and does not mention her usage of the term): what cosmopolitans have in common lies not at the level of the content of their ideas, but at the level of form – a 'kind of interruption' (Ingram 2013: 7), since cosmopolitanism emerges inevitably as an interrogation of the given meanings and understandings, a disaffiliation and disidentification from the local and the given, a negation of the particular, a challenge to constituted forms of authority, legitimacy and belonging.

Reclaiming the Cynics' legacy and the recent rediscoveries of the radical logic of cosmopolitanism, this book advances a radical and militant cosmopolitics with four components: *cosmopolitan*, since it refers to the entire world; *radical*, since it contains a radical critique targeting the roots of the existing world order; *political* (not moral or cultural), because it envisages political transformation of the world both from below through contestatory practices and from above by rethinking the idea of a World Republic in the spirit of a radical cosmopolitics; and *militant* – by reclaiming the Cynic militancy which is a 'militancy addressed to absolutely everyone' (Foucault 2011: 285) and presupposes a militant life which 'aspires to change the world'. Thus, radical cosmopolitics cannot be otherwise than 'an overt, universal, aggressive militancy; militancy in the world and against the world' (Foucault 2011: 285).

The radical and militant cosmopolitics is constituted as well as a critique of adjectival cosmopolitanisms. In the last three decades there has been an avalanche of adjectival concepts of cosmopolitanism, in different sub-fields of humanities and social sciences, such as 'rooted' (Cohen 1992), 'discrepant' (Clifford 1992), 'vernacular' (Bhabha 1996), 'patriotic' (Appiah 1997), 'moderate' (Scheffler 1999), 'post-colonial' (Mignolo 2000a), 'anchored' (Dallmayr 2003), 'situated' (Baynes 2007), 'embedded' (Erskine 2008), 'indigenous' (de la Cadena 2010), 'statist' (Ypi 2012) and many others.[2] In the increased global interconnectedness from the last three decades of neoliberal globalisation, a cosmopolitan theory that would reflect this interconnectedness appeared necessary, but paradoxically in a theoretical context marked by the end of grand narratives. Thus, the adjectival cosmopolitanisms could be considered an expression of sensibility to criticism of grand narratives. The scholars advancing an adjectival cosmopolitan approach attempted to make it compatible with the plurality of social, cultural and political standpoints in the contemporary world, thus they were looking to avoid the primacy of the West, to reject the European analytical and temporal frameworks usually thought as structuring cosmopolitanism, and to advance non-totalising, non-European, non-Western, non-liberal, non-normative and historically situated forms of cosmopolitanism. As a rule, adjectival cosmopolitanisms postulate two sets of values and practices: enlightened, universalist, elitist, modernist and Western ones, and local, parochial, rooted values and practices, and the local set of values and practices is considered the most authentic mode of implementing cosmopolitanism. While attempting to reconcile local attachments and global obligations, these approaches are self-congratulatory in their display of an implicit virtue of moderation, an epistemic and motivational realism, plus the benefit of bringing cosmopolitanism closer to the everyday life of individuals, by 'counteracting' its alleged abstract dryness. The notion of cosmopolitics was used as well to indicate situations characteristic for adjectival cosmopolitanism: inspired by Stengers's work, authors introduce different 'earth-beings' into the situation (de la Cadena 2010; Blaser 2016), which play the role of the idiot or of Bartleby, that is, have the power to activate our thinking, and calling the situation 'indigenous cosmopolitics'.

However, these conciliatory approaches of cosmopolitanism do not impress its most coherent critics who see it as 'oxymoronic cosmopolitanism' betraying the very idea of cosmopolitanism as a theory for living in one world (Mouffe 2005: 105–7). In different chapters, this book shows that the oxymoronic cosmopolitanisms preserve methodological nationalism, reproduce the status quo, and end up supporting practices that reproduce world inequalities, while vehiculating respect to multicultural differences. While the earth-beings point to the other ways of existing that are viable but excluded from constructing the common world, there is a permanent risk to 'romanticising' the indigenous and the Aboriginal, to legitimising different ways of living as being equally cosmopolitan. Treating others with respect and some curiosity is simple, while imagining a more just way of living in the world for everyone requires more substantial approaches: 'When people suggest that there is vernacular cosmopolitanism among immigrants situated in various places, either paperless or papered, I think there is something questionable in it. It is an abdication of responsibility' (Spivak 2012: 111). As Spivak remarks,

> to suggest now that global minorities, labour export, paperless immigrant women achieve cosmopolitanism is to forget that they must exist in race-class divided situations where it is impossible to feel or exercise the sense of general equality that must be the definitive predication of epistemic cosmopolitanism. (Spivak 2012: 111)

Thus, we have to construct cosmopolitanism differently: 'We must train our imaginations to go into a different epistemological performance when it comes to the idea of cosmopolitanism' (Spivak 2012: 112). The radical and militant cosmopolitics is a proposal for a different epistemological performance – it is an invitation to think beyond nation-state, beyond empire, beyond status quo, beyond West, through peculiar but the only reliable cosmopolitical 'instruments': 'alter the values of all currencies', 'permanent questioning' and 'life in problematicity'. These instruments cannot be 'from above', male, Western, white, European, since the very adjectival cosmopolitanisms make use of these instruments in their necessary critique of the narrow European framework of Enlightenment cosmopolitanisms, but they stop at a certain point by postulating a 'rooted' cosmopolitanism, while the militant cosmopolitics continues the permanent questioning.

In this permanent questioning, the radical and militant cosmopolitics is a critique both of the nation-state and of capital. Capitalism in its global expansion continually produces protests and revolts worldwide, not only from a local perspective, but also from a global one, which have been case studies for testing the concept of cosmopolitanism of dissent (see Chapter 1). Capitalism in its global expansion generates a global agency from below speaking in the name of and addressing the entire world, looking to counteract the global unjust and exploitative nature of globalisation from above and, as the Zapatistas say, pointing out that there is a global powerful class of 'those above, who globalize conform-ism, cynicism, stupidity, war, destruction and death' (EZLN 1996) and those below who 'globalize hope'. The struggles against capitalism can-not be otherwise than within capitalism's amplitude and globality, and the theoretical equivalent of this struggle has to be the radical and mili-tant cosmopolitics, otherwise a cosmopolitan perspective on the world risks being reduced to local rooted or vernacular forms, while globally there will be only a cosmopolitanism of elite with its glamorous lifestyle and consumption. Marx was the first to observe that 'The bourgeoisie has through its exploitation of the world market given a cosmopolitan character to production and consumption in every country' (Marx and Engles 1978: 488). He famously criticises the bourgeois hypocritical cos-mopolitanism of political economy that 'displays a cosmopolitan, uni-versal energy' which, however, 'must throw aside this hypocrisy in the course of its further development and come out in its complete cynicism' (1975: 291) and the cosmopolitanism of the possessors of capital: 'As money develops into world money, so the commodity owner becomes a cosmopolitan' (Marx 1976: 384). Marx's critique of bourgeois cos-mopolitanism was not formulated from a local or national perspective, but from a radical cosmopolitan perspective: despite its brutality, global capitalism fulfils a progressive historical role, eliminating all sorts of bar-riers erected between human beings in previous epochs and laying the groundwork for a higher level of universalism and emancipation, so that the struggle could become a universal human struggle. For Marx the fight against hypocritical and exploitative bourgeois cosmopolitanism should be from a cosmopolitan perspective from below, from the prole-tariat, which is 'the expression of the dissolution of all classes, nation-alities, etc.' (Marx and Engles 1974: 94), since working men 'have no country' (Marx and Engles 1978: 500). For the obvious reasons of size, this book does not focus on the potential for thinking about a radical cosmopolitics starting from Marx's work or on a separate critique and opposition to the universality of capital, but it envisages capital as knot-ted in the trinity nation–state–capital, which reproduce each other. The book focuses mainly on the critique of the nation-state which, through appeals to emotions of national unity, tames the excesses of the world market (for example, through redistribution) and is the last resort for the survival of capitalism, while continuing to reproduce inequalities between countries – one of the most recent expressions of this inequality being 'vaccine nationalism'.

This book was written during the pandemic caused by Covid-19. Apparently, nothing around justified writing it: national lockdowns, bor-ders closing, nation-states becoming stronger and exercising tight control over borders and over anything else, and the shameless 'vaccine nationalism'. So, were not the political theorists arguing for the importance of nationality right all along? Should not all be nationalists at heart, seeking to protect their country and co-citizens to survive the pandemic? Are not the political theories that caused my 'theoretical trauma' valid? The answer to all these questions is that the responses to the Covid-19 pandemic could not have been different. The assumption beyond these questions is that there was a more cosmopolitan alternative in terms of institutions and infrastructure, and it collapsed during the pandemic leading to the triumph of local petty nationalisms. On the contrary, the pandemic revealed the real infrastructure that was supporting an apparently 'cosmopolitan' world from the last three decades of neoliberal globalisation: the trinity of nation, state and capital. The pandemic just blew away the glossy layer of lifestyle choices that passed as 'cosmopolitanism'.

I already knew before the pandemic that radical protests with radical claims such as 'No One Is Illegal' and 'No Borders No Nations' 'disappear' into the nation-states, since there is no institution – and not even a hint of an institution – that will be up to these mottos. I knew already that the World Social Forum's (WSF's) vision that 'Another World Is Possible' could be taken down by a country that does not give visas to the members of WSF from the Global South to attend the only WSF meeting that took place in the Global North (2016 in Canada, see Chapter 3). The world was profoundly nationalistic before the pandemic, the pandemic only showed it once again. The pandemic was sudden, requiring prompt responses, and the approaches have been those already existing. A very significant failure for cosmopolitan theories or cosmopolitan-oriented theorists was the moment when half the people of some countries were 'taking their country back', as happened in the case of Brexit, an option taken in normal non-pandemic times, when there was time to reflect and the alternative of not taking 'the country back'.

Also, we have known since the Zapatistas said it that there is a 'world war of the powerful who want to turn the planet into a private club' (EZLN 1996). And these powerful did not stop privatising the planet and colonising space even during the pandemic. For many, the borders have been closed and access to other countries denied, while for a privileged few there were 'No Borders No Nations', and for them even the borders of the planet Earth became porous. Some billionaires flew to outer space, to the edge of the outer hemisphere, on private spacecrafts, marking a new era of 'space tourism'.[3] Closed borders in a pandemic, but not for all. Mega corporations and powerful states with all their administrative apparatuses and services cooperated in this 'historical' conquest of space by a pair of billionaires in the time of pandemic.

And mega corporations and powerful states cooperated undisturbed in producing 'vaccine nationalism'. The governments of the countries from the Global North signed agreements with pharmaceutical manufacturers and, through advance purchase commitments, purchased many more vaccines than the size of their populations, from five to ten doses for each citizen, Canada being top with about ten vaccine doses per resident. Meanwhile, in the Global South even those people at greatest risk, the elderly and the healthcare professionals involved in patient care, were still unable to access vaccines. The 'vaccine nationalism' provoked revulsion and waves of revolt and it was rightly described as a 'catastrophic moral failure',[4] and it remains a moral catastrophe. But again, for someone who for years was reluctant to move beyond the theoretical confines of the nation-state, vaccine nationalism appeared as the only plausible scenario. If people behave nationally in day-to-day interaction, how could they behave otherwise in a sudden pandemic affecting everyone?

The impression that there was a cosmopolitanism in practice before the pandemic was just a conflation of cosmopolitanism with globalisation. Globalisation itself was an economic process – it consisted of the economic interdependencies of the world, which were neither just nor correct, just the result of the alleged invisible hand of the market that indeed cannot be stopped at the borders of a nation-state. The renewal of cosmopolitanism as a theoretical approach in the 1990s was a reaction to globalisation, attempting to clarify how we should live in a just way in the world as a whole. Theories of cosmopolitanism failed to address this adequately, playing with 'moderate', 'vernacular', 'statist' and other adjectival cosmopolitanisms. Thus, what the pandemic revealed was not the failure of some inexistent cosmopolitan framework, but mainly the failure of political philosophers to think more deeply about cosmopolitanism, to go beyond the methodological nationalism of their theories and to endorse a cosmopolitan position. Not only did what was happening during the pandemic not discourage the writing of this book, on the contrary, everything justified writing it. And this was not the assumption made by some sociologists who considered the pandemic one of the most cosmopolitan events in human history, since it was the first global phenomenon in which the majority of the world's population was experiencing a similar event at the same time, having the same conversations and sharing the same fears.[5] Locked in our apartments, spending countless hours in front of computers and TV screens, we allegedly experienced what it feels like to live in One World. This cosmopolitanism may be sociologically plausible, but a sociological cosmopolitan moment is not enough. And it did not last for the whole pandemic: when vaccines started to be available, the solidarity with the others having the same experience ended and 'vaccine nationalism' took the place of the cosmopolitan moment. The pandemic, by showing once again the man-made, unjust and shameless nationalistic arrangements of the world, encouraged further the affirmation of a radical and militant cosmopolitics.

NOTES

1. See Lampedusa Charter (2014).
2. Any search in the academic journal database will turn out expressions such as 'urban cosmopolitans', 'rural cosmopolitans', 'upper-class cosmopolitan', 'middle-class cosmopolitan', 'working-class cosmopolitan', 'peripheral', 'subaltern cosmopolitanism', and many others whose examination is beyond the aim of this book.
3. Available at <https://www.wsj.com/articles/richard-branson-races-jeff-bezos-to-space-as-covid-19-hits-business-back-on-earth-11625753740> (last accessed 30 November 2021).
4. Available at <https://www.theguardian.com/commentisfree/2021/mar/05/vaccination-covid-vaccines-rich-nations> (last accessed 30 November 2021).
5. Available at <https://www.europeansociologist.org/issue-45-pandemic-impossibilities-vol-1/being-cosmopolitan-and-anti-cosmopolitan-covid-19-pandemic> (last accessed 30 November 2021).

Chapter 1

COSMOPOLITANISM OF DISSENT

My research on cosmopolitanism started only when I found the resources to confront the fear of a new grand narrative. I could finally address the criticisms and questions that were stopping me from having a cosmopolitan position within political theory, such as how should we conceive of cosmopolitanism after the scepticism towards the grand narratives of modern ideologies? Can cosmopolitanism avoid being a new grand narrative? How can one justify cosmopolitan values without falling back on certain conceptions of a fixed human nature or a shared system of belief? What does it mean to be cosmopolitan today, given the plurality of the interpretative standpoints in the contemporary world? How should a cosmopolitan project look in the alleged post-metaphysical and post-universalistic theoretical framework? My invaluable resources in confronting these questions and many potential criticisms were the concepts of 'permanent questioning', 'living in problematicity' and 'shaken solidarities' advanced by Jan Patočka, in which I identified a minimalist framework for conceiving a non-totalising cosmopolitan theory.

'PERMANENT QUESTIONING' OF THE EASTERN EUROPEAN DISSIDENCE

Jan Patočka (1907–77) was a Czech philosopher, considered the most important and influential thinker from Eastern Europe of the twentieth century. He studied philosophy with Husserl and Heidegger, in the 1930s, and his phenomenological approach, which was his main contribution to philosophy, is understood as a continuation, development and critique of what he considered to be un-thought by his masters. After the Second World War, he refused to join the Communist Party and was banned from academia, except for a few years after the Prague Spring of 1968. In 1977, he founded and was one of the spokespersons of *Charta* 77, a human rights movement in Czechoslovakia. In this context, Patočka was arrested by authorities. He died after a prolonged interrogation by the secret police. His death suggests an analogy to the fate of Socrates, because Patočka lent to the Charter the sense that it was led by a figure committed to truth (Tucker 2000: 3; Falk 2003: 242). The influence of Patočka and, through him, of philosophy on Václav Havel, on the Chartists, on the Czechoslovak dissidence, and on the Velvet Revolution of 1989 in general is considered to be decisive (Tucker 2000: 3–5; Falk 2003: 242–7).

Patočka did not elaborate a political philosophy; however, his entire work contains an implicit political philosophy (Caraus 2016e). He has not written anything on cosmopolitanism, but this was not an impediment for me in identifying a resource for thinking cosmopolitanism in his thought. Obviously, my approach was not an interpretation of Patočka's text, but a certain 'use' of his ideas, mainly of three elements from Patočka's philosophy, which I postulated as grounding elements of a political philosophy of cosmopolitanism: 'permanent questioning', 'living in problematicity' and 'shaken solidarities'.

Permanent questioning is Patočka's 'negative Platonism'. For Patočka, the story of metaphysics begins with Socratic knowledge described as 'a learned ignorance, that is, a question' (Patočka 1989a: 180). Socrates permanently challenges his interlocutors through questioning their and his knowledge, but he does not formulate the newly gained knowledge in objective, factual, positive assertions but again, indirectly, in the form of a new questioning, the 'Socratic question' being 'a question which claims to do without a response or to be itself better than a response' (Patočka 1989a: 195–6). The essence of metaphysics, as Plato and Aristotle formulated it, consists in offering an answer to the Socratic question, an answer that philosophers seek to derive from the question itself. In this way, 'Ignorance became a form of knowledge . . . more secure than anything on the earth' (Patočka 1989a: 181). Philosophy started to be portrayed not only as a movement towards transcending the sensible, but also as a movement towards an ideal being. In Patočka's view, 'The integrity of human life is broken. Man becomes one of the beings ruled by ideas; ethics and politics as a grand unity take on the task of discovery of the inner ideal law of a humanly perfect life' (1989a: 182). Patočka's interpretation of metaphysics reconsiders one of the common objections to Platonism: critics have found the radical separation of two worlds implausible and impossible to reconcile with the claim that ideas shape and guide the order of things and events from the empirical world. Patočka takes seriously the very possibility of thinking this separation: 'The separation is identical with freedom' (1989a: 192). Patočka's Platonism is a negative philosophy in the sense that, instead of positing a certain positive content, it takes as point of departure 'the negative character of a distance, of a remove, of an overcoming of every objectivity' (1989a: 193). The possibility of questioning is in this very separation between the world of Ideas and the real world. The world of Ideas does not stand as a ground for the real world, but both worlds are grounded and de-grounded in the experience of questioning. The question does not require an answer, at least not a permanent one. Each answer will be temporary, since what an answer can offer is just a perspective of another question, and humans have to learn to live in problematicity.

'Living in problematicity' is the second element of Patočka's philosophy that I found suitable for grounding a theory of cosmopolitanism. Patočka examines humans as 'being in and of the world' (Patočka 1998: 155) in three movements: the movement of anchoring in corporeity and in the world, the movement of self-projection and the movement of breaking-through. In this third movement, man confronts his finitude and by virtue of this confrontation politics, philosophy and history are born: 'The reason for this special position of politics is that political life in its original and primordial form is nothing other than active freedom' (Patočka 1996: 77). Politics is born with the experience of freedom as distancing, removing and shaking up the given meaning and should not be identified with the administrative organisation of life.

Politics starts in the movement of shaking the naive, given meanings and, concomitantly, starts the experience of meaninglessness. For Patočka, the question of an absolute/final meaning of existence cannot be answered because meaning does not pre-exist as a (metaphysical) origin and meaning did not pre-exist prior to the question of its possibility: 'the shaking of the naïve meaning is the genesis of a perspective on an absolute meaning' (Patočka 1996: 77). Patočka argues that meaning will not be given after formulating the question, because what the entire question offers is just a perspective with the inevitability of another question. 'Humans cannot live without meaning', admits Patočka (1996: 75), but this does not mean that they should live with an unproblematic meaning. Humans have to be prepared 'to give up the hope of a directly given meaning and to accept the meaning as a way' (1996: 77), that is, meaning as a quest for meaning. What man fails to comprehend is that 'history is nothing other than the shaken attitude of pre-given meanings. It has no other meaning or goal' (1996: 118), and entire modern civilisation fails to understand that 'the problem of history may not be resolved; it must be preserved as a problem' (1996: 118). Human beings should learn to live in problematicity.

Living in problematicity might sound like living in permanent conflict but, on the contrary, living in problematicity makes possible an unprecedented solidarity: the solidarity of the shaken which is 'the solidarity of those who are capable of understanding what life and death are about, and so what history is about' (Patočka 1996: 43). The solidarity of the shaken is not a solidarity of king-philosophers, an elitist solidarity inaccessible to most human beings. It is a solidarity of those who resist any monolithic programmes and ideologies: 'The solidarity of the shaken can say "No" to the measures of mobilization that makes the state of war permanent. It will not offer positive programs, but will speak, like Socrates' *daimonion*, in warnings and prohibitions' (Patočka 1996:135).

Patočka admits that permanent questioning, living in problematicity and solidarity of the shaken are not easy tasks, and asks if 'a conversion of historic proportions' (Patočka 1996: 77), which would make humans capable of accepting responsibility for the meaninglessness, is possible. The possibility of a conversion depends essentially on the capacity to live with problematicity, and in a 'self-denial demanded by the state of uprootedness in which alone a meaningfulness, both absolute and accessible to humans, because it is problematic, might be realized' (1996: 75–6).

I selected these three elements – permanent questioning, problematicity of meaning and shaken solidarities – as a minimal set for a theory of cosmopolitanism. Nevertheless, how can these assumptions help to formulate a cosmopolitan theory and eventuality to ground a practice? The 'secret' is that these elements came already embodied in a practice – the dissident movement of *Charta 77*. My first published paper on cosmopolitanism (Caraus 2013) was mapping in Patočka's philosophy a potential cosmopolitan theory and in his founding of the *Charta 77* a cosmopolitan practice.

The declaration of the *Charta 77* was published on 6 January 1977, along with the names of the first 242 signatories. That document described the *Charta 77* as a 'loose, informal and open association of people . . . united by the will to strive individually and collectively for respect for human and civil rights in our country and throughout the world' (*Charta 77* 1977). *Charta 77* criticised the government for failing to implement the human rights provisions from a number of documents it had signed, mainly the Final Act of the 1975 Conference on Security and Co-operation in Europe (Part III of the Helsinki Accords), and the United Nations covenants on political, civil, economic and cultural rights. The text of the charter was considered illegal, and its dissemination was a political crime. Signatories were punished through different means characteristic of the Communist regime: dismissal from work, forced exile, loss of citizenship, forced collaboration with the Communist secret police, detention, trial and imprisonment. Despite unrelenting harassment and arrests, the charter continued to issue reports on the government's violations of human rights until 1989 (Falk 2003: 88–92). *Charta 77* produced 572 documents over the decade and a half of its existence, considered the collective oeuvre of Chartists who monitored the injustice committed by Communist authorities in everyday life, the relations between dissident organisations in Central and Eastern Europe, and the human rights abuses around the world (Falk 2003: 251–4).

Patočka's two *Charta 77* texts – 'The Obligation to Resist Injustice' and 'What We Can and Cannot Expect from Charta 77' (Patočka 1989b: 175–206) – made more real the cosmopolitan event of the *Charta 77*. Without using the words 'cosmopolitan' or 'cosmopolitanism', these texts express a cosmopolitan viewpoint. First, the texts showed that the values that legitimated the protest of the charter signatories and their contestation of the political regime were universal, unconditional values. For Patočka, all *raison d'être* of a state – the so-called national interest, the collective well-being, the appeals to a common identity, religion or ideology as foundations of a state – are irrelevant. The sovereignty of states should be subordinated to a higher sphere, above or outside politics, and this is the realm of morality: 'No society . . . can function without a moral foundation' (1989b: 341). Sovereign states are obliged to respect the elementary fact that our humanity has precedence over any political role we may be assigned to or pressed to play as citizens: 'Humankind needs to be convinced of the unconditional validity of principles which are, in that sense, "scared", valid for all humans and all times and capable of setting out humanity's goals' (1989b: 340).

Second, Patočka's *Charta 77* texts made a difference between the sphere of international relations and a new realm of the world created by the Declaration of Human Rights:

> We consider a time when it became possible to sign a Declaration of Human Rights a new historical epoch, the stage of an immense outreach, since it represents a reversal of human consciousness, of the attitude of humans to themselves and to their society. (Patočka 1989b: 342)

Those who have signed *Charta 77* are convinced that 'this Act is far more significant than the usual treaties among nations, which deal only with the interests of countries and powers' (1989b: 341). Therefore, to the extent that the action of the individual is at the heart of the cosmopolitan project, Patočka affirmed a cosmopolitan point of view while defending the necessity of the *Charta 77* movement.

Third, the texts emphasised the role of clear consciousness of those who signed and followed the charter, which amounts to a role of transparency and publicity in creating a cosmopolitan public sphere. By explaining 'What we can and cannot expect from *Charta 77*', Patočka clarifies first of all what the expectations were of those who signed the act, on both sides. The representatives of East European countries 'signed expecting that nothing will change in the way the powerful treat the public, that all will go as before' (Patočka 1989b: 345), while the other side signed in hopeful expectation that there would be no repetition of the events from the 1920s and 1930s in the Soviet Union and from the 1950s in Eastern Europe. What *Charta 77* has already achieved is the fact that 'It has shown that carrying out the Helsinki agreements will not be as effortless as some had thought' (1989b: 345). The actions of the government and of the opponents of *Charta 77* 'have won us more sympathy at home and abroad that we dare to expect' (1989b: 344). An incontestable achievement of the *Charta 77* is that it drew attention to what happens in Eastern Europe to the entire world: 'the positive achievement of the *Charta* is that all of this has been revealed' (1989b: 345), and that 'Clear conscience and decency have proved to be also a powerful factor of political reality' (1989b: 344).

Finally, an interesting aspect is the emphasis that the *Charta 77* expected nothing more than to educate citizens to act as free persons beyond the sovereignty of the nation state: 'It is the hope of *Charta 77* that our citizens may learn to act as free persons, self-motivated and responsible' (1989b: 346). The respect of human rights is also something that should be learnt and requires a permanent awareness:

> The *Charta* will unceasingly remind us how far we fall short of those rights belonging to our citizens by law; it will not cease to remind both our and the foreign public of it, regardless of the risks of such activity. (Patočka 1989b: 347)

Thus, *Charta* envisages a global awareness, both of 'our citizens' and of 'the foreign public'.

Therefore, Patočka's *Charta 77* texts helped to see how this concrete event of dissidence qualifies as a cosmopolitan practice. The dissidents' contestation of the imposed meanings in the concrete political regime of socialist Czechoslovakia was legitimated by values that are universal, not local or national. *Charta 77* resistance to a hegemonic ideology and to a totalising system was possible through the appeal to unconditional universal values – human rights – and to a cosmopolitan vision that considers that individual human beings are ultimate units of moral concern, not states, specific regimes, or particular forms of human associations. In Patočka's argumentation, persons speaking out for themselves, and joining *Charta 77*, taught those in power that individual persons, empowered by the Declaration of Human Rights, can change the world around them and, indirectly, the entire world.

But where are the 'permanent questioning', 'living in problematicity' and 'shaken solidarities' in this invocation of human rights? How are these elements embodied in the practice of claiming human rights? And is not here a contradiction in Patočka's thought since his philosophy speaks of the problematicity of all meanings, but his final texts invoke human rights, morality, an obligation to oneself to resist injustice. The question of compatibility of this 'absolute morality' with Patočka's previous philosophy has been justly raised, some commentators seeing a late 'Kantian turn' in Patočka's thinking (Tucker 2000; Mensch 2011). However, permanent questioning and human rights are not necessarily in contradiction:

> From the moment when the rights of man are posited as the ultimate reference, the established right is open to question. It becomes still more so as the collective wills or, one might prefer to say, social agents bearing new demands mobilize a force in opposition to the one that tends to contain the effects of the recognized rights. Now, where right is in question, society – that is, the established order – is in question. (Lefort 1986: 258)

According to Lefort, human rights are the generative principle of politics; they are not grounded in a metaphysical principle and are not a pre-political condition for politics. The 'ultimate markers of certainty' are destroyed and at the same time there is born a new awareness of humanity in all the varieties of its figures, and this awareness is expressed in the claim for new rights. The fact that more and more rights can be claimed means that human rights, as a product of past struggles and the object of the present ones, are 'perpetually opened to questioning' (Marchart 2007: 105). Political movements arise to win new rights or to expand the existing ones, and this has deep effects on the political imagination and practice: they create a new 'awareness of rights'. Patočka himself expressed a similar view on human rights in a text from 1968:

> The intellectuals of the West have become accustomed to seeing the liberal principles of human rights and freedoms as nothing more nor less than the ideological camouflage of bourgeois regimes, and therefore accord them no importance. The intellectuals of the East, on the contrary, see them as a condition of their own effectiveness as a force of reason penetrating a whole and non-alienated society. Perhaps they overrate them, *since none of these principles has an absolute character*, and are successful only in a historical situation determined by a new structural form of the forces of production. What is important is that we are talking here of different principles; not the abstract principles of supposedly natural freedoms, but principles that, after having been negated, are reborn – born again as conditions under which the government of reason

in a totally emancipated society finally becomes possible. (Patočka 2016: 19; emphasis added)

The practice of claiming rights expands their inscription and transforms the idea, the engine of human rights being in their experimental activation, and this conception of rights allows the conceiving human rights as a contestatory politics and a practice of cosmopolitanisation. But the tension should not be dissolved entirely: Patočka's 'radical negation' should not be overshadowed by the affirmation of human rights. This tension should be preserved, and it was the core of Patočka's thought that 'inspired' me to detect here a resource for cosmopolitanism.

Patočka's involvement in the dissidence movement of *Charta* 77 amounts to a political decision resulting concomitantly from the concrete historical circumstances and from his philosophy. This 'spirit' of dissidence was taken over by other dissidents who defined themselves not primarily as a political avant-garde advancing a positive programme, but as those who say 'No' to power and 'shatter the world of appearances and unmask the real nature of power' and with this 'No' to 'expand the space available for life' (Havel 1978).

COSMOPOLITANISM OF DISSENT: THREE PATTERNS

This rediscovery of the legacy of Eastern European dissent took place in the context of protests against global political-economic systems, international institutions or against local political regimes, such as Occupy and Arab Spring. My hypothesis was that if Eastern European dissidence had a cosmopolitan dimension that legitimated dissent, then it is worth seeing whether other episodes of dissent and resistance had a cosmopolitan dimension as well. So, in mapping the legacy of dissent for a theory of cosmopolitanism, several clusters of questions have been advanced as landmarks: What legitimated the dissidents' questioning and contestation of imposed meanings in a political regime? Were the values invoked by dissidents local, national or universal? Is there a dialectics between the universal and the particular in a concrete case of dissent? Do dissident movements in different contexts manifest a cosmopolitan solidarity with other dissidents? Are dissidents 'rooted' or 'rootless' cosmopolitans?

Enthusiastic as a result of my initial findings, I tried to inspire other scholars with my enthusiasm and to delineate the cosmopolitan dimension in different episodes of dissent around the globe. The methodology consisted in close-reading of the discourses and texts of dissident thinkers and movements: manifestos, declarations and other texts explaining the necessity of dissent (for example, autobiographies, memories etc.) from the perspective of a possible cosmopolitanism. The readings looked into motivations and justifications for engaging in an act of dissent, that is, the dissenter's cause, reasons for defending that cause and for engaging in this form of protest, and so on.

To avoid an essentialist view and a grand narrative of dissent, I identified three historical patterns of dissent as cosmopolitan practice: dissidence, civil disobedience and global resistance (Caraus 2014a). These case studies could qualify as forms of historical cosmopolitanism producing cosmopolitan events, that is, appealing to and receiving the support and solidarity of the entire world through the content of their claims and their practices of opposition. Concomitantly, these three historical patterns also bring conceptual clarification to the specifics of contestation: dissidence in authoritarian regimes, civil disobedience in democratic or 'reasonably just' regimes, and resistance in the globalised context of power. The historical situatedness of dissent also avoids projecting one image of dissent to the detriment of another, by moving from paradigmatic 'heroes' of dissidence towards anonymous or collective dissenters within the global resistance.

The main legacy of *dissidence* for cosmopolitanism of dissent is its 'tradition' of resistance to authoritarian rule. The shift from mass terror to selective repression is the first precondition for the possibility of dissent – in the Stalinist era the dissenter was executed before articulating a sustained criticism of the regime. The Eastern European dissidence was possible only after the Eastern European states signed the Helsinki Agreements on Human Rights in 1975. The forms of resistance that existed before the Helsinki agreements are usually called revisionism and were mainly attempts by members of the communist parties to reform the party according to communist ideals. Human rights formally endorsed by these states opened new possibilities for a critique of regimes and set certain limits to the repression against dissidents, reducing the individual risks of oppositional engagement. Protesters turned away from the attempt to reform the party system from inside and used the formally valid constitutional principles, claiming, in particular, the right to freedom of expression. But the exercise of formally existing rights was nevertheless forbidden and persecuted by the authoritarian states: the signatories of *Charta 77* in Czechoslovakia were persecuted, the text of the charter was considered illegal and its dissemination a political crime (Falk 2003: 88–92). Similarly, the signatories of *Charter 08* in China have been interrogated by police, applications to travel abroad rejected, newspapers and publishing houses ordered to blacklist anyone who had signed *Charter 08*, and Liu Xiaobo, a key drafter of the charter, was arrested and sentenced to eleven years in prison (Xiaobo 2012; Beja et al. 2012), although the Chinese state signed the International Covenant on Civil and Political Rights in 1998, and an amendment to the Constitution in 2004 added the provision that '[the State] respects and guarantees human rights' (*Charter 08* 2008).

The main characteristic of dissidence as a historical pattern of dissent is the attitude of dissidents towards the political regime, which they consider entirely unjust, and which they demand to be replaced with a democratic regime guaranteeing human rights; thus the resources legitimating dissidence coincide with its goals. For example, *Charta 77* comes into being to ensure the respect for rights assumed by signing the Helsinki Agreements: 'We accordingly welcome the Czechoslovak Socialist Republic's accession to those agreements. Their publication, however, serves as a powerful reminder of the extent to which basic human rights in our country exist, regrettably, on paper alone' (*Charta 77* 1977). The Chinese dissident *Charter 08* points to the fact that 'the government has promised to formulate and implement a National Human Rights Action Plan. But so far, this political progress has largely remained on paper' (*Charter 08* 2008).

Obviously, dissidence is not exclusively used for achieving human rights and democracy. There are cases of dissidence that do not require their government to implement human rights and democracy, the most famous example being Alexander Solzhenitsyn's opposition to the communist regime in the USSR in the name of religious Orthodoxy and the national values of the 'Russian soul', while Andrei Sakharov opposed the same regime in the name of universal human rights. Despite exceptions, the most paradigmatic cases of dissidence confirm the cosmopolitanism of universal rights and freedoms as necessary for expanding the space available for life.

While dissidence takes place within an authoritarian society, *civil disobedience* takes place within a more or less just democratic state. The concept of civil disobedience assumes that, in democratic societies, people have an obligation to follow the law, but sometimes, in order to make the law more just, it should be disobeyed. The resistance to British rule in India led by Gandhi, the US civil rights movement led by Martin Luther King Jr, and student sit-ins against the Vietnam War are the historical cases most frequently associated with the idea and practice of civil disobedience (Bedau 1991: 2–3). In *A Theory of Justice*, Rawls defined civil disobedience as 'a public, non-violent, conscientious yet political act contrary to law usually done with the aim of bringing about a change in law or policies of government' (Rawls 1971: 320) and identified criteria that make a breach of law an act of civil disobedience, such as conscious intent, clear injustice addressing the public conception of justice, the difference between broken law and wrong law, publicity, non-violence and fidelity to law. Therefore, the dominant feature of civil disobedience is that the disobedient protester considers the prevailing system as 'reasonably just' and looks only for limited reform, not radical change. The assumption that the 'paradigmatic' practitioners of disobedience regarded the prevailing system as 'reasonably just', seeking not radical but limited change, could be a false picture of historically significant resistance, for example it is not very plausible to claim that Luther King regard the system as 'reasonable just'. Nevertheless, the difference between an authoritarian regime denying rights/freedoms to all members of the society and a system protecting basic rights/freedoms at least for a part of the population is essential for differentiating between these two historical patterns of dissent.

This feature also points to the 'content' of this form of dissent: Luther King declared that 'What the Negro wants – and will not stop until he gets – is absolute and unqualified freedom and equality' (King 1991: 353). The fact that rights and freedoms are granted only to a part of population is perceived as an injustice by those to whom rights are not granted. In rejecting injustice, civil disobedience takes place in the name of the universal, demanding the same (justice) for all: 'We are appealing to others to reconsider and to put themselves in our position and to recognize that they cannot expect us to acquiesce indefinitely in the terms they impose on us' (Rawls 1971: 335–6). The universalist content of civil disobedience is the appeal for the same (rights, freedom and justice) for all. Asking for the same rights and justice for all is a cosmopolitan emphasis on human beings as ultimate units of concern.

The third historically situated pattern of dissent is *global resistance*. The specific feature of this pattern is also in the nature of power and regime, which changes substantially. There is no sharp opposition between ruled and rulers, and the 'headquarters' from which power is exercised and injustice produced are multiple and diffuse, and the agents, practices, sites and targets of global resistance are multiple as well (Mittelman 2000). The agents of global resistance are assumed to be those discontent with globalisation, for example by financial globalisation creating inequality and exclusion, and the most visible acts of protests are those against the World Bank, International Monetary Fund and World Trade Organization, and against corporation and trade agreements. The protests are known by such names as Seattle 1999, Genoa 2001, Quebec City 2001, Porto Alegre 2002 and so on (Amoore 2005: 99–209). Some practices of resistance reaffirm historical forms – protest, demonstration, public statements, declarations – while other forms of resistance are diffuse and less institutionalised. Even everyday activities such as what one wears, and what one buys or consumes, might qualify as resistance as much as strikes and boycotts. Old/existing frameworks are adjusted to explain global resistance, new approaches are advanced, some celebrating the 'multitude against empire', while other approaches are advanced through the activist stance of the authors themselves. The authors frame global resistance as multiple, situated, mobile and transitory, and confirm Foucault's insight:

> Points of resistance are present everywhere in the network. Hence, there is no single locus of great Refusal, no soul of revolt, sources of all rebellions, or pure law of the revolutionary. Instead, there is a plurality of resistance, each of them a special case: resistances that are possible, necessary, improbable. (Foucault 2005: 88)

What therefore is the cosmopolitan potential of global resistance? It is important to note that being global or transnational does not mean being cosmopolitan. For example, religiously exclusivist global movements, such as al-Qaida, that espouse a single truth and demonise the others, at times violently, are anti-cosmopolitan despite these movements' transnational networks and global aspirations. Movements of global resistance claim to speak for all: 'We come together again to continue our struggles' (WSF 2002: 627). The global resistance movements speak in the name of the entire world, as in the mottos 'Another World Is Possible' from the World Social Forum, 'Our World is Not For Sale' originating in the 1999 Seattle protests against the World Trade Organization, 'You G8, we 8 billions' from the Genoa protests in 2001, and the famous 'We are the 99 percent' of the Occupy movement. The mottos and slogans connect 'we' and 'you' to 'world', 'Earth', 'planet' and 'humanity', and by this making a cosmopolitan statement. Protesters speak about and address the 'people of the world' or 'brothers and sisters from all five continents' (EZLN 1996), although there is no presence of all humans or of 'our world' on a global scale protest that would justify the representative claim. The cosmopolitan representative claims speak as if all of us and the entire world are present in the event of protests (Caraus 2017). The specific solidarity of the '99 per cent', without ever taking place or being even desirable as a physical solidarity, displays a world view of individuals aware of others' needs and situation.

Thus, each pattern of dissent displays different degrees of cosmopolitanism, but there are some common aspects that justify advancing the notion of cosmopolitanism of dissent as a novel and original concept. Cosmopolitanism of dissent is a practice and action rather than an idea. The practices of contesting the unjust forms of power expand the space of life beyond the confines imposed by a certain political regime and express cosmopolitan aspirations, sometimes without directly professing a cosmopolitan vision. Cosmopolitanism of dissent is an action from below, not from above, by this avoiding the main criticism of cosmopolitanism from above, that point to the lack of a cosmopolitan agency who would like to bring cosmopolitanism and cosmopolitan institutions into being. Dissent takes place in a certain concrete place and emerges as a rejection of injustice in this specific context. It shows that although the human being is in these circumstances, through dissent she puts into question all attempts to confine her locally or to confine her as a fixed entity, for example as a Negro in a certain part of the bus in the paradigmatic example of Rosa Parks. Thus, cosmopolitanism of dissent is not a 'rooted' form of cosmopolitanism, but an uprooted one. Dissent takes place in a certain place and historical context but, by dissenting, a person refuses to be confined to local practices or values. Unlike 'rooted', 'vernacular' and other 'situated' cosmopolitanisms,[1] which combine apparently contradictory opposites – local and universal values – into dialectics, cosmopolitanism of dissent is not dialectical for obvious reasons. As a reaction against injustice, it does not retain injustice and combine it with rights and liberties, resolving them into a 'synthesis'. Injustice must cease, as all dissenters ask.

This moment of transcending the local and the given through an act of dissent demanding the end of the injustice is a cosmopolitan moment and event. The image of the collapse of the Berlin Wall, of a single individual standing up to the tanks in Tiananmen Square, or other images of resistance all around the world, are moments of common humanity. These images are cosmopolitan events not because they radiate across the globe as an effect of mass media, but because they affirm the common bonds of humanity through vulnerability to injustice and the capacity of human beings to have the courage to reject injustice. Through acknowledging common vulnerability in a common world, a 'solidarity of the shaken' is initiated. Instead of a global community, monolithic and uniform, cosmopolitanism of dissent projects a world of plural and partial solidarities, a world that recognises its problematicity and vulnerability.

Therefore, cosmopolitanism of dissent is a *practice and action* rather than an idea; it is a practice and action *from the below, not from above*; it is a *political* form of cosmopolitanism not a moral or cultural one, and which has a temporality of *event*, and displays a 'solidarity of the shaken'. Cosmopolitanism as a practice of dissent allowed me to overcome the fear of criticisms of cosmopolitanism that were impeding me in having a cosmopolitan positioning. Equally important is the fact that cosmopolitanism of dissent allowed me to re-examine the foundations of cosmopolitanism from a new perspective.

DISSENT AS FOUNDATION: POST-FOUNDATIONAL COSMOPOLITANISM

Dissent itself is part of the modern story of the death of God. Dissent was not possible when life was governed by laws that lay beyond human capacity to change them, when everything was in the hands of God and his quasi-divine earthly embodiments. The possibility to withdraw consent to voluntary servitude was a radical element of the humanist world view, combining free will, human agency, a strong belief in autonomy and in the subject endowed with capacity to shape the world. The rebellious (and sometimes Romantic) individual becomes the foundation of dissent, shaping a grand theory and practice of non-violent resistance. And we (still) associate dissent with images of heroic rebellion and social change through great events, though this image of dissent diminishes the possibilities of seeing domination and resistance in different ways. This vision of dissent permits dissent only once: the hero inaugurated the new world and man was placed (by himself) at the centre of the world. But dissent continues. From heroes and icons of human rights to anonymous protesters in the grey zones of global resistance, dissent becomes perpetual.

Therefore, dissent was born by contesting power, being at the same time a contestation of the foundations of that power. Dissent challenges not only a form of power but the instituted ground beyond it, which is dismantled as contingent or unjust. Since dissent becomes perpetual, the contestation of the grounds becomes perpetual as well, so dissent pointed to a new way of conceiving foundations of cosmopolitanism, and especially of addressing and overcoming cosmopolitanism 'temptations of foundationalism' (Hayden 2013: 196). Traditional grounds of cosmopolitanism, like the laws of the cosmos, humanism, teleology of reason, universal history, progress, human rights and global justice express ideas that pertain to foundationalism, which posits some basic beliefs as infallible. Although the terms 'foundation' and 'foundationalism' only rarely find expression in discussions on political theory of cosmopolitanism, the authors, while not explicitly invoking the term 'foundations', postulate cosmopolitan principles, cosmopolitan norms, cosmopolitan right, ultimate units of concern and so on, assuming some basic justified beliefs, both about human beings and about the world.

Cosmopolitanism's implicit or explicit foundationalism involves some risks, as critics or even sympathisers of cosmopolitanism have noticed, pointing again and again to the omnipresent risk of a new totalising grand narrative and to the 'oppressiveness of abstracted universalism' (Harvey 2009: 80) or to 'the constant risk of transmuting from an inspiring vision into an inviolable doctrine of universal salvation. In this way, cosmopolitanism could be yet another threatening modernist ideology of human betterment – a new political religion of immutable truth' (Hayden 2013: 196). Given the temptation of foundationalism inherent in cosmopolitanism, one has to ask how it is possible to formulate theories of cosmopolitanism after the critique and deconstruction of foundations, or how is it possible to think about cosmopolitanism after the critique of foundations. Can cosmopolitanism be conceived without an ultimate ground? Can we construct theories of cosmopolitanism without some certainties about the entire world or about the cosmos? Should we continue to look for foundations of cosmopolitan rights, norms and values? Alternatively, should we aim towards cosmopolitanism without foundations or towards cosmopolitanism with contingent foundations?

The concept of the cosmopolitanism of dissent helps to escape cosmopolitanism's temptations of foundationalism (Caraus 2016a). The whole argument of rescuing cosmopolitanism from foundationalism has to be resumed here briefly. Foundationalism is a view about the structure of justification of knowledge, which posits some basic beliefs as *prima facie* justified or even infallible. The whole idea of foundationalism is that justificatory claims in a certain domain terminate in a single unified foundation (Fumerton and Hasan 2010). The concept of foundations was always at 'the centre' of Western thought; however, the postmodern critique questioned it, and foundations themselves have been questioned. No one is prepared to defend any longer a strong foundationalist position, à la Descartes for example, where the cogito constitutes basic innate knowledge and the centred self is seen as the foundation of all conscious experience. The most direct stance of critique of foundations is the anti-foundationalist position, meaning 'no foundations', that is, no fundamental belief or principle which is the basic ground or foundation of inquiry and knowledge. Anti-foundationalism describes a constellation of approaches that shares some common features, like anti-essentialism, historicity, contingency, anti-totalisation, oppressiveness of foundations and so on. In political theory especially, anti-foundationalism considers foundations a threat to otherness, particularity and individuality and, therefore, emancipation can occur only by resisting foundational claims (Marchart 2007: 11–13). Most frequently, anti-foundationalism in political theory is associated with the work of Rorty, Lyotard, Baudrillard and Foucault in some interpretations.

Cosmopolitanism cannot be anti-foundational. A potential anti-foundational cosmopolitanism would have to stress the ineluctability of pure differences and the impossibility of totality or universality. A cosmopolitanism of pure differences, without a minimal 'common bond of humanity' has not yet been formulated because cosmopolitanism depends upon some constellation of assumptions attributed to all human beings. Cosmopolitanism cannot avoid positing some grounds about all human beings or about the world as a whole, but this does not mean that grounds postulated by cosmopolitanism are inviolable or non-contestable. On the contrary, the grounds of cosmopolitanism have to be opened to 'permanent questioning and 'life in problematicity', and cosmopolitanism of dissent offers a glimpse of how this happens.

Dissent says 'No' to the power and to its foundations, and usually advances a new ground for 'Another world'. But one cannot dissent once and for all, and the new ground will not be the ultimate one – it will be contestable as well. Dissent as permanent questioning can be articulated exactly because contingent foundations are created or posited as 'absolute' over and over again. Accepting the contingent character of foundations does not render dissent impossible; on the contrary, it enhances dissent and makes it perpetual, as a 'permanent questioning'. Cosmopolitanism of dissent presupposes a contestation of the power and withdrawal of the ground of any political power and, indirectly, of any ground. The crucial step here is that cosmopolitanism reveals itself as grounded in dissent. Through questioning of the given, the local and the particular, cosmopolitanism keeps open the possibility of 'true' universality and points to the human subject's fundamental openness.

Cosmopolitanism grounded in dissent 'qualifies' as a post-foundational approach to foundations (Caraus 2015a, 2015b, 2016a, 2016b), that is, a constant interrogation of metaphysical figures of foundation, such as totality, universality, essence and ground. For the post-foundational perspective in political theory exemplified by a variety of contemporary authors, mainly in the continental tradition – Claude Lefort, Jacques Derrida, Ernesto Laclau, Chantal Mouffe, Jan Luc Nancy, Alain Badiou, Georgio Agamben, Jacques Rancière, William Connolly, Stephen K. White, Étienne Balibar and other authors (Marchart 2007) – the function of grounding does not disappear, nor is the ground negated as in some versions of anti-foundationalism. The grounding still occurs by way of a constant withdrawal of ground, and the moment of a definite and final foundation will never be achieved. Post-foundationalism still stresses the necessity for grounds, but every ground will necessarily fail to be an ultimate ground, because the very absence of an ultimate ground makes possible a plurality of foundational attempts. If withdrawal of the ground means that the ultimate ground will never be achieved, this does not impede the plurality of foundational attempts to become grounds. It is exactly the absence of an ultimate ground that makes grounds in the plural possible. This shift in analysis is from the 'actually existing' foundations to their status and conditions of possibility. What is problematic is not the existence of foundations in the plural, but their ontological status, which is seen now as 'necessarily contingent' (Marchart 2007: 15). The concept of 'necessary contingency' means that society is always constituted in the eternal move between attempts at some form of grounding and the failure of such efforts due to the radical contingency underlying all experiences. Contingency, argues Marchart, is part of our intellectual horizon marked by an increased 'awareness of contingency', and the key operational term within the theoretical paradigm of post-foundationalism (2007: 26–30). From this perspective, cosmopolitanism cannot be otherwise than post-foundational: it cannot be advanced without assuming a universal ground, although the assumed universal ground will fail or will be contingent. At the same time, cosmopolitanism cannot be reduced only to this failed ground; it is co-substantial with freedom that makes possible the plural attempts to offer an 'ultimate' cosmopolitan foundation.

Apparently, there is nothing particularly new in the concept of post-foundational cosmopolitanism or in the concept of post-foundationalism in general. Virtually all late twentieth-century thought is post-foundational, in the sense of a rejection of absolute foundations for ethics, science, truth and so on. Indeed, the post-foundational stance might appear as the 'natural' precondition of carrying on the task of much of what is currently going on in the humanities and social sciences. Currently, most of us believe that our social and political order is the outcome of a contingent series of events without higher purpose, direction or meaning. Like Molière's character who discovers that he was speaking in prose all his life without knowing it, we realise that we are all post-foundational now and, indeed, there may be a 'banality' of post-foundationalism in our theoretical and existential endeavours. Apart from this 'discovery', cosmopolitanism could have been thought of in a post-foundational manner from inception. Unlike any other concepts within the field of political philosophy, cosmopolitanism, in its expressions during history since the Ancient Cynics, had an unmistakable function of de-grounding the order of society in the name of the ideal order of the cosmos. From its very first stance, cosmopolitanism was a dissenting gesture; however, this original dissent of cosmopolitanism was well hidden, as the next chapter will show.

WHEN PERMANENT QUESTIONING STOPS

In testing the concept of cosmopolitanism of dissent in different episodes of dissent around the world, a particular case could not be left out of the picture: that of Aung San Suu Kyi's protests against military rule in Burma (Caraus 2014b). It was a non-Western case of dissent performed by a woman – two powerful reasons to include the case in the research conducted. Aung San Suu Kyi (hereafter referred to as Suu Kyi) was under house arrest for fifteen years between July 1989 and November 2010 and has been called a 'national hero' in her country, but also a global 'human rights icon' and 'goddess of democracy' (Kyaw 2007). In 1991, she received the Nobel Peace Prize for 'her nonviolent struggle for democracy and human rights', 'profound simplicity', 'visionary idealism' and 'fearlessness' and for symbolising and mobilising what is 'the best in us'. Vaclav Havel considered that by dedicating her life to the fight for human rights and democracy in Burma, Suu Kyi spoke out for justice not only in her own country, but 'for all those who want to be free to choose their own destiny . . . whether the cry for freedom comes from Central Europe, Russia, Africa or Asia, it has a common sound: all people must be treated with dignity' (Havel, in Suu Kyi 1991: xiii).

Suu Kyi's 'revolution of the spirit' confirms the plausibility of cosmopolitanism of dissent as a practice of contesting unjust political regimes: 'When I speak about a spiritual revolution, I am talking about our struggle for democracy' (Suu Kyi 1991: 82). Her revolution, like all revolutions, aims to replace the existing law and order with a new order that will secure justice for all. The change is not required only in law and order, but in the spirit as well: 'The quintessential revolution is that of the spirit, born of an intellectual conviction of the need for change in those mental attitudes and values which shape the course of a nation's development' (1991: 183). The revolution of spirit has to be carried daily through specific means: courage, sacrifice, nonviolence and the questioning mind. Suu Kyi explains to 'her people' that 'If we want democracy, we need to show courage' (1991: 219). One of her famous quotes is that 'it is not power that corrupts but fear' (1991: 180). Courage is a synonym for 'freedom from fear', an expression which Suu Kyi takes from the Preamble to the Declaration of Human Rights, and which does not mean fearlessness, which might be a gift, but courage acquired through endeavour, and which could be a precondition for the willingness to sacrifice oneself required to inaugurate democracy. Another compulsory ingredient of the revolution of spirit is nonviolence. Suu Kyi objects to the use of violence because 'it would perpetuate a tradition of changing the political situation through force of arms' (Suu Kyi 2008: 114). The revolution of spirit as non-violence does not mean passivity, but ongoing activity through questioning: 'Our principal task is to encourage the need in people to question the situation and not just accept everything' (2008: 167). Thus, courage as the absence of fear is expressed through questioning. Many people just accept things out of either fear or inertia, says Suu Kyi but 'the readiness to accept without question has to be removed. And it's very un-Buddhist. After all, the Buddha did not accept the status quo without questioning it' (2008: 167). Her argument that questioning is a Buddhist activity might not be doctrinally correct, but it confirms the 'permanent questioning' of an act of dissent.

The revolution of spirit is Suu Kyi's vision of dissent. Dissent coincides with the revolutionary call towards the radical change of the spirit and of the existing order. If implementing democracy and rights requires courage, sacrifice and a questioning mind, in other words, a demanding revolution of the spirit, then the legacy of this concrete episode of dissent for a possible theory of cosmopolitanism is the claim that cosmopolitanism requires a change of attitude and a permanent questioning. As well, cosmopolitanism can be detected at the 'content' of her views: 'The challenge we now face is for the different nations and peoples of the world to agree on a basic set of human values, which will serve as a unifying force in the development of a genuine global community' (Suu Kyi 2008: 270). By affirming the necessity of universal principles, Suu Kyi maintains that these are not just the West's values, although human rights were quite recently enforced in a Western world that had suffered devastation from the Second World War. Her argument is that, in its most basic form, the concept of human rights is not just a Western idea but common to all major cultures. Not only can the values that democracy and human rights seek to promote be found in many cultures, but also the 'support for strong government and dictatorship can be found in all cultures both Eastern and Western' (2008: 266).

Suu Kyi generalises the significance of her struggle in cosmopolitan terms: 'the quest for democracy in Burma is the struggle of a people to live whole, meaningful lives as free and equal members of the world community' (Suu Kyi 1991: 200). She explains that she sees the award of the Nobel Peace Prize as recognition that 'the oppressed and the isolated in Burma were also a part of the world . . . recognising the oneness of humanity' (Suu Kyi 2008: 93). She has seen herself as 'part of a procession, a dynamic process, doing all that we can to move towards more good and justice'. For Suu Kyi, our duties go beyond duties to our fatherland: 'Since we live in this world, we have the duty to do our best for the world' (2008: 91). Similarly, 'the world's population could be made to realise that self-interest (whether of an individual, a community or a nation) cannot be divorced entirely from the interests of others' (Suu Kyi 1991: 244). The activities of governments and institutions that influence public opinion and set international standards of behaviour must lead to the understanding that 'No country can survive by itself. No country can be an island unto itself. We know that. And we want to live in a world where each country is linked to the others through bonds of humanity' (Suu Kyi 2008: 109).

However, once seen as a symbol of hope by the entire world, in the last few years the human rights icon has been criticised for her reluctance to condemn the offensive against Kachin civilians and the actions against Rohingya Muslims in Burma's Rakhine state that have resulted in a humanitarian crisis in the region.[2] She was accused of failing to protect Myanmar's Rohingya Muslims from persecution and of 'legitimising genocide' in Myanmar, and all her explanations of the situation have been criticised as insincere.[3] Critics remind her exactly of the cosmopolitan stance she had in the dissent period: 'Lady, you no longer belong only to the NLD or to "Burma". Speak for all humankind. So that all concerned will be touched by the better angels of our nature.'[4] Different awards and honorary positions held by Suu Kyi were withdrawn as a punishment for her 'betrayal' of the ideals she once vehiculated. Critics urge her to return to dissent: 'Go back to your models, Mahatma Gandhi and Martin Luther King Jr. You know in your heart what they would do in your situation'.[5] Suu Kyi's dissent revealed the incontestable capacity of dissident practices to affirm universality and common bonds of humanity. But cosmopolitanism is a fragile stance: a word, or sometimes the reluctance to say a word – but mainly to address a question – might compromise it. When permanent questioning stops, the 'Another World' seems less possible.

With this acknowledgement of the fragility of a cosmopolitan stance, my journey into searching and affirming a cosmopolitan position continued, concomitantly acknowledging other fragilities. Studying further dissent and protests movements which (apparently) confirmed my approaches of cosmopolitanism of dissent, I obviously acknowledged that movements end and even vanish. It is not plausible to expect a movement to exist forever – it is an action of protest, and it has a temporality of event. But what happened to the cosmopolitanism that I identified in an event? Did it disappear with the event as well? Or did it generate fidelity of participants that will reaffirm further the cosmopolitan moments created through protests? What happened to the radical cosmopolitics of Zapatistas or World Social Forum, whose cosmopolitanism was especially powerfully expressed (Caraus 2017; Caraus and Parvu 2017a)? Is it possible to live as before after such events for those who experienced them? One of the answers to my questions – and which even preceded them – was that movements constitute a prefiguration whose main task is 'to create and sustain within the live practice of the movement, relationships and political forms that "prefigured" and embodied the desired society' (Breines 1989: 6). But can one prefigure a cosmopolitics and then to go back affirming a local allegiance and living it? This is a painful question which prefiguration cannot appease.

The question of where and how cosmopolitanism of dissent disappears is different from a question such as 'When are activist campaigns successful?' Activist movements are successful in many cases and situations, achieving some real legal and societal changes, such as the historical precedents of abolitionist and women's suffrage movements. And even most of the cases I considered to be 'cosmopolitan dissent' were successful – the dissidents achieved regime changes, sometimes they even became presidents. But with these achievements, the cosmopolitan idea that animated their struggles was tamed, and went so far as to vanish completely. One can argue that cosmopolitanism was not the movements' direct aim, but one that I detected in them, so its vanishing should not be regarded as a contradiction of the movement itself. But then is cosmopolitanism just an invocation for achieving other more local aims?

On the other hand, the argument goes, one should not expect the cosmopolitanism of, for example, anti-neoliberal global justice movements to be successful instantaneously. These movements should be regarded as a long-term endeavour which may displace the borders of legitimacy over time and create a 'cosmopolitical horizon'. As it was argued (Arrighi et al. 1989), the events of 1848 constituted nothing short of a first world revolution, with the events of 1968 constituting a second one, spanning a geographical continuum from many European countries to the United States and to parts of Latin America and Asia, while the revolts of 2011 – with occupations emerging all over the globe, from Cairo to New York, from Barcelona to Istanbul, from Tel Aviv to Santiago de Chile – constituted another democratic 'world revolution' (Marchart 2016). However, a world revolution is not necessarily a cosmopolitan one – the 1848 as a world revolution also consolidated nation-states, while in other parts of the world created nation-states. The fact that democratic movements sometimes go beyond the nation-state does not mean than they do not come back, sometimes fortifying it. Too often the protest movements are captured by the logic and practices of state sovereignty, re-enacting sovereignty of the nation-state. When cosmopolitanism of dissent disappears, it disappears in the logic of the nation-state which acts as a countervailing force for radical democratic movements, dissolving the cosmopolitan potential. But another way of disappearing, which remains almost invisible, is the disappearance in the way we look, detect and approach it. Different approaches see in the same movement an international or transnational manifestation, while only in a very few approaches is seen a cosmopolitan expression. An event cannot plausibly be at the same time international and cosmopolitan, since 'international' presupposes the allegiance to a nation, while 'cosmopolitan' an allegiance to the world – an elementary difference but which is nevertheless overlooked, and the cosmopolitan claims are often described as international or transnational. The way of looking at and examining a nascent cosmopolitan stance is determined by the confines of the nation-state and preserves the status quo. Thus, cosmopolitanism disappears both in the logic of the nation-state and in the theoretical approaches that are not able to see beyond the international and transnational dimensions. Cosmopolitanism disappears even in the approaches that declare themselves cosmopolitan but tame the radical core inherent in the fact of being and living as a citizen of the world. Reclaiming the radical core of a cosmopolitan stance should be the task of each cosmopolitan theory since cosmopolitanism was born radical, as the next chapter 'discovers'.

NOTES

1. See Introduction, the section entitled 'Cosmopolitics'.
2. Available at <https://www.hrw.org/tag/rohingya> (last accessed 9 December 2021).
3. Available at <https://www.nytimes.com/2017/10/31/world/asia/aung-san-suu-kyi-myanmar.html> (last accessed 1 December 2021).
4. Available at <https://yourviet.blogspot.com/2012/07/indonesia-ladys-dilemma-over-myanmars.html> (last accessed 9 December 2021).
5. Available at <https://yourviet.blogspot.com/2012/07/indonesia-ladys-dilemma-over-myanmars.html> (last accessed 9 December 2021).

Chapter 2

BORN RADICAL. THEN WHAT HAPPENED?

The concept of cosmopolitanism of dissent sounded novel, pointing to a cosmopolitan practice previously unexamined. Permanent questioning and life in problematicity were plausibly leading to the concept of post-foundational cosmopolitanism. The audiences to whom I presented my findings were confirming – or at least it seemed so to me – the originality of my approach. However, soon I realised that my approach was not so novel: cosmopolitanism of dissent reiterated the first cosmopolitan stance of the Ancient Cynics who performed a sustained critique of every aspect of life, of all customs, rules, habits, unveiling the roots of every convention of life in the Greek antiquity, rejecting the polis itself as the ultimate convention and declaring themselves 'citizens of the world'. What a joy to discover that your 'novel' approach reiterates the birth of cosmopolitanism! But the joy was short and my approach susceptible to some academic malpractice: should not one look firstly at the birth of cosmopolitanism and only after that to advance 'novel' concepts? The bizarrerie is that I looked at the history of the idea of cosmopolitanism and at its birth, but dissent, negativity and radicality of the first cosmopolitan stance were not easy detectable – all were well hidden under other less dissenting accounts of the idea of cosmopolitanism. But if cosmopolitanism was indeed born through dissent, then what happen to the dissenting element, why was it so difficult to 'detect' it?

THE ANCIENT CYNICS AND THE FIRST
COSMOPOLITAN DISSENT

Cosmopolitanism was born in the Greek antiquity, in the fourth century BCE, when Diogenes the Cynic, one of the founders of Cynic philosophy, was asked where he came from, and he replied, 'I am a citizen of the world [*kosmopolitês*]' (DL 6.63), and when he said that 'The only true commonwealth' is 'as wide as the universe' (DL 6.72). Some Cynics declared themselves 'citizens of the Diogenes' (DL 6.93), while others emphasised their rootlessness: 'My homeland is not one tower, nor one roof, but the citadel and home of the whole world is ready for us to inhabit' (DL 6.98).

Diogenes was the first to declare himself a citizen of the world, a position also explained through the real facts of his life. Diogenes was born in Sinope and died at Corinth in 323 BC. His father minted coins for a living and, according to the legend, Diogenes falsified some coins. His father, as the person responsible for minting coins, was imprisoned and died. Diogenes was sent into exile, as a punishment, and was living in Athens as a stateless and exiled person (Branham and Goulet-Cazé 1996; Desmond 2008). Thus, these two facts – exile and the defacing of the value of currency – are considered the circumstances that determined the birth of cosmopolitanism.

Exile was a significant punishment in the Greek antiquity, since it prevented the condemned person from using the law courts, temples, agora, and assembly and public buildings. The exiled could not buy and sell in the marketplace or transact business, he could not vote, defend himself in court, and he could not offer sacrifice to the gods, thereby angering them (Desmond 2008: 113–15). According to the exegetes, Diogenes' own experience of exile is transformed into the foundation of his liberty. When someone reproached Diogenes with his exile, he replied: 'No, it was through that, you miserable fellow, that I came to be a philosopher' (DL 6.49). Or when someone reminded him that the people of Sinope had sentenced him to exile, 'And I them', said he, 'to home-staying' (DL 6.49). The acceptance of exile as a way of life appears a crucial component of the first cosmopolitan stance. His freedom from conventions and local identity implies freedom of movement across different types of borders, physical and moral. Diogenes' capacity to act and speak freely is achieved by liberating himself from conventions of the polis, by refusing to accept their authority, and this is as well a result of not having a shelter, a home and a city (Gebh 2013: 73–5). Thus, his condition of exile and statelessness turned into a condition for affirmation of a broader citizenship – the cosmopolitan one.

The other crucial condition for the birth of cosmopolitanism comes from the fact of altering the value of coins. According to one legend, Diogenes went to the Delphi oracle and asked 'what he should do to gain the greatest reputation' (DL 6.21). The answer he received from gods was to alter the currency (*nomisma*) (DL 6.20–1). In deciphering the oracle, Diogenes assumed further and endorsed philosophically his action of falsifying coins. The principle 'Alter the currency' or 'Change the value of the currency' is regarded as the most fundamental Cynic principle (Branham 1994). *Nomisma* means not only 'currency', but also nomos, law, custom, so the principle implies changing the custom, rules, habits, conventions, laws and the polis itself, as the ultimate convention. The change implies adopting a critical standpoint towards all these conventions, which have to be criticised in order to clear the way for a 'life according to nature' (DL 6.71).

Cynics' life according to nature rather than to nomos has been described as simplicity of natural desire, the bounty of the natural world and man's natural fitness for his environment (Desmond 2008). The natural life of the Cynic is the life of a dog (*kynikos*), which does in public, in front of everyone, what only dogs and animals do. In their deeds and behaviour, Cynics performed private activities assigned to the household, like eating, sleeping, urinating and so on, in the public space and under the eyes of the others, challenging the social norms and the order of society. However, the Cynic bare life is not a life that has embraced animal embodiment. It is not an animal life, generating an 'animal cosmopolitanism' (Haslanger 2015), but it is a form that the Cynics give to their life through poverty, humility and destitution. The Cynic's dog life is a life of a guard which barks at enemies, which knows how to distinguish the good from the bad and the true from the false.

Through a sustained critique of every aspect of life, Cynics unveiled the roots of every convention of life in the Greek antiquity. Metaphorically speaking, cosmopolitanism in its first instance was a total and radical defacing of the 'political currency' (Gebh 2013). Cosmopolitanism was born in a sustained act of unveiling and shaking the roots, and the radicality of this act generated a dispute as to whether Diogenes proposes a merely dismissive and negative account of cosmopolitanism or an affirmative one.

The scholars who claim that Cynic cosmopolitanism was a form of nay-saying argue that when Diogenes claimed to be 'a citizen of the world', he allegedly just said 'I am not a Sinopean, or an Athenian, or an Elean, or a Theban, or a citizen of any particular polis' (Baldry 1965: 108) or in other words, the Cynic is '*apolis* before he is a *kosmopolitês*' (Baker 2018: 616). Allegedly, the Cynics just try to see 'how far their Natural Man was also Universal Man' (Baldry 1965: 101), without proclaiming a universal polity. The Cynic as the natural man is a vagabond with no fixed abode, and even if nature is his only address, 'he is not at home in every city, on the contrary he is indifferent to them all' (Baldry 1965: 108). Thus, one cannot ascribe to the Cynics the vision of all mankind living together 'like a flock', 'an all-embracing society of all men' (Baldry 1965: 101). Finally, the Cynic cosmopolitanism cannot unite the human race given their 'community of wise'. Although the Cynic, in advance of most fourth-century thought, ignores the traditional barriers that make female inferior to male, slave to master, foreigner to Greek, the Cynic draws a single great dividing line separating 'the few wise men from the many fools' (Baldry 1965: 110).

There are reasons to doubt that Cynic cosmopolitanism was merely a form of nay-saying, or one separating the few wise men from the many fools. If Diogenes' point were merely negative, he could have said, 'I am without a city [*apolis*]' but he affirmed a wider allegiance (Moles 1995, 1996) and 're-stamp[ed] law as the law of the cosmos' (Paone 2018: 492). Also, Diogenes' saying was not formulated in a vacuum but in a tradition of authors from antiquity who also rejected the fatherland and the polis, while Diogenes went further by affirming that he was a citizen of the cosmos. Further, the Cynics' critique of the polis was a necessary step towards affirming their 'freedom from inessentials' as 'a condition of positive freedom' (Moles 1996: 109). Finally, the accusation of elitism and of the division between a handful of wise men and the majority of fools is easily rejected given the Cynics' attempt to achieve a reputation for *philanthropia*, benevolence towards their fellow men, in spite of the general contempt for the mob (Moles 1996: 119), which is part of their critique of what it means to be human. The dispute is ongoing and the question of how a total critique of every aspect of the Greek polis could lead to the statement, 'I am a citizen of the world', still does not have a final answer.

Foucault in his famous reading of the Cynics as heroes of *parrhesia* (Foucault 2011) offered a plausible unravelling of this dispute, although not directly engaging in it (Caraus 2021). Foucault finds a positive side in taking all negations to their extreme consequences: for the Cynic, the negations are necessary in order 'to exercise, in a positive way, the positive mission he has been given' (2011: 301). The negativity of the initial condition which comes from the principle 'Alter the currency!' turns into positivity the mission to care for humankind. In their ways of life, Cynics construct bonds with the whole of humanity and become militants which act as 'functionar[ies] of humanity in general' and 'functionar[ies] of ethical universality', effects which for Foucault are 'nothing other than the reverse, positive side of his necessary detachment' (Foucault 2011: 301).

For Foucault, the Cynics' negation of this life and this world is the condition for another life and another world. The alteration of the currency and the change of its value mean that the forms and habits of existence must be replaced, that 'life led by men in general and by philosophers in particular should be *an other* life' (2011: 244). Further, the principle of an other life becomes an 'aspiration for *an other* world' (2011: 278) as the objective of the Cynic practice:

> The Cynic addresses all men. He shows all men that they are leading a
> life other than the one they should be leading. And thereby it is a whole

other world which has to emerge, or at any rate be on the horizon, be the objective of this Cynic practice. (2011: 315)

The content of another life and another world is never specified by Foucault's Cynics – their militancy aims to raise in all men an awareness similar to the famous World Social Forum's call that 'Another World Is Possible'. And in this awareness, the negation of the current world becomes an affirmation of the horizon of another world. Thus, from Foucault's perspective, the militant Cynic concomitantly negates this world and affirms *an other* world, making a negative-affirmative stance. However, the Cynic positivity is not dialectical – we do not have in Cynics a negation of the negation mediated by the universal. There is no transition of opposites into each other and no universal manifestation of the law of the unity and struggle of opposites. In assessing a wrong and an injustice in the existing polis, one cannot reconcile it with justice. Similarly, when detecting a vice or a fault in the local customs, one cannot reconcile it with a virtue. It is more plausible to argue that the Cynic arrives at his mission to care for humanity by a continuous 'affirmation of the negation' (Baker 2018: 618), otherwise, looking for a balance of negative and positive one risks eliminating the negative radical core of the birth of cosmopolitanism, a core which needs to be retained.

This discussion about the negative or positive cosmopolitanism of the Cynics reiterates the tension between the permanent questioning and the affirmation of human rights that many commentators identified in Patočka's philosophy (see Chapter 1). But this is not the only common feature of cosmopolitanism of dissent and Cynics' cosmopolitanism.[1] 'Permanent questioning', 'living in problematicity' and 'shaken solidarities' – all my Patočkian inspired elements of the minimalist framework for conceiving a non-totalising theory of cosmopolitanism – were already present in the first cosmopolitan stance.

The 'Alter the currency!' principle performs the permanent questioning motive. The alteration of the currency and its values is an ongoing de-grounding move of all conventions of life in the polis. The alteration of values leads to the shaking of the 'naïve given meaning' (Patočka 1996: 77), and the Cynics' way of life is an outstanding example of living in and with problematicity of meaning. Even more, the Cynics uncover the problematicity of all meanings with their own life by practicing endurance, poverty, self-renunciation, destitution. By accepting destitutions, insults and blows, the Cynics appear stronger than the others who live in the comfort of conventions. In order to be able to accept the meaning as a quest for meaning, both the Cynics and the Eastern

European dissidents aim to live a 'life in truth'. And in both cases the 'true life' is not a life with a finally found absolute meaning, but a life in a perpetual quest for meaning and the 'care for the soul', achieved only through a radical transformation, a 'conversion of historic proportions' (Patočka 1998: 77).

Another crucial common feature is the fact that cosmopolitanism was born as a practice from below, and dissent is also a practice from below. The Cynics had a broad presence in society. Cobblers, joiners, fullers and wool carders, if they decided to become philosophers, could join the Cynic school, although one qualifies as a Cynic only after a long series of tests of endurance, not theoretical or doctrinal tests. The theoretical poverty of the Cynic doctrine, its thinness and the banality of its doctrinal teachings, made it easy to recruit people to Cynicism (Foucault 2011: 231–3). Similarly, dissent movements are inherently from below and include all 'who find themselves in open conflict with the regime' and who become so 'through the inner logic of their thinking, behaviour, or work', and through finding the 'courage of truth' to 'expand the space available for life' (Havel 1978).

Despite similarities, I had to acknowledge a rather significant difference between cosmopolitanism of dissent and the first cosmopolitan stance: cosmopolitanism of dissent is less radical. Unlike the Cynics, dissidents do not reject entirely their allegiance to a particular polis – they usually aim at a recalibration of the existing polis in order to make it just for all its citizens. However, targeting different unjust regimes of power, cosmopolitanism of dissent may leave intact the polis and the world order based on nation-states. In the historical episodes of dissent, the dissidents invoke universal values to justify their critique of the unjust power and political regimes but, unlike the Cynics, they do not declare themselves citizens of the world. And unlike the Cynics, dissent does not state that the 'true commonwealth' is the one 'in the cosmos' (DL 6.72).

Cosmopolitanism was born radical. The etymological meaning of the word 'radical' is derived from the classical Latin word *radix* meaning 'root' (as in the root of a plant). Thus, that which is 'radical' pertains to the 'root' of something. In its development in political thought, the meaning of 'radicalism' referred to the 'roots', 'foundations' or 'origins' of something – 'To be radical is to grasp things by the roots', as Karl Marx famously wrote (Marx and Engels 1978: 60). The grasping is not for the sake of grasping roots, but to change them; thus, in its modern usage, radicalism means as well a fundamental change, especially in the political domain (McLaughlin 2012: 18). Roots, to the extent that they are not normally visible, imply an element of concealment and radicalism implies a dismantling and making visible the invisible roots, uncovering them. Therefore, some kind of destruction is always implicit in reaching the concealed roots (and radicalism has negative connotations in everyday use). Thus, to be radical is to seek to uncover the roots, foundations or origins of something, and radicalism is mainly a logic not a content.

The Cynics performed a cosmopolitical act through a radical critique which aimed at the roots of the existing polis. Radicalism might have its origins in the principle of 'Alter the currency', the Cynics being considered not only the first cosmopolitans but also the first radicals and the first anarchists (Desmond 2008: 184–8).[2] But if cosmopolitanism was born radical, then what happened, where did radicalism disappear to?

BORN RADICAL, BUT THEN WHAT HAPPEN?

My findings about cosmopolitan aspects of different dissenting episodes sounded 'new' on the background of a general understanding of cosmopolitanism mainly as 'cosmopolitan', both as a noun: 'someone who has experience of many different parts of the world' and as an adjective: 'containing people and things from many different parts of the world, or having experience of many different places and things'.[3] The academic dominant approach of cosmopolitanism is not very different from this traditional understanding. The birth of cosmopolitanism through radical dissent and negativity seems forgotten: 'cosmopolitanism has been identified with a great variety of positive visions that, despite their many differences, share a forgetting of the negations of Cynicism that enabled cosmopolitanism' (Baker 2018: 620). Why was the birth of cosmopolitanism 'forgotten'? And how was it possible to ignore the Cynics' birth of cosmopolitanism?

It is plausible to affirm that the 'forgetting' started with the cosmopolitan stance expressed after the Cynics, that of the Stoics (Baker 2018: 620). Stoicism acquired cosmopolitanism, amongst many other doctrines, from the Cynics, transforming it in the process (Dudley 1937; Pangle 1998; Sellars 2007; Bosman 2007; Desmond 2008; Dobbin 2012; Paone 2018; Allen 2020). What exactly happened in the passage from the Cynic to the Stoic cosmopolitanism is a topic of research for the scholars of the respective periods and for the historians of the ideas and political thought. Here, the passage could only be approximated in an attempt to understand how the 'forgetting' of the Cynic radicalism and negativity was possible by focusing on a particularly influential Stoic text, Cicero's *De Officiis*, considered 'foundational' for Kant's cosmopolitanism (Nussbaum 1997).

To admit that the passage itself is a legitimate object of study, one should give justice to the Cynics by admitting their inaugural moment of cosmopolitanism, which is not necessarily the case in all accounts of the idea of cosmopolitanism.[4] The commentators who credit the Cynics with an account of cosmopolitanism admit that Stoics drew heavily on Cynicism but smoothed out its radical iconoclasm (Bosman 2007; Ingram 2013; Baker 2018; Paome 2018; Nederman 2020b). The smoothing and extirpation of radicalism took place in stages, which correspond to the early and late Stoics. The early Stoics still retain (some of) the Cynics' radicalism (Pangle 1998; Paome 2018). Thus, Stoic cosmopolitanism was set out by Zeno (*c.*336–254 BC) in his lost book *Politeia/Republic* which 'considered all men to be of one community and one polity' with 'a common law and an order common to us all':

> All the inhabitants of this world of ours should not live differentiated by their respective rules of justice in separate cities and communities, but that we should consider all men to be of one community and one polity, and that we should have a common life and an order common to us all, even as a herd that feeds together and shares the pasturage of a common field. This Zeno wrote, giving shape to a dream or, as it were, shadowy picture of a well-ordered and philosophic commonwealth. (Plutarch quoted in Heater 1996: 13)

The very fact of conceiving a World Republic was radical then, as it is now. The lost book, as Plutarch said, gave shape to a 'dream' and a 'shadowy picture' of a well-ordered and philosophic commonwealth that still haunts political thought, while the image of all humans as a herd in the same pasture turns out to have a peculiar relevance in the current concerns for the environment and the future of the planet. Two concerns could be raised about whether Zeno's book has completed the Cynics radical cosmopolitanism with a theory of cosmopolitan institution or diminished its radicalism. First, Zeno's cosmopolis may appear as diminishing Cynic radicalism since imagining all people grazing in the same pasture could be a more consensual and less confrontational approach. Could the radical cosmopolitics of the Cynics be completed with a theory of institutional cosmopolitanism without losing its 'permanent questioning' dimension? (This worry has to wait to be addressed until Chapter 4 of this book.) The second concern is that although Zeno is credited with effectively inventing the concept of the cosmopolis, there are worries that 'the patent was transferred, as it were, from Zeno to Alexander' (Heater 1996: 13). The accusation of the 'transfer of the patent' from a philosophical approach of a World Republic to a concrete Empire have their origins in this apparently first immediate transfer: 'Zeno's "Cosmopolis", the world which is all one city, was, seemingly for Zeno himself and certainly for most other Greeks, the Greek polis extended to non-Greeks' (Pagden 2000: 5). Could a World Republic be advanced without being an Empire is, again, a question to be explored further in this book.

Interesting enough, the accounts of the history of the idea of cosmopolitanism that dismiss the legacy of the Cynics, dismiss the legacy of Zeno's cosmopolitanism as well, and the foundational role of cosmopolitanism is attributed to the Roman Stoics – early Roman (Cicero), and late Roman (Seneca, Marcus Aurelius). For example, Martha Nussbaum reclaims cosmopolitanism exclusively from the Stoics. For her, Cicero's work is the paradigm for the ancient Greco-Roman world, while *De Officiis* has a foundational value for cosmopolitanism. 'We know', affirms Nussbaum,

> that Cicero's *De Officiis*, a pivotal text in the moral philosophy of the period, was especially important to Kant at the time when he was writing the *Grundlegung* and the later ethical/political works . . . [T]the argument of the *Grundlegung* follows Cicero closely, especially in its way of connecting the idea of a universal law of nature with the idea of respect for humanity. (1997: 5)

Nussbaum is sure that

> Although Kant characteristically discusses Stoic ideas only in a brief and general way, without precise textual detail, he seems nonetheless to have been profoundly shaped by them, or at least to have found in them a deep affinity with his own unfolding ideas about cosmopolitan humanity. (1997: 5)

But Nussbaum is not just a 'for example' – she is credited with initiating the Renaissance of cosmopolitanism in political theory in 1990s,[5] and she initiated it by making Cicero the source of inspiration for Kantian cosmopolitanism, currently still dominant in political theory.

If *De Officiis* is 'foundational' for cosmopolitanism, then what can be noticed on the very first reading of Cicero's text is that there is no trace of cosmopolitan radicalism in it, or almost no trace of cosmopolitanism. But what is gained instead? What is new in the cosmopolitanism of this 'pivotal' text? Without attempting to present an exegesis of *De Officiis*, or a statement about Cicero's political philosophy in general – in the last two decades the exegesis of Cicero's work has flourished[6] – this reading aims to answer only one question: if this text is taken, as Nussbaum does, as a foundational text for cosmopolitanism, then what is in it new and different compared to Cynic cosmopolitanism? *De Officiis* (Cicero 1913) was written in 44 BC, Cicero's last year alive, when he was still trying to be active in politics. The essay was published posthumously following his assassination. The text is written in the form of letters to his son Marcus who was studying philosophy in Athens, or as the genre is called today, 'an open letter to my son'. Cicero urged his son to follow nature and wisdom, and warned against pleasure and indolence, but nonetheless it reads as if Cicero wrote with a broader audience in mind. Cicero stresses that he is writing not as a political philosopher but, rather, as a former victorious commander of Roman legions, as a former leading metropolitan statesman and successful provincial governor and as the orator of Rome (Long 1995)

De Officiis has three parts. Book I treats what is honourable in itself, and in what true manner our duties are founded in honour and virtue. Book II elaborates on duties which relate to private advantage and improvement of life, such as political advancement, attainment of wealth, power and popularity. Book III discusses the apparent conflict between virtue and expediency, and if true virtue can be put in competition with private advantage. Apparently, nothing should be accounted useful or profitable if not strictly virtuous. However, at the beginning of the third part, Cicero discloses clearly that his treatise does not in fact have as its theme true virtue practised only by the wise, but instead treats a 'second rank' of virtue or 'mean duties' (Cicero 1913: III.13.14) that makes its practitioners 'resemble' the truly moral or virtuous men in the eyes of 'the multitude' or 'the common crowd' that do not, as a rule, comprehend how far it falls short of real perfection (III.3.15). If a book on virtue admits that, in fact, it treats 'only a semblance of it' (III.14), then it is already on the other end of the spectrum of the Cynics' rejection of the semblances and conventions in the name of a 'true life' and cosmopolitanism of this treatise announces itself 'only a semblance of it' (III.14). But let's not anticipate the conclusions.

One of the main elements of Cicero's cosmopolitanism is considered to be his view on nature (see Alonso 2013) that ordains that every human being should promote the good of every other human being: 'we are all subject to a single law of nature, and if this is so we are bound not to harm anyone' (III.27–8) and which established the 'ultimate sources of the principles of fellowship and society' (I.50). So, nature establishes:

> the connection subsisting between all the members of the human race; and that bond of connection is reason and speech, which by the processes of teaching and learning, of communicating, discussing, and reasoning associate men together and unite them in a sort of natural fraternity. In no other particular are we farther removed from the nature of beasts; for we admit that they may have courage (horses and lions, for example); but we do not admit that they have justice, equity, and goodness; for they are not endowed with reason or speech. (I.50)

Another cosmopolitan element attributed to this treatise is the treatment of foreigners, leading to the idea of the brotherhood of mankind: 'who say that regard should be had for the rights of fellow-citizens, but not of foreigners, would destroy the universal brotherhood of mankind; and, when this is annihilated, kindness, generosity, goodness, and justice must utterly perish' (III.28). This is the only fragment where Cicero uses the expression 'universal brotherhood of mankind' and is considered the most cosmopolitan fragment of *De Officiis*.

The cosmopolitanism of concentric circles is considered another famous 'cosmopolitan innovation' of *De Officiis*:

> There are a great many degrees of closeness or remoteness in human society. To proceed beyond the universal bond of our common human-ity, there is the closer one of belonging to the same people, tribe, and tongue, by which men are very closely bound together; it is a still closer relation to be citizens of the same city-state; for fellow-citizens have much in common – forum, temples, colonnades, streets, statutes, laws, courts, rights of suffrage, to say nothing of social and friendly circles and diverse business relations with many. But a still closer social union exists between kindred. Starting with that infinite bond of union of the human race in general, the conception is now confined to a small and narrow circle. (I.53)

According to Nussbaum, here Cicero argues that we should regard our-selves not as devoid of local affiliations and that our task as citizens of the world will be to draw the circles somehow toward the centre 'making all human beings more like our fellow city dwellers' (Nussbaum 1997: 9). The direction of concentric circles is usually from a concrete small point – a stone thrown in the water – to larger concentric circles. In Cicero's fragment, the movement of concentric circles is in the opposite direction: it starts from the bond of human race and ends in the 'small and narrow circle' where one has stronger moral duties:

> If a contrast and comparison were to be made to find out where most of our moral obligation is due, country would come first, and parents; for their services have laid us under the heaviest obligation; next come children and the whole family, who look to us alone for support and can have no other protection. (I.58)

The concentric circle image is the basis for Cicero's view on justice and especially duties of justice that we owe to the others, both close and distant. Cicero's duties of justice are considered another element of cosmopolitanism, especially by Nussbaum, who had nevertheless to acknowledge its 'problematic legacy' (Nussbaum 2019: 18–64).

These three elements – the universal reason, the brotherhood of man-kind and concentric circles of allegiance – identified by part of the Cice-ronian scholarship as the cosmopolitan dimensions of his thinking might sound cosmopolitan but only taken from the context of the entire world view expressed in *De Officiis*. Read as a whole, *De Officiis* does not offer a cosmopolitan view on the world. Even if a fragment appears as affirming a cosmopolitan view, in the next fragment this affirmation will be contradicted by an opposite one. The passages considered cosmopoli-tan from Book I, such as I.50–1 may articulate a society of all human beings united by justice and common advantage, while the very next fragments, I.51–7, suggests that a citizen's greatest allegiance should be to his own *res publica*.[7]

All cosmopolitan elements of *De Officiis*, approached not as separate fragments but in conjunction with other fragments, have a very precari-ous cosmopolitan status. The famous 'universal brotherhood of man-kind' itself appears as a precondition for the local allegiances to flourish, because if brotherhood of humanity is destroyed, the kindness, gener-osity and goodness at the local level will be annihilated. The famous human treatment of the foreigner by Cicero is also ambiguous:

> It may not be right, of course, for one who is not a citizen to exercise the rights and privileges of citizenship; and the law on this point was secured by two of our wisest consuls . . . Still, to debar foreigners from enjoying the advantages of the city is altogether contrary to the laws of humanity. (III.46–7)

This ambiguity is fully fledged in the contemporary political philoso-phy's provisions on the foreigner: it firstly subscribes to the whole politi-cal and legal arsenal making the foreigners 'illegal', and then it adds a 'still . . . [it] is altogether contrary to the laws of humanity'.

The famous concentric circles are intricate, ambiguous and contra-dictory, but the general tone is nevertheless to focus them on the closest relationship. When the circles move beyond the extended families, these end in 'common blood bonds' and in 'ancestral tombs': 'The bonds of common blood hold men fast through good-will and affection; for it means much to share in common the same family traditions, the same forms of domestic worship, and the same ancestral tombs' (1.54) When the concentric circles go to allegiances beyond the blood bonds, they do not go beyond the community of friends since we owe 'the com-munity of living, giving counsel, speeches, exhortations, consolation, and sometimes even reproof, most to friends' (I.50). The special status of friends in Cicero's other writings[8] have an echo in *De Officiis*, and while Cicero's view on friendship as a complex system of relations that

condition who we are and how we can act is worthy of full consider-
ation, seen from the perspective of cosmopolitanism, friendship does
not have cosmopolitan potential. Apparently advancing a cosmopolitan
argument on how nature produced all things for the common use of
mankind, Cicero reduces mankind to friends:

> Since the resources of individuals are limited and the number of the needy
> is infinite, this spirit of universal liberality must be regulated according to
> that test of Ennius – 'No less shines his' – in order that we may continue
> to have the means for being generous to our friends. (I.52)

The non-cosmopolitan topics and arguments of *De Officiis* are overwhelmingly more numerous than the cosmopolitan ones. It is more plausible to see in *De Officiis* an incipient theory of international relations
than a theory of cosmopolitanism, since several international relations
topics originated in this book (I.34–8), for example it is credited with the
invention of just war theory (Pangle 1998). For Nussbaum (1997: 11),
the discussion on just war is part of the Stoics' cosmopolitanism that
'requires certain international limitations upon the conduct of warfare
in general, the renunciation of aggression and the resort to force only
in self-defence, when all discussion has proven futile'. But this confuses
the attribute 'cosmopolitan', which sees humans as citizens of the world,
with 'international', which see humans as citizens of a nation. Thinking
'just war' regulations presupposes an entirely non-cosmopolitan view
on the world divided into separate units ready to go to war for different warriors' reasons, with one quite important reason specified in
De Officiis being the war for glory. The term 'the law of nations' that
appeared firstly in *De Officiis* – *natura, id est iure gentium* (III.23) –
confirms the default non-cosmopolitan vision of the text: the 'law of
nature', considered an element of Cicero's cosmopolitan, reveals itself to
be no more than the law of nations (Pangle 1998). Cicero's expression
was extensively discussed by Hugo Grotius, Samuel von Pufendorf and
other international relations theorists who drew on *De Officiis* in their
work. The ambiguous and contradictory affirmations of cosmopolitanism converge naturally and plausibly in an incipient international relations treatise. The problem is that this work passed as 'foundational' for
cosmopolitanism, and in this way, it not only eliminated the radicalism
of the cosmopolitanism birth but damaged the idea of cosmopolitanism
for two millennia.

If *De Officiis* is to be taken as a 'pivotal' moment for cosmopolitanism, as Nussbaum does, then only as a reaction against cosmopolitanism as it was born, transforming it in such a way as to make the initial
idea unrecognisable. It is plausible, as Pangle (1998) notes, that Cicero

distanced himself from the earlier versions of cosmopolitan Stoicism, and even looked to eradicate completely the legacy of the Cynics, by addressing aspects previously rejected by the Cynics and earlier Stoicism: denigration of the virtues of local citizenship, statesmanship and patriotism (Pangle 1998). Now cosmopolitanism is associated more with the Ciceronian murky waters of concentric circles of allegiance than with the fact of being a citizen of the world by altering its 'currency' and 'living in truth'. The transformations of the initial idea are significant and could be presented in terms of a 'before' and 'after' picture.

In the 'after' *De Officiis* picture, the Cynic cosmopolitan agency from below disappears and it is replaced by an agency from above, represented by the addressees of this text – the young Romans who are about to begin their careers as administrators of the imperial system. Goodness requires serving other human beings as best one can, but serving all human beings equally well is impossible, since the 'resources of individuals are limited and the number of the needy is infinite' (I.52). The motivating idea is to help human beings, and sometimes the best way to do that is to serve as a teacher or as a political advisor in some foreign place. In this fashion, 'the Stoics introduce clear, practical content to their metaphor of the cosmopolis: a cosmopolitan considers moving away in order to serve, whereas a non-cosmopolitan does not' (Kleingeld and Brown 2019). In this way, the cosmopolitanism of travelling elite was born, and it will be always a 'stain' on every attempt to think about and advance a cosmopolitan view of the world. The original cosmopolitical agency from below has been resurrected very rarely, but in a powerful way, as happened in the emergency of the proletariat, described in Marx's (not Marxist) texts, and, in some degree, in the cosmopolitanism of social movement from the last three decades, which I examined from the perspective of cosmopolitanism of dissent. Marx considered the proletariat an expression of the dissolution of all classes and nationalities:

> The communist revolution is . . . carried through by the class which no longer counts as a class in society, is not recognised as a class, and is in itself the expression of the dissolution of all classes, nationalities, etc. within present society. (Marx and Engels 1974: 94)

The Cynics and the proletariat share the same material preconditions for their action. The Cynics have to renounce everything and accept poverty and destitution, while 'The proletarians have nothing to lose but their chains', as the *Communist Manifesto* says (Marx and Engles 1978: 500). The proletariat constitutes the universal non-class of history – a negative universality invoked by the Cynics and which made possible their identification as citizens of the universe.[9]

Another transformation is the fact that the public nature of the Cynics' cosmopolitanism is replaced by a more private pursuit. Acquiring a Cynic cosmopolitan stance is not an act of individualism or private advantage for at least two reasons. First, the Cynics contest all conventions, including the difference between public and private: the Cynics live in the public space and perform in public all the activities deemed for the private space. It is less plausible to consider a Cynic act as a private, individual act since it is not made only for the individual single experience but for the experience of all, be it only the experience of provoking or disgusting the others. Second, the Cynics' main stake, as defined by Foucault, is to live in truth, *parrhesia*, which is not an individual or private stake: *parrhesia* takes place in public space. Therefore, cosmopolitanism could not be born otherwise than through an enlarged intersubjective stance, and it is exactly this intersubjectivity as an extended self that is presupposed every time cosmopolitanism is considered very demanding, or is associated with philanthropy and charity, or with responsibility towards the other (see Chapter 7). The addressees of Cicero's 'letters to his son' also need the others, but for their own glory. The young Romans need the state where they can perform the services to bring glory, and for greater glory the state has to be bigger, thus expandable in to an empire:

> Those, then, whose office it is to look after the interests of the state . . . must strive, too, by whatever means they can, in peace or in war, to advance the state in power, in territory, and in revenues. Such service calls for great men; it was commonly rendered in the days of our ancestors; if men will perform duties such as these, they will win popularity and glory for themselves and at the same time render eminent service to the state. (II.85)

Another change that happens in the transition from the Cynics' cosmopolitanism to Cicero's 'pivotal' text is the move from a cosmopolitanism of 'having nothing' to a pursuit of advantages. The Cynics have to renounce everything – no clothes, no shelter, no family, no native land – all these have to be renounced in order to be able to care for the others, since the Cynics care for the self only to the extent they care for the others. Cicero's addressee, on the contrary, should keep everything he has:

> Everything assigned as private property by the statutes and by civil law shall be so held as prescribed by those same laws, everything else shall be regarded in the light indicated by the Greek proverb: 'Amongst friends all things in common.' (I.51)

Even what is not private property is not for all, but for friends only. Cicero's cosmopolitanism appears as the first instance of what Marx will call 'bourgeois cosmopolitanism' – one of consumption and indulgence, and of 'new needs for the products from new lands and climes' (Marx and Engels 1978: 476). The young Roman administrators also need new lands and properties, for the glory of the state and for their own glory since they 'must strive, too, by whatever means they can, in peace or in war, to advance the state in power, in territory, and in revenues' (II.85). The expansion of the market, as Marx argues, gave birth to the hypocritical 'bourgeois cosmopolitanism' that exploits the entire world, less for the glory of the bourgeois, more for the inner logic of the capital itself, but the augmentation of the republic in territory, and in revenues is done precisely for the personal glory of 'great men' serving a 'great republic'.

The augmentation of the republic in territory and in revenues brought another transformation to Cynic cosmopolitanism which will be a large, ugly stain on each cosmopolitan approach: a shift from rejection of every convention of your own polis towards affirming and expanding the conventions of your polis to the entire world. The Cynics dismantled every convention of the city, so they could make an allegiance with the cosmos. Only by rejection of the polis could the cosmopolis be imagined as a just polis for everyone. Stoicism as it emerged from Cicero's works or from Seneca's varied corpus explicitly acknowledges that obligations to Rome are far more important than obligations to the cosmos. The young Roman administrators should not reject anything from their polis; on the contrary, they have to expand and multiply it for 'popularity and glory for themselves' and 'eminent service to the state' (II.85). Nussbaum tries to justify Cicero's augmentation of the republic with an Empire as a 'political side' of cosmopolitanism: 'In the Roman world the directly political side of cosmopolitanism could come into its own in a very practical way as Roman Stoic philosophers had a major influence on the conduct of political life' (Nussbaum 1997: 11). However, even she admits that Cicero did not escape the imperial idea: 'the Stoics did not and could not conclude, as Kant does, that colonial conquest is morally unacceptable. Cicero tries to moralize the Roman imperial project but without much success' (Nussbaum 1997: 14). Legitimated by philosophers such as Cicero, it was very easy for many Romans to identify the Roman *patria* with the cosmopolis itself (Kleingeld and Brown 2019), and this is the anti-cosmopolitan legacy of Cicero and the Stoics that overshadows all other alleged cosmopolitan elements. Thus, if one maintains that *De Officiis* is a 'pivotal' text for cosmopolitanism, as Nussbaum does, then it can be done only by reversing the Cynics' idea of a citizen of the universe into a private pursuit of the elite looking to exploit the world for their own benefits and, under a disguised cosmopolis, to extend their country into a universal empire.

Therefore, cosmopolitanism attributed to Cicero inaugurated a very serious problem for the political theory of cosmopolitanism – its association with imperialism. If today cosmopolitanism can be defined without hesitation by some authors in terms of imperialism – '[I]f we wished to capture the essence of cosmopolitanism in a single formula, it would be this. It is a discourse of the universal that is inherently local – a locality that is always surreptitiously imperial' (Brennan 1997: 81) – then one has the measure of the degree of 'forgetting' that cosmopolitanism is possible only by negating and rejecting the local and that it was born this way.

The bewildering question 'If cosmopolitanism was born radical, then what happened?' has an answer: then Cicero's *De Officiis* came, which was considered a foundational text for cosmopolitanism. However, the fact that *De Officiis* is considered foundational for cosmopolitanism is the 'achievement' of its readers, not of the text itself.[10] The huge influence of *De Officiis* through the centuries[11] and the lack of other sources elaborating on how to live in the world as a whole could have made this text appear to have a 'cosmopolitan' ingredient, among many other ingredients. The fact that the *fin de siècle* Renaissance of cosmopolitanism in political theory was inaugurated by Nussbaum's writings declaring Cicero's and the Stoics' texts 'foundational' for cosmopolitanism points again to the same need to clarify how we should live in a just way in the world as a whole. This became urgent at the end of the Cold War, and political theory was unprepared to address it. So, the invocation of the Stoic origins had to fill the gaps and veil the poverty of political philosophy, and it appeared credible to many. It is not by accident that all the 'spirit' the Stoic cosmopolitanism could inspire recently were oxymoronic, patriotic, statist and moderated versions of cosmopolitanism. There were nevertheless voices pointing out that the current various revivals of Stoic cosmopolitanism cannot but help the criticism of cosmopolitanism (Pangle 1998: 261). Perhaps, 'Cicero's quasi-cosmopolitanism' (Nederman 2020b: 3) is still a too generous label, since Nussbaum herself, after more than two decades, discovered the 'problematic legacy' of Cicero's *De Officiis* and the 'two tensions' in Stoic cosmopolitanism (Nussbaum 2019: 18–64, 65–97). This discovery of tensions in Stoic cosmopolitanism entitles Nussbaum to declare cosmopolitanism 'a noble but flawed ideal' (Nussbaum 2019), which reveals that for her there is no other cosmopolitanism except the Stoic one, and if this fails, then all cosmopolitanism is 'flawed'. After two decades of positioning herself – and being considered by others – as a cosmopolitan author, Nussbaum declares it 'flawed', and this label has the action of a boomerang coming back to cover the entire work of a 'cosmopolitan' author that enunciates it. Now it is time to get rid of the Nussbaum–Ciceronian legacy and to think again about how to live in one world.

Cosmopolitanism was born radical, and the original negative core of Cynics – contestation of the polis and of all its conventions – was tamed, ignored, hidden and finally 'forgotten'. But the 'forgotten' radical cosmopolitics of the Cynics resurrects in the very logic and ontology of cosmopolitanism.

COSMOPOLITAN ONTOLOGY OR THE COSMOS 'HAUNTING' THE POLIS

Cosmopolitanism was born radical, and it could not be otherwise. Only a naked, homeless and profoundly anti-social exiled Cynic could be the first to call himself a citizen of the world (Baker 2018: 620). Cosmopolitanism could not have come into being without this first negation of the polis, without distancing from the current polis perceived as unjust or corrupt. If the polis – as the Stoics' *patria* – is perceived as great and one attempts to shine in its glory, the contestation of the polis is less probable. Starting with the first stance, cosmopolitanism is enabled by a certain degree of negation of the polis and of its conventions. This core of the Cynic cosmopolitics is in every instance of cosmopolitanism, both as its logic and its ontology. As Ingram argued, what cosmopolitans have in common lies not at the level of the content of their ideas, but at the level of form – a 'kind of interruption' (Ingram 2013: 7). In its theoretical or practical instantiation, cosmopolitanism emerges inevitably as a disaffiliation and disidentification from the local and the given, a negation of the particular, a challenge to constituted forms of authority, legitimacy and belonging. A cosmopolitan stance interrogates given meanings and understandings, calling for another type of politics with higher standards of justice. Starting with its Cynic origins, this act of disruption, which for Ingram constitutes the logic of cosmopolitanism, is displayed in the Christian, Enlightenment, economic, Kantian and revolutionary versions of cosmopolitanisms, through its post-Second World War revival and *fin de siècle* renaissance in the 1990s (Ingram 2013: 48–51). The denigratory views of cosmopolitans as 'rootless, non-patriotic profiteers with no roots and no conscience', 'damaging the unity of the nation' and 'poisoning our culture'[12] confirm the fact that an affirmation of cosmopolitanism causes a disruption of the life in polis.

I 'detected' this disruption at the core of each cosmopolitan stance while trying to map the cosmopolitan ontology (Caraus 2016b). Ontology traditionally referred to Being – the idea of Being-as-ground – and was remote from political concerns. The 'turn to ontology' in contemporary political theory argues that there is an inevitable ontological dimension in every theoretical endeavour to construct a political theory (White 2000). In our theorising we do not stop making ontological commitments, by advancing a set of entities assumed as basic. This set of entities, called an 'ontological constellation' or 'ontological template' (White 2000: 45, 49), is different from author to author. Although the set of entities postulated by 'weak ontologies' (White 2000) does not include human nature, God, universal reason, telos and so on as 'strong' traditional ontologies did, the weak versions of ontology nevertheless contain some existential realities that are not simply a matter of choice (White 2000: 8–9), since we are in a world that is not entirely our choosing, such as possessing a language or being mortal. The turn to ontology is part of the post-foundational political theory which regards foundations as 'fundamental and contestable' (White 2000: 6). The 'fundamental' dimension allows us 'the affirmative gesture of constructing foundations', while the contestability 'prevents us from carrying them in [a] traditional way' (White 2000: 8).

If in affirming a theory one makes a commitment to the existence of certain entities, then what are the ontological commitments made by theorists of cosmopolitanism? If all political theories contain an ontology, then what is the ontology of cosmopolitan political theories? What are the basic entities that these theories assume to exist? The answer to these questions should be found in the theories of cosmopolitanism which, as in all political theories, cannot avoid 'secreting' a cosmopolitan ontology, while theorists cannot avoid making ontological commitments. However, theorists of cosmopolitanism do not state explicitly what their 'ontological templates' are, with the exception of Benhabib who asks what the ontological status of cosmopolitan norms is (Benhabib 2006: 26). Her answer is that such norms and principles create a 'universe of meaning, values, and social relations that had not existed before . . . They found a new order – a *novo ordo saeculorum*' (Benhabib 2006: 72). However, Benhabib's concern is less with the 'kind of ontological universe in which cosmopolitan norms can be said to "exist," but more with how these norms, whatever their ontological status, can shape, guide, and constrain our political life' (Benhabib 2006: 26). The exercise of stating how cosmopolitan norm can guide the political life is the usual one, while the question of what the basic entities are that theorists of cosmopolitanism are committed to in their theorising is still not addressed. Thus, I aimed to find what entities are considered basic for theories of cosmopolitanism by looking at these theories and their ontological template (Caraus 2016b).

The Cynics' statement, 'I am a citizen of the world', points to a minimal set of entities: the human being and the world. However, there are very few affirmations of cosmopolitanism containing this ontological set and usually these affirmations are not made by political theories, but by writers, artists and individuals who declared themselves citizens of the world (see Chapter 4). The contemporary array of approaches calling themselves 'cosmopolitan' do not postulate this minimal ontological set – the world and the human being – but have instead a plurality of elements such as states, nations, citizens, migrants, 'foreigners', international sphere and the West. These entities serve as well for a national ontological template; so what makes them cosmopolitan? Scrutinising theory after theory to identify what exactly makes a theory cosmopolitan from an ontological point of view, the 'discovery' was that in a cosmopolitan theory the usual set of elements – states, nations, citizens, migrants, the world – are in a different relation from those in non-cosmopolitan theory. Concomitantly, the interaction of these elements as it supposedly happens in the real world is doubled by a picture of how these elements ought to interact in a just and ideal way.

Thus, the ontological dimension of cosmopolitan theories is 'detectable' in three entities: a set of elements as currently configured in the 'real' world, a reconfiguration of these set of elements in a (more) just/ ideal way, and the interaction between these two sets. Looking for a cosmopolitan ontology, I detected it not in an immutable set of entities but in an interaction, and I called it the interaction of the ideal *cosmos* and the current order of the *polis*. This relation is suggested by the terms *cosmo-polis* or *cosmo-poli*-tanism: the interaction of cosmos and polis,[13] and this interaction contains the tamed radical core of the first cosmopolitan stance of the Cynics that still 'haunts' all political philosophy.

For the Cynics, the relation between cosmos and polis was one of a total negation – a possibility that did not occur to earlier political philosophers. Zeno's World Republic was as well an unprecedented idea of the ideal cosmos haunting the current polis. As Plutarch remarked, 'This Zeno wrote, giving shape to a dream or, as it were, shadowy picture of a well-ordered and philosophic commonwealth' (quoted in Heater 1996: 13). The quality of being 'dream' and 'shadowy picture' point precisely to the mode of existence of a World Republic in political philosophy: its realm of existence is that of dreams, shadows and spectres. But as each spectre, the spectres of a World Republic and of the citizen of the world 'haunt' and return with the power of a dream. The idea of the citizen of the world, once 'discovered' by the Cynics, did not disappear. Although tamed, ignored or 'repressed', it came always back to 'haunt' the theories and theorists. Thus, the radical core of the Cynics' cosmopolitanism did not disappear – it shaped cosmopolitan ontology, whose main ontological set and template is an interaction that can also be called a relation of 'haunting'[14] – the cosmos 'haunting' the polis. This 'haunting' dimension is especially visible in the accounts of cosmopolitanism that emphasise the role of the stranger, the foreigner and of the uncanny other (Kristeva 1991; Derrida 2001) in challenging the given meanings and allegiances.

The mapping of the interaction between cosmos and polis in contemporary political theories of cosmopolitanism revealed different intensities and degree of tension between cosmos and polis. Thus, in theories of global justice, there is a higher degree of tension between cosmos and polis, since the cosmopolitan view of global justice was advanced by counteracting the main theses of Rawls's domestic theory of justice concerning the scope, content, duty and nature of justice (Beitz 1979; Pogge 1989). A weaker tension between cosmos and polis is displayed by theories of cosmopolitan democracy posited not instead of but concomitant with other forms of democracy (Archibugi and Held 2011). The tension between cosmos and polis is less intense in the approach of cosmopolitanism developing the theoretical framework of discursive ethics and deliberative democracy (Habermas 2001; Benhabib 2006), which do not limit the scope of *moral conversation* to those who reside within nationally recognised boundaries, but the discursive approach aims to dissolve fluidly the tension between cosmos and polis. Adjectival cosmopolitanisms[15] attempt to counteract the alleged abstract dryness and moral demands of cosmopolitanism and claim that the demands of rootedness and of equal cosmopolitan regard can coexist smoothly, which is nothing less than an attempt to reconcile the cosmos and the polis, while clinging to the polis.

The cosmopolitan ontology reveals that the radical core of cosmopolitanism did not disappear but is continuously tamed. The tamed radicalism and negativity come back in each cosmopolitan stance. Cosmopolitanism is not and never was an ideal of the peaceful unification of the world, but a dynamic vision in a certain agonistic relation with the current order. However, to say that the tamed radicalism and negativity come back in each cosmopolitan stance in different degrees and intensities does not mean to justify everything that claims to be a cosmopolitan theory. Does it not mean accepting that everyone who claims to be a cosmopolitan is a cosmopolitan, even the 'patriotic cosmopolitans' that continuously try to dissolve the tension, and to claim that the polis as it is now can be accommodated with the cosmos? Is not the concept of cosmopolitan ontology a conciliatory one?

The elaborations on the ontology of cosmopolitanism does not intend to justify everything that was asserted in the name of this idea, but to show and to reassure that radicalism did not disappear, that it is in its ontology as the cosmos 'haunting' the polis with all the pressure of a spectre. Even the most conciliatory approaches cannot avoid entirely the pressure of the spectre, otherwise they will be content in their *patria* without bothering to elaborate on 'patriotic cosmopolitanism'. The history of the idea of cosmopolitanism contains different affirmations of cosmopolitanism which cannot be ignored or deleted, but this does not mean that we should not go back to the birth of cosmopolitanism and to reaffirm it in a current context where the idea of a citizen of the world is still so radical that theorists feel the need to tame it. Radical cosmopolitan claims are made more often than we acknowledge, as the next chapter shows, concomitantly reaffirming the radical cosmopolitan core once again.

NOTES

1. For similarities between the Eastern European dissidence and the Cynics' *parrhesia* see, among many others, Szakolczai (1994); Prozorov (2017).
2. Allen (2020) writes that as a result of recent scholarly interest in the phenomenon of Cynicism, there is a growing list of so-called inheritors of Cynic philosophy, from comedians and satirists, to tricksters, street artists and political activists, which points towards a 'inevitability of Cynicism', see the chapter entitled 'Coda'.
3. Available at: <https://dictionary.cambridge.org/dictionary/english/cosmopolitan> (last accessed 9 January 2022).
4. Some consider that there is also a Socratic cosmopolitanism, since Socrates was sensitive to a cosmopolitan identification with human beings. Whether Socrates was self-consciously cosmopolitan or not, there is no doubt that his ideas accelerated the development of cosmopolitanism and that he was in later antiquity embraced as a citizen of the world (Kleingeld and Brown 2019).
5. 'Exaggerating only slightly, we can trace the re-emergence of cosmopolitanism in the English-speaking academy to a single event: the 1994 publication of a short essay by Martha Nussbaum in a fledgling American cultural journal, the Boston Review' (Ingram 2013, Chapter 1, section 'A Fin De Siècle Renaissance').
6. Steel (2013); Atkins (2013); Nicgorski (2016); Schofield (2021).
7. For a recent revaluation of Cicero's republicanism see Smith (2018).
8. Cicero writes: 'For this reason, friends are together when they are separated, rich when they are poor, strong when they are weak, and – a thing even harder to explain – they live on after they have died, so great is the honour that follows them, so vivid the memory, so poignant the sorrow' (1971: 56).
9. The logic of a cosmopolitanism as non-elitist and from above is also restated from a normative tradition; see the notion 'humble cosmopolitan' in Cabrera (2020).

10. 'Cicero does not so much argue for patriotism as assume it in his reader' (Atkins 1990), and the same can be said about Cicero's 'cosmopolitanism'.

11. For the legacy of Cicero in the period 1100–*c.*1550 see Nederman (2020). See also Steel (2013: 231–373).

12. A quote from a *Pravda* article that dates from the time of Stalin's anti-Zionist campaign between 1948 and 1953. In the article, the author speaks about 'unbridled, evil-minded cosmopolitans, profiteers with no roots and no conscience . . . Grown on the rotten yeast of bourgeois cosmopolitanism, decadence and formalism . . . non-indigenous nationals without a motherland poison with stench . . . our proletarian culture' (quoted in Rapport 2012: 199).

13. For the 'cosmos' and 'polis' distinction as components of cosmopolitanism, see Bosman (2007: 27–8).

14. This haunting of the polis by the cosmos as an ontological dimension has similarity with 'hauntology' as originated from Derrida's discussion of Karl Marx in *Spectres of Marx*. The reading of Marx's proclamation that 'a spectre is haunting Europe – the spectre of communism' from 'The Communist Manifesto' (Marx and Engels 1978) and of the phrase 'the time is out of joint' from Shakespeare's *Hamlet*, revealed that ghosts cannot properly be said to belong to the past, since they determine the future. The idea of a World Republic, described by Plutarch as 'dream' and 'shadowy', determines the future; however, the cosmos haunting the polis is not necessarily similar to hauntology as a cultural trend of recycling and incapacity to escape the past, since cosmopolitanism and a World Republic did not have configurations in the real world in order to be 'recycled'.

15. See Introduction, the section entitled 'Cosmopolitics'.

Chapter 3

MIGRANT RADICAL COSMOPOLITICS

My concepts of cosmopolitanism of dissent and post-foundational cosmopolitanism have been tested once more, this time in the migrants' protests and resistance all over the world, such as *Sans Papiers*, No One Is Illegal, No Borders, A Day Without Us marches, migrant protests related to Lampedusa and Calais camps, anti-deportation campaigns and others. Since these actions were taking place all over the world and the 'content' of their claims – such as 'No One Is Illegal' or 'No Borders No Nations' – sounded radically cosmopolitan, it became imperative for me to study migrants' protests. Apart from testing the concepts once more, I had one more crucial motive to study migrants' movements: to test the hypothesis, deduced from Diogenes' cosmopolitanism born in the condition of exile and statelessness, that migration and cosmopolitanism are consubstantial and, therefore, every approach of cosmopolitanism has to provide an account of migration. Consubstantiality of cosmopolitanism and migration has a structure which sounds like a syllogism: cosmopolitanism means to be a citizen of the world, with no borders. Migration means to move from one place to another. Thus, migration, without impediments, appears to be the natural starting point for a cosmopolitan view. A syllogism which turns out to be a theoretical impossibility and a scandal both for the current approaches of migration and for cosmopolitanism, and which almost shattered my two 'novel' concepts.

MIGRANT PROTESTS AS RADICAL COSMOPOLITICS

To re-establish the consubstantiality of cosmopolitanism and migration, the research turned from the perspective of the citizen, traditional for existing theories of migration, to the perspective of the migrant by analysing migrant protests from the last decades (Caraus 2018a, 2018b, 2018c; Caraus and Parvu 2018). As in the previous research on dissent and protests, at stake was to identify the intersection between this form of protests and cosmopolitanism: are migrants' protests a political avant-garde, in terms of identifying new possibilities for politics? Is this avant-garde a cosmopolitan one? How are cosmopolitan subjectivities constituted through migrant protests? Is there any link between the alleged illegality of migrants and a cosmopolitan stance? As in the previous analysis of different patterns of dissent, the methodology implied a close reading of discourses produced by migrant protest movements: manifestos, declarations, websites and other texts explaining the necessity of protests. A minimal background of each case was provided, describing the context generating the protest and the main outcomes of this form of action.

Some of the structural features of migrant protests were similar to the features of protest and activism of non-migrants: occupation of public and symbolic spaces, marches, blockades, rallies, tours, demonstrations, direct action, horizontalism and leaderless, use of technology and social media, and so on. As well, the transnational dimension, cross-border coordination, networking, petitions, boycotts and non-cooperation, are features common to the forms of protest by non-migrants. Apart from these, there are features characteristic only to migrant protests, such as resisting deportation, targeting the airlines, collaboration of migrant and pro-migrant activists, camp resistance and the practice of lip-sewing. As well, migrant manifestations are considered illegal because they are enacted by persons considered irregular/illegal. The illegality is produced by the laws and the order of the nation-state, and the protests contest exactly this order, by rejecting their own illegality.

By coming out from illegality and by acquiring visibility, migrants reject the immobility and invisibility imposed by the lack of legal status. This visibility carries a great risk, but it is a necessary condition for migrants to position themselves as subjects having a political agency. Coming out from invisibility, migrants occupy public and symbolic places to create a stage and framework that can provide validity for their claims. In these public spaces, migrants present themselves as political subjects capable of acting and speaking on their own and attempting to intervene in the processes and decisions that affect their lives. Also, the process of coming out from illegality presupposes coining names either by inventing a name for themselves or by identifying with existing denigratory names, such as *Sans Papiers*. Through all these means and manifestations of migrant activism, a global political subject with a radical political agency emerges that is a real challenge for political theory and migration studies, because it requires acknowledging its radicality which cannot be otherwise than a radical cosmopolitics (Caraus 2018a, 2018b, 2018c).

Migrant protests instantiate radicalism according to the etymological meaning of the word 'radical', derived from the classical Latin word *radix*, meaning 'root', 'foundations' or 'origins' of something, in this case the roots of the current world order. So, migrant activism displays clear features of a political radicalism. It starts with the experience of the borders of the nation-state and of all obstacles to mobility as a wrong, which is a moral intuition. It dismantles and makes visible the invisible roots of the current world order – the nation-state and its borders considered as natural – and it implies a destruction of the world order constructed on those roots: the order of the nation-states. As well, migrant activism implies a fundamental change, viewed as utopia – 'No Borders No Nations' – but which already happens every day for people crossing borders in spite of obstacles and surveillance. These radical features of migrant activism have been described as radical cosmopolitan attitude, radical cosmopolitan action and radical cosmopolitan ends (Caraus 2018a).

The radical cosmopolitan attitude that emerges from migrant protests is mainly based on the intuition of the wrong of borders: 'Those subject to immigration control are dehumanized, are reduced to non-persons, are nobodies. People are thus punished not for anything they have themselves done, but for what others might do in the future' (No One Is Illegal 2001). The moral wrong of the borders is obvious, as the manifesto of the No Border (2002) movement emphasises:

> Borders create misery and death. They are a cruel fiction, a weapon of divide and rule. They serve the rich, who use them to protect the wealth hoarded by colonialism and capitalism, and to turn the rest of us against each other.

Migrants' manifestos articulate a critique of foundations of the current global order, of capitalism and colonialism, and of practices based on this order: border system control, global division of labour, exploitation of cheap labour and so on. The intuition of the wrong determines the conviction that the wrong should be righted. The critical attitude is the starting point for articulating new rights and making new claims, such as 'No One Is Illegal', 'Papers for All or No Papers at All!', 'No Borders, No Nations, No Flags, No Patriots', and other claims that became mottos.

The radical cosmopolitan action is mainly expressed through the very fact of mobility and the very fact of protests. There is a cosmopolitan potential in the very fact of mobility beyond and across borders, an empirical 'real feeling' of being on move: the transgression of state borders in times where citizenship is exclusively defined by territorial affiliation can be interpreted as a protest and critique per se of the existing borders of the nation-state (De Genova 2013). By exercising mobility, the whole panoply of the nation-state laws is contested, and especially the very law that produced migrant illegality, the immigration law: 'Under all other laws it is the act that is illegal, but under immigration law, it is the person who is illegal . . . There are no illegal or undeserving human beings, only inhumane and immoral laws' (No One Is Illegal 2003). By exercising mobility, migrants take back from the nation-state the legitimate political subjectivity. The nation-state has monopolised political subjectivity to the extent that political expression of individuals was and still is legitimated only in the nation-state, but migrants exercise it across and beyond borders. Protesting migrants enact the rights as if these were indeed the rights of the man, not of the citizen, and so they bring into view the possibility of instituting rights for a global citizen.

The radical cosmopolitan ends are mapped in the transformations that the very fact of mobility and the very fact of protests bring to the current norms, practices and institutions. By overcoming or ignoring the obstacles for free movement, protesting migrants make the first step towards a cosmopolitan restructuring of the world, but mainly this is a first step in restructuring subjectivity. Migrants, by moving illegally, confront the current world order directly, even if unwillingly, and this is a cosmopolitan experience in its 'abject' form (Nyers 2003). The experience of protesting, of occupying public/symbolic spaces and acquiring visibility carries a great risk, but it is a significant experience towards acquiring a new political subjectivity. Although the protests are broken up and the occupied public spaces cleaned, the migrant who leaves the public space of protest is different from the person who entered it (Beltrán 2009). This transformation is from a (formal) subject of a particular nation-state towards a subject speaking and acting beyond and across the borders. As well, by protesting, migrants claim and enact rights that they do not officially have. These rights are claimed not as citizens of a particular state but as human beings, that is, protesters perform and behave as if they have rights simply because of being in the world, 'being there', or in other words, they behave in that very moment as cosmopolitan citizens. Those making the demands and acting in the name of the world act already *as if* the world already exists as One World.

My concept of cosmopolitanism of dissent was confirmed immediately by migrant protest, but it was also denied immediately, since migrant protests with their radicalism go beyond the cosmopolitanism of dissent as identified in other form of protests. The radical attitude, radical actions and radical ends converge into a more radical form of cosmopolitanism – a radical cosmopolitics that contests the existing political world order based on the nation-state and formulates radical political demands concerning the whole world. However, the radical attitude, radical actions and radical ends make migrant protests the most radical cosmopolitan protest, but also the most fragile one.

THE 'DOUBLE BIND' OF MIGRANT PROTESTS

When I started to study migrant protests and resistance, I was already aware that cosmopolitanism of dissent is a powerful but also a fragile stance, that dissent and resistance may vanish, and sometimes even the ideas that animated them vanish. Nevertheless, I did not foresee the degree of fragility of migrant radical cosmopolitics. Migrants' and refugees' protests are the most radical expression of cosmopolitanism and the most evanescent one. What exactly is this fragility, from where does it come? To identify the causes of fragility, the power of a cosmopolitan migrant stance has to be identified first.

The powerfulness of this stance comes from migrants' view of a world without borders, as expressed in slogans and manifestos: 'No One Is Illegal', 'Papers for All or No Papers at All!', 'No Borders, No Nations, No Flags, No Patriots', 'Justice and Dignity for Everyone', 'We Are Here and We Will Fight. Freedom of Movement Is Everybody's Right!, and others. Coming out from invisibility and illegality, protesting migrants speak in the name of all – 'There are no illegal or undeserving human beings, only inhumane and immoral laws' (No One Is Illegal 2003) – suggest new ways of being in the world, 'No Borders No Nations', and remind us that we 'all inhabit the planet Earth as a shared space' (Lampedusa Charter 2014). The migrant view of the world compels us to move towards an idea of membership of a global political community, where all will be free and equal members:

> We demand status for migrant workers and all those who have been deemed illegal . . .
>
> We seek an end to detentions and deportations and the violence of all forms of control.
>
> No One Is Illegal means what it says – anyone in the entire world who wishes to come or remain should have the right to do so.
>
> No One Is Illegal, No Exceptions, No Concessions, No Conciliation! No immigration controls! No Need For Justification of Presence! (No One Is Illegal 2003)

This vision of a world without borders is a powerful cosmopolitical stance, but is subverted by migrants' own actions. Thus, protesting migrants formulate radical claims and end up asking for legalisation in one nation-state or another, thus reconfirming the very institutions that they contest. The fragility of the migrant cosmopolitan stance was noticed by many scholars who asserted that the claims of protesting migrants both challenge and re-inscribe existing political arrangements: 'Migrants contests the exclusivity of citizenship as a measure of political inclusion.

Yet their call for legalization simultaneously reinforces the authority of citizenship as the foremost measure of belonging' (McNevin 2007: 670). Indeed, some of the protests ended with many protesters receiving legalisation, such as the Berlin Refugees Movement (2012), Vienna Votive Church Refugees Protest (2012) and the 'inaugural' movement of the *Sans-Papiers* (1996) in France.[1] Scholars plausibly notice that migrant activism is captured by the logic and practices of state sovereignty and, in this way, migrants re-enact the sovereignty of the state. Protesting migrants reaffirm the international regime of sovereign national state with closed borders and the constitutive dualisms of modern politics: included/excluded, vocal/silent, visible/invisible (McNevin 2007, 2013; Marciniak and Tyler 2013; Ataç et al. 2016). Thus, migrants become a 'reinforcing supplement' to the nation (Honig 2001), confirming the countries of destination status as a choice worthy.

The radicalism of migrant protests, as argued above, is defined both by the act of protest, but also by the content of their manifestos that, as all manifestos, not only describe a state of affairs but mainly tend to produce an effect, to make us recognise the situation described in the manifesto and to act accordingly. Thus, the manifestos create a horizon of expectation that those drafting it will act according to their letter and spirit. Indeed, in the case of migrants protesting illegality and stating that 'There are no illegal or undeserving human beings, only inhumane and immoral laws' or that 'Modern states try to turn movement into a right that is granted or denied according to economic and political power' (No Border 2002), the request for legalisation in a particular nation-state comes across as a betrayal of the 'spirit' of the manifesto. Thus, since citizenship is both the regime of exclusion which they are protesting and the goal many migrant protesters are striving to achieve, the migrant activism is caught in a 'double bind' (McNevin 2013). However, who is entitled to ask an illegal migrant to remain illegal in order not to betray a manifesto? On the other hand, should scholars try to save the promised cosmopolitics in migrant activism or they should just notice the contradictions of migrant protests? This question is a real dilemma, a 'double bind' for scholars of migration. Without hesitation, I tried to overcome the dilemma by trying to rescue the promised radical cosmopolitics, making at least two attempts.

To rescue the promised radical cosmopolitics, I argued that the migrant protests are already performing acts of cosmopolitan citizenship (Caraus 2018c). I started my argument from the recent conceptual innovations about citizenship as an act (Isin and Neilsen 2008). According to this conceptual innovation, an act of citizenship enacts a political subjectivity, acting beyond and against law, formulating and enacting new claims and rights, performing an event. In migrant resistance movements, all these aspects of an act of citizenship have a cosmopolitan dimension, since protesting migrants express a political subjectivity that goes beyond the confines of the nation-state, they act beyond and against law of the nation-states, and enact new claims concerning the whole world, while the event is performed as well beyond borders, on a world stage. All these dimensions converge into a radical cosmopolitical stance, which crucially 'reiterates' the primordial act of the birth of cosmopolitanism when Diogenes asked where he came from and said, 'I am a citizen of the cosmos', which revealed that cosmopolitanism was born as an act of citizenship. Therefore, the act of cosmopolitan citizenship perspective is one of the lenses through which migrant protests could be examined academically, without accusing protesting migrants of contradiction, double bind and even pragmatic uses of protests in order to receive legalisation.

I made one more attempt to rescue the promised radical cosmopolitics. I asked myself if in their public, visible actions, the protesting migrants end up asking for papers and receiving some form of legalisation, by this confirming the very institution they are contesting – the nation-state with its borders and sovereignty – maybe they are more subversive in their invisible resistance (Caraus 2018b)? Diverse forms of migrant struggles take place by avoiding the dominant regimes of visibility through escape, falsification of papers, destruction of identity documents, destruction of fingertips, false documents, false identities, false marriages, false visas, overstaying visas, concealment of illegal status from employees, and other forms of everyday resistance by which migrants render themselves unclassifiable, imperceptible and unidentifiable. There is an assumed radicalism of the 'invisible' resistance in general, such as in underground cultural and political resistance, and invisible migrant resistance has its subversive power as well. However, the power of resistance does not rest univocally either within visibility or within invisibility. Some other aspects of migrant existence are made 'invisible' by the way knowledge on migration and migrants is produced. State officials managing migration and the academic production of knowledge about migration make some aspects of migration exposable and apprehensible and, at the same time, leave other aspects as unseen or unperceivable, like the migrant clandestine labour that is convenient to states, companies and individuals from the host countries, everyone keeping the 'secret' of using the 'illegal' cheap labour (De Genova 2013). On the other hand, for the population at large, there is a supra-visibility of migrants in mass media: migrants portrayed as 'criminals', as 'abusive of social benefits' or in a humanitarian frame as 'victims'. Thus, invisibility is both empowering and disempowering for migrants and it is neither inherently liberating, nor inherently oppressive. However, if there is a subverting power in migrant invisible resistance, where is it? What are the implications of migrant invisible resistance for the state's exercise of sovereignty? How do these practices question and subvert the borders and order of nation-states? I identified migrant invisible power in four types of subversion: 'taking back the means of legitimate movement', 'tying the hands of the state, 'creating a new ontology' and 'working towards the shipwreck of the state'.

The nation-state monopolised the legitimate 'means of movement' (Torpey 2000) and took the freedom of movement away from human beings by making passports and visas the prerequisite for the legal cross-ing of borders. Migrants' hidden resistance comes exactly from this 'resource' – false passports, false documents, fake visas, overstaying visas and so on. In other words, migrants take back the means of legiti-mate movement. The modern state made the people legible (Scott 1998: 2) through registration and documentation which serves to govern and control its population. The people who move around escape legibility and undermine one of the founding activities of the state. Although reg-istration, surveillance and fingertips have become instruments of control and of the fight against illegal migration, when the persons are undocu-mented and fingertips are destroyed, they constitute an attack on some of the founding pillars of the nation-state, making it, temporarily or partially, inoperative.

When disappearing beyond and across borders, migrants do not express an argument against the state or a vision of a world without borders; nevertheless, in doing so, they create a new ontology, or a new world. The new world is invisible to those who are not experiencing illegal mobility and contains a set of entities that are basic for migrants and to which they make a commitment by the very fact of moving in spite of the restrictions, such as knowledge of mobility that circulates between the people on the move (knowledge about border crossings, routes, shelters, hubs, escape routes, resting places; knowledge about policing and surveillance, ways to defy control, strategies against biosur-veillance, etc.); an infrastructure of connectivity which is crucial to dis-tributing such knowledge; a multiplicity of informal economies in which the migrants are involved; and diverse forms of transnational communi-ties of justice and support actions, created by migrants and pro-migrant activists (Papadopoulos and Tsianos 2013). Thus, through their clandes-tine actions, migrants create a new world in the heart of the old world. Finally, migrants do not hold a place in history, because from the nation-state's point of view, migrants are not perceived as a political subject, hence the clandestine presence and new ontology do not interfere with the 'naturalised' ontology of the nation-state and citizenship, causing one day, as other invisible forms of resistance do, a 'shipwreck' of the state (Scott 1985: 36). When migrants clandestinely defy the borders, they expose the limits of citizenship without ever intending it. While aiming at survival or at a better life, migrant invisible resistance produces a cosmopolitan framework – that of a world without borders. By exercising mobility, unauthorised migrants seek to implement the promises that stand at the foundations of the international/global normative order, like free movement of human beings, through disobeying and challenging a system that they perceive as unjust. In other words, they implement, although 'illegally', the cosmopolitan promise of universal and equal human rights.

My attempts to rescue cosmopolitics of migrant protests and resistance were theoretical attempts. Where some authors were seeing a contradiction in migrant public protests, I tried to see an act of cosmopolitan citizenship. Where some authors were seeing migrants as victims to be imprisoned, detained, deported or managed in a camp, I was trying to see the subverting effects of the migrant illegality on the nation-state. This does not mean that I have not seen as well that migrants 'betray' the spirit and the letter of manifestos. But again, can a scholar ask (theoretically) an 'illegal' migrant to remain illegal in order not to 'betray' a cosmopolitical manifesto? Or, in fact, the protesting migrant ask the scholar of migration to give up their ways of approaching migration? And the crucial question about the perishability of cosmopolitan dissent must be asked again: where does cosmopolitanism go when the manifestos are 'betrayed'?

WHERE DOES RADICALISM GO WHEN IT DISAPPEARS?

Radical cosmopolitics of migrant protests disappears in migrants' further actions, but equally it disappears in theoretical approaches of migrant activism that fail to see it. They are not supported in their attempts by political philosophers who refuse to think beyond the container of the nation-state and to provide a glimpse of what the world in which No One Is Illegal would look like. On the contrary, political philosophy, as it currently exists, contributes to the framing of some human beings as 'illegal'.

While I was looking for manifestations of cosmopolitanism in migrant protests, many other scholars were examining protests from different perspectives, most of them interesting and creative, but missing a crucial feature – radical cosmopolitics. An extensively covered perspective is citizenship studies, which points to the ways in which migrant protests open new spaces of citizenship by enacting new rights (Nyers and Rygiel 2012; Marciniak and Tyler 2013; Ataç et al. 2016). However, with few exceptions (Nyers 2003), this approach sees the acts of citizenship as taking part mainly in the nation-state. A cluster of approaches identify new and creative ways of protesting in migrant activism, such as migrant and non-migrant solidarity grief activism, migrants' biopolitical arsenal of lip-sewing, and others.[2] The identification of novelty in expressing a protest is considered sufficient, thus there is no attempt to go further and to unfold the cosmopolitan potential of these new forms of protest. An interesting perspective is that of the autonomy of migration. Inspired by the Italian tradition of *operaismo*, the autonomy of migration considers that migration is a social fact that mobilises a full spectrum of creativity in the human agency (Mezzadra 2004; Mezzadra and Neilson 2013; Papadopoulos and Tsianos 2013). The autonomy of migration tends to liberate research on migration from some of the prevailing frameworks in migration studies, such as humanitarianism, securitisation, migration management, labour market and so on, and refuses to frame migration within the discourse of victimisation (migrants are powerless) or security (migrants are dangerous), privileging instead the voice and subjectivity of migrants. The autonomy of migration is as well an activist–research nexus that has developed primarily in Europe, connecting the scholarly and activist worlds. It sees the migrants as an avant-garde; however, it does not go further in exploring the cosmopolitan potential of the very fact of mobility.

For many theorists, migrant activism instantiates two main Arendtian motives – the 'right to have rights' and 'spaces of appearance'. The 'right to have rights' sheds light on the new rights claims made by undocumented immigrants (for example, Gündogdu 2015). However, while rights claimed by the undocumented migrants offer a plausible instantiation of 'the right to have rights' beyond the border of the nation-state, the cosmopolitan nature and legitimacy of these claims is ignored. Arendt's insights about the lack of human rights in the cases of those who need them desperately – the refugee and stateless people – apparently make an approach critical and self-reflexive. Arendt signalled the paradox and avoided taking a cosmopolitan position, preferring the authenticity of the paradox, which is reiterated every time by all those who want to criticise human rights and their inability to protect refugees, but without exiting the structure of exclusion of the nation-state (Caraus forthcoming). The paradox itself is possible only in the frame of the exclusionary structure of the political form that is the nation-state and of the theory that takes the nation-state as a building block. There are some five decades of signalling the paradox under Arendtian auspices, but few theoretical attempts of thinking a way out of the paradox. As well, Arendtian 'spaces of appearing' is a fruit-ful perspective for capturing one of the main features of migrant activ-ism – becoming public and coming out from invisibility (Beltrán 2009). However, these approaches do not take into consideration the fact that the appearance is not only in the public space of a nation-state but on the world stage.

The approaches to migrant protests that attempt to map its cosmopol-itanism are rare and with unequal premises. In some attempts, cosmopol-itanism is reduced to a kind of multiculturalism of migrants' coexistence within the host country, which is a very infelicitous way of understand-ing cosmopolitanism. Equally infelicitous is the reiteration of the idea of sanctuary spaces as a type of cosmopolitanism, taking Derrida's short text on sanctuary (2001) as a legitimating frame, although the idea of sanctu-ary keeps intact the structure of exclusion of the state by marking a place for all excluded to be separated further. The approaches that identify the genuine link between migrant protests and cosmopolitanism and their consubstantiality are unique (Nail 2015). So, the pro-migrant activists who are willing to make sacrifices of time, energy and personal resources to protect vulnerable non-compatriots are presented as instances of 'indi-vidual cosmopolitanism' (Cabrera 2008). The anti-deportation activism of undocumented persons was insightfully named 'abject cosmopolitan-ism' which 'contest[s] and reshape[s] the traditional terms of political community, identity and practice' (Nyers 2003: 1075). The 'abject' cos-mopolitanism captures very plausibly the radical cosmopolitan potential of migrant acts, but why do only a few scholars see cosmopolitanism which is more than explicit in some of the migrant protests? The plurality of approaches – all plausible, relevant and creative – is an indisputable academic principle; nevertheless, the failure to see cosmopolitanism more than explicit in migrant protests is a sign that theory is caught in the trap of methodological nationalism.

Methodological nationalism is a cognitive bias in which researchers subsume society under the nation-state and presuppose basic dualisms such as domestic/foreign or national/international. As Ulrich Beck argues in most of his works, methodological nationalism naturalises the bound-aries of nation-states, views it as a necessary container and functions as an unrecognised mental block (for example, Beck 2004; Beck and Szneider 2006). Within the framework of methodological nationalism, migration is regarded as an exception to a sedentary rule and as a problem that hap-pens at the border of the Western/European states. So, political theory, as well as migration studies in general, is mainly an approach of *im*migration in the Western states (Cole 2000: 43–60), while migration is a 'total fact' (Sayad 2004) implying not only *im*migrants at the border of the Western states, but the world as a whole – the countries of origin, the countries of destination, the countries of transit, the routes taken, the agency of migrants, the causes of migration and many other aspects. Within liberal political theory, methodological nationalism determines both the closed borders and open borders approaches, although these are considered to be in opposition to each other. The 'closed borders' approach starts from the presumption that states have the right to discretionary control over their borders, and advances arguments for closed borders: preserving culture, sustaining the economy, distributing state benefits, political functioning, establishing security and so on (Miller 2016). 'Open borders' claims that immigration restrictions are inconsistent with basic liberal egalitarian values, including freedom and moral equality, and that affluent, liberal democratic societies are morally obliged to admit immigrants as a partial response to global injustices, such as poverty and human rights violations (Carens 2013). Nevertheless, 'closed borders' and 'open borders' differ only by a matter of degree. The open borders approach is more generous, and discusses the brain drain, the conditions for guest workers, the fair criteria for recruiting immigrants or what to do with the undocumented persons already in and so on. Thus, the 'open borders' approach does not mean a world without borders – it just points to the attempts of some political theorists to change something in political theory but without changing anything. So, staying within methodological nationalism and using nation-state categories that classify persons as legal and illegal, scholars of migration and political theorists themselves more or less directly 'make people illegal' (Dauvergne 2008).

Although criticisms of methodological nationalism are being increasingly accepted within migration studies (Wimmer and Glick Schiller 2002) – but less so in political theory (Sager 2018: 17–37) – there is still a lack of systematic reflection on how to approach migration differently. Migration is therefore an epistemic challenge and a methodological task, which presupposes at least three exits that political theory has to perform: from the structure of exclusion of the nation-state, from the Kantian legacy and from the perspective of the citizen, exits that are the preconditions for building political philosophy anew.

The first exit means abandoning methodological nationalism and the perspective of the nation-state in approaching migration. The nation-state excludes outsiders, and political philosophers search for a justification for exclusion, often on the grounds that it is a widely accepted practice in liberal democratic states. Thus, a justification must be possible and, by providing a justification, political philosophy reveals its structure of exclusion (Cole 2000). Exiting methodological nationalism means that theorists need to inquire into the production of knowledge about

migration and how power and interests have shaped dominant categories of approaching migration. The second exit is from the approaches
that do not resolve the structural political exclusion of migrants, but only
alleviate it temporarily, and this is the Kantian legacy. For Kant, migrants,
nomads and other non-citizens are only allowed the right of visitation not
residence, that is, temporary access to the territory of a state (Kant 1991:
105–8), so the Kantian right of cosmopolitan hospitality protects migrants
and refugees but only through their perpetual displacement. The Kantian
inspired United Nations' framework defines the right to leave a territory
as a human right, but not the right to enter a territory. Following this
provision, political theory asserts that there is a fundamental human right
to emigration but hesitates to argue for a right to immigration, showing a
conceptual incoherence (Cole 2000).

The third exit is from a political theory that privileges the voice of the
citizen. Political theory has been an 'insider theory', a body of theory that
privileges the voice of the insider, the one who possesses statehood, the
citizen. Migrants and refugees are excluded from the theory – they appear
as a residual both of the state and of the theory, a 'problem' to be solved
or managed in the interests of the citizen (Cole 2014, 2016). As well,
political theory ignore that the migration regime plays a role in maintaining extreme inequalities of wealth across the globe, since there is a global
migration regime through which a block of powerful capitalist states control access of the poor and unskilled while exploiting their labour at cheap
costs and illegally (Mezzadra and Neilson 2013), and also actively seeking
out 'human capital' considered economically valuable from all over the
world provoking 'brain drain'. A body of theory constructed in the space
of migrancy might look radically different from that constructed within
the privileged space of the academia of the developed North (Cole 2014:
515). Even though migrants do not have the instruments and concepts
of political philosophy, they have the manifestos and statements which
are *in nuce* a political philosophy.

A political philosopher honestly confronting the problem of migration
and examining the possibilities of political theory in the face of migration
cannot but arrive at the conclusion that the entire theoretical arsenal has
to be rethought. Bizarrely, this conclusion is very rare, and when such
conclusions are voiced, they remain somehow inaudible. For example, in
1993, in a text entitled 'Beyond Human Rights', Giorgio Agamben made a
call to rethink political philosophy starting from the figure of the refugee:

> Given the by now unstoppable decline of the nation-state and the general
> corrosion of traditional political-juridical categories, the refugee is perhaps
> the only thinkable figure for the people of our time and the only category

in which one may see today – at least until the process of dissolution of the nation-state and of its sovereignty has achieved full completion – the forms and limits of a coming political community. It is even possible that, if we want to be equal to the absolutely new tasks ahead, we will have to abandon decidedly, without reservation, the fundamental concepts through which we have so far represented the subjects of the political (Man, the Citizen and its rights, but also the sovereign people, the worker, and so forth) and build our political philosophy anew starting from the one and only figure of the refugee. (Agamben 2000: 18).

To whom was the call addressed? To all political philosophers, or to Agamben himself? While Agamben's philosophy might be considered the one that attempted to renew political categories and advance a political philosophy that many others fail to recognise as political, the scholars of migration were keen to prove his other insights that the refugee is an embodiment of the 'bare life' to be managed in a camp.[3] Almost three decades later migration is approached with the same categories that produce the refugees.

Another rather unique call to rethink political philosophy was formulated from the inside of liberal political theory by Philip Cole in *Philosophy of Exclusion*: 'The migration of peoples therefore calls for a re-shaping of the political order, and a re-shaping of political theory itself' (Cole 2000: 11). Confronted with the 'problem' of migration, 'liberal theory cannot address the membership question without addressing itself, and cannot answer it without radically transforming itself' (Cole 2000: 202), and starting again with only two building blocks: the human being and the world as a whole (Cole 2014, 2016). This call to rethink political philosophy was heard even less than that of Agamben's, liberal political theory being incapable of going beyond the 'open borders' approach, which stands for a 'cutting-edge' approach within this tradition of doing political philosophy.[4] But does the political philosopher have an obligation to build political philosophy anew? Obviously, the political philosopher does not have an obligation to think in one way or another – he should be free to think. The bizarrerie is that while being free to think, he/she stops the thinking at the borders . . .

'NO ONE IS ILLEGAL': WHAT IF WE TAKE THE MOTTO SERIOUSLY?

After taking up migration as an epistemological task and challenge, I had to acknowledge that although my concept of the cosmopolitanism of dissent is confirmed in migrant protests, it keeps and perpetuates the status quo. In other words, my concept of cosmopolitanism of dissent although confirmed, nevertheless fails in the case of migrant protests. How is this contradictory performance possible? The migrant protests are a form of dissent that expresses a strong cosmopolitan stance. However, migrant radicalism goes beyond the concept of cosmopolitanism of dissent as elaborated previously. A case that makes my peculiar achievement clearer is that of the World Social Forum meeting in 2016 that took place in Canada.[5] Seventy per cent of activists were denied visa entry to Canada. Many activists from Latin America, Africa and Asia received a negative response to their visa requests based on 'unacceptable, exclusionary and discriminatory arguments', as the organisers said in a statement. Activists expressed outrage and shock.[6] However, the difficulty of obtaining visas, Canada being especially restrictive, was one of the initial arguments against holding it there in the first place, but it turned out that the impediment of visas was underassessed. The result was a forum composed mainly of Quebecois activists. The WSF was one of the main cases studies that confirmed my cosmopolitanism of dissent in the global social movements. In its statements and positions, WSF was incontestably radical, and its motto 'Another World Is Possible', launched in 2001 in Porto Alegre, embedded the whole cosmopolitical vision of the beginning of the millennium. But WSF cosmopolitanism was halted and shattered by some bureaucracies refusing to give visas to the WSF activists. And so was shattered the relevance of my cosmopolitanism of dissent in different countries and political regimes. The WSF 2016 meeting in Canada shows that in order to be truly cosmopolitan, a motto like 'Another World is Possible' has to be issued concomitantly with 'No Borders No Nations' and 'No One Is Illegal'.

It has to be noted here that the 2016 WSF, in its failure, brings into view a necessary confluence of decolonisation struggles and radical cosmopolitics. The activists who did not receive visas were from the former colonial regions, currently called the Global South, and who continue the decolonisation struggle in the current situation, under the motto 'Another World Is Possible'. Thus, this WSF meeting shows that in order for decolonisation struggles to achieve their initial aim of liberation, the obstacle of nation-state and its borders have to be eliminated, and this is not only a point of confluence between the decolonisation stance and the cosmopolitical one: it shows that decolonisation struggles in order to achieve their aims have to also be cosmopolitical.

The decolonisation through movements of national liberation and self-determination was described mainly as a failure, starting with 1970s. For example, Elie Kedourie's *Nationalism in Asia and Africa* (1970) situated the deviations of anti-colonial nationalism within an account of the inherently pathological character of nationalism as a dangerous romantic fantasy that naturalised the nation and falsely equated the realisation of the national principle with political liberty and just government. David Scott's *Conscripts of Modernity: The Tragedy of Colonial Enlightenment* (2004) described how anti-colonialists narrated the transition from colonialism to post-colonialism as a story of overcoming and vindication, of salvation and redemption, and how the transition ended in tragedy. Paul Gilroy calls *Postcolonial Melancholia* (2005) a 'structure of feeling' associated with the deep disappointments, disillusionments and disenchantments accompanying the growing expropriation and exploitation practiced by post-colonial nation-states, that followed the initial and deeply felt euphoria that many experienced with the end of imperial rule. However, despite acknowledging the tragedy of national liberation, it did not result in a cosmopolitan stance in post-colonial and decolonial theoretical approaches, or when this did happen, it resulted in moderate cosmopolitanism, the latest being Adom Getachew's *Worldmaking after Empire* (2018). Getachew contrasts her approach with the type of analysis viewing anti-colonial movements of national self-determination as tragedy and argues that in aiming for a transition from empire to nation, the anti-colonial nationalists were not solely concerned with national self-determination and the establishment of nation-states but were committed to a 'worldmaking'. Although anti-colonial nationalism was bound to the institutional form of the nation-state, its vision of the world order went beyond this, pursuing a reinvention of the legal, political and economic structures of the international order. An example of 'worldmaking' is the Pan-Africanism movement as it developed after the Second World War, especially through the activity of the Black Atlantic leaders, and mainly of Kwame Nkrumah, the anti-colonial activist and first Prime Minister and President of Ghana, and a major advocate for Pan-Africanism. Another worldmaking strategy was the New International Economic Order (NIEO), also put forward by the Black Atlantic leaders who in the 1960s–70s, confronted by declining terms of trade in primary commodities that devastated many post-colonial economies, combined with the failure of federalist initiatives, identified post-colonial nations as the 'workers of the world' and demanded the redistribution of wealth from the Global North to its producers in the South.

Although the Pan-Africanism movement and the NIEO failed – both are presented through the narrative of 'rise and fall' – the author considers that a post-colonial cosmopolitanism emerges from the conceptual and political innovations of anti-colonial worldmaking as a 'normative orientation that retains the anti-imperial aspiration for a domination-free international order' (Getachew 2018: 11). This proposal of post-colonial cosmopolitanism is the latest in the series of political theorists exploring the legacy of anti-colonialism, but it is only a version of conciliatory moderate cosmopolitanism. Thus, it envisages a crucial role for the nation-state: 'this model of cosmopolitanism is less aimed at the limits of the nation-state and more concerned with the ways that relations of hierarchy continue to create differentiated modes of sovereignty and reproduce domination in the international sphere' (Getachew 2018: 32). The role attributed to the state is explained by the fact that it is 'premature' to give up the self-determination and state sovereignty, otherwise 'cosmopolitans risk becoming apologists for neo-imperial projects' (Getachew 2018: 34) – a new reiteration of the old fear of cosmopolitanism as an imperial project. On the other hand, although the author claims that 'the anticolonial account of self-determination marked a radical break from the Eurocentric model of international society' the book shows how federalists like Kwame Nkrumah and Eric Williams 'positioned the United States as a model of postcolonial federation' (Getachew 2018: 12), so we have a cosmopolitanism of non-domination trying to implement a Western model.

While Getachew still sees an emancipatory power of national self-determination for a post-colonial cosmopolitanism of non-domination, Nandita Sharma's book *Home Rule: National Sovereignty and the Separation of Natives and Migrants* (2020) sees the persistence of domination. Although not formulated from a cosmopolitan perspective, this book shows the consubstantiality of decolonisation and radical cosmopolitics. For Sharma, the anti-colonisation movements, including Pan-Africanism movements and Non-Aligned Movement (NAM), created in 1955 in Bandung, to promote Afro-Asian economic and cultural cooperation, to oppose colonialism, and to avoid alignment to the Western or Eastern Bloc, were instruments for normalisation of post-colonial power, for instituting a global governmentality through the nation-state and for cementing the trinity nation-state-capital. *Home Rule* argues that the new post-colonial world of nation-states implemented nationalist forms of regulating capitalism, containing and diverting the revolutionary and liberatory demands of people across the globe. According to Sharma, when the first doubts about liberation through nationalism appeared, including the observations that the local elites hijacked the national liberation, the discourse of neocolonialism was formulated. The term 'neocolonialism' appears for the first time in the 1963 preamble to the Charter of the Organization of African States that Nkrumah helped to create and advanced further in his book, *Neo-colonialism: The Last Stage of Imperialism* (1965). The thesis of neocolonialism was that national self-determination was not being achieved because of the actions of external forces that were thwarting national aspirations, and that independence and sovereignty are only 'in theory', while in reality its economic system and thus its political policy were directed from outside. According to Sharma, the neocolonialism was based on two false assumptions: first, that the post-colonial new world order of nation-states could somehow be made equal at an international level and, second, that the continued existence of class relations prevailing in every nation-state was compatible with calls for equality. The neocolonial discourse did not allow the acknowledgement that nation-states and global capital were uninterested in achieving *liberation* for those who were longing for it: the (ordinary) people: 'the identification of the problem as one of (neo)colonialism or (neo)imperialism offered *more nationalism* as the solution' (Sharma 2020: 156). In this context, as Sharma argues, the discourse of self-determination became a discourse of the National-Natives as the ultimate source of law and the grantor of rights. Since all claimants to national sovereignty imagine themselves to be engaged in anti-colonial resistance against a 'foreign invader', it produced the figure of the Migrant, defined as the quintessential outsider to national rule. While capital was given greater ability to penetrate previously closed imperial economies, each new nation-state enacted exclusionary citizenship and immigration controls for anyone not deemed to be a national citizen. Thus, in this new post-colonial world order, the borders became an instrument of control and exploitation, as the migrant protests movement analysed in this chapter show.

Recognising that national sovereignty has not met – and cannot meet – the dream of decolonisation is not an argument for a return to empire, argues *Home Rule*. It is a call to reject the post-colonial system of nation-states and build social relationships, social bodies and practices of social reproduction able to meet liberatory demands. Although Sharma, unlike Getachew, does not use the expressions 'cosmopolitanism' or 'cosmopolitics', Sharma's approach to decolonisation is the true post-colonial cosmopolitanism, and the solutions provided by Sharma are consubstantial with the radical cosmopolitics. Thus, 'Only after the death of the national liberation project can we renew our commitment to decolonization' (Sharma 2020: 276), and the first key to this is a rejection of the politics of nationalism with its basis in discourses of autochthony and nativity. 'If we want a decolonized world', argues Sharma, 'we will need to achieve it against national sovereignty, not through it. Otherwise, we will be left with a nationalist, racist politics of anti-mobility that rests on the separation of Natives and Migrants' (Sharma 2020: 407). The solidarity of the decolonisation struggles, as the WSF in Canada shows, can be achieved not across but mainly against the nation-states and their borders, dismantling barriers to people's free mobility.

A liberatory politics of 'No Borders' is thus central to collective liberation from colonialism and neocolonialism. Rejecting all nationalisms is critical to anti-colonial struggle. As long as those who gained their national liberation and self-determination remain 'illegal' in the most parts of the world, decolonisation is a failure. Thus, radical cosmopolitics is not part of any imperial project; on the contrary, it is consubstantial with the decolonisation project.

As the decolonisation struggles are half emancipatory if conducted through national means, so any radicalism and any cosmopolitics that does not envisage going behind the confinements of the nation-state are only half-radical and half-cosmopolitan. My concept of cosmopolitanism of dissent was half-radical and quasi-cosmopolitan. It was still somehow captive in methodological nationalism since it could take place plausibly in the confines of the nation-state, eventually with some transnational solidarity with dissidents and protesters from other parts of the world.

Thus, migration showed that my concepts need to be radicalised and updated as radical cosmopolitics. Radical cosmopolitics of a world where 'No One Is Illegal' is the only way for political philosophy to avoid producing 'illegal' beings and, obviously, to avoid the 'double bind' of migrant activism. Migrant activists end up asking for some kind of legalisation since there is no alternative non-statist institutionalised way of addressing their claims. This contradiction of migrant activism shows the necessity of bringing back the idea of a citizen of the world and of a World Republic as a *telos* of cosmopolitanism. These findings determined my future research – rethinking and advancing a new concept of a cosmopolitan institution, which is nothing other than the gesture of taking seriously the motto 'No One Is Illegal'. Without an account of cosmopolitan institution, every theory of cosmopolitanism is only half-cosmopolitan. A political theory of cosmopolitanism has to include the idea of a cosmopolitan institution that will make all humans citizens of the world. It would be a world with, at least, one exclusion less. So, the next chapter takes the motto 'No One Is Illegal' very seriously.

NOTES

1. Information about the results of the protests cab be found the movements' web pages: <https://oplatz.net/>; <https://refugeecampvienna.noblogs.org/post/2012/11/25/urgent-demands/>; <https://transversal.at/transversal/0313>; <https://www.histoire-immigration.fr/collections/28-juin-23-aout-1996-les-sans-papiers-de-saint-bernard>; <https://openborders.info/> (all last accessed 3 December 2021).
2. For a more extensive analysis of the state of the art in approaching migrant protests see Caraus (2018a).

3. On Agamben's attempt to follow his own call to think about political philosophy in a new way starting from the refugee and on the confirmation of his concepts 'bare life' in the 'camp' through empirical evidence about biopolitical management of refugees, see Caraus (forthcoming).

4. For an overview of approaches of liberal political theory on migration see Fine and Ypi (2016).

5. Available at <https://www.opendemocracy.net/en/openglobalrights-open-page/right-place-for-left-world-social-forum-in-montreal/> (last accessed 3 December 2021).

6. Available at <https://theconversation.com/world-social-forum-is-another-world-being-constructed-without-africa-46997> (last accessed 3 December 2021).

Chapter 4

THE INSTITUTION OF 'PERMANENT QUESTIONING' OR THE IDEA OF A WORLD REPUBLIC

═══════

A political theory of cosmopolitanism that will live up to the motto 'No One Is Illegal' has to endorse the idea of a cosmopolitan institution. A very difficult task. I had to overcome a threefold initial reluctance. First, the reluctance to think about institutions and thus to think institutionally. Since institutions presuppose power, hierarchy, control and discipline, critically thinking theorists want to be anti-institutional and to advance arguments enhancing freedom not power and control. The second reluctance was the notorious reluctance to think about a cosmopolitan institution usually regarded as a global Leviathan. The third reluctance was conditioned by the assumption that radical cosmopolitics could not be completed by an institution without losing its 'permanent questioning' dimension. The motivation and the courage to go further have been found in the very protests and social movements that instantiated the concept of cosmopolitanism of dissent and which not only contested the existing institutions, but advanced institutional experiments from below. So, I 'embarked' on my study of the idea of a cosmopolitan institution from the institutional experimentations from the bottom up, but alone – those scholars who joined me in researching cosmopolitanism of dissent, post-foundational cosmopolitanism and migrant protests withdrew from the prospect of such a radicalisation of research. However, there was nothing heroic in that lonely scholarly stance confronting the spectre of a global Leviathan and attempting to address a set of questions: Are cosmopolitan institutions from the bottom up possible? How can the concept of an institution that would embody a post-foundational cosmopolitanism with a 'groundless ground' be thought about? How can cosmopolitan institutions be constructed and legitimated? Is a world state inevitable when thinking about cosmopolitan institutions?

THE INSTITUTION AS A 'MEANING–STRUCTURE'

The first step in the confrontation with the global Leviathan was to examine the fear of institutions. Fear and distrust in institutions come from the everyday experience of institutions and functionaries that 'populate' them. Described as a necessary feature of modernity that brings rationalisation and efficiency to everyday life, bureaucracy permeates almost every aspect of modern life, concomitantly generating innumerable criticisms: excessive regulations and paperwork, obscure rules and procedures, hierarchies and power structures, duplicated tasks, lack of accountability, impossibility of dissent and so on (see Graeber 2015). The distrust in institutions is expressed by individuals for whom to be a twenty-first-century critically thinking individual means to be rational, liberated and authentic, or to be anti-institutional (Heclo 2011), and by theory itself, one of the most recent famous expressions of the distrust in institutions is the gathering of all institutions under the category of 'police' (Rancière 1999).

In the background of this general distrust in institutions, the fear of an institution for the world as a whole is even stronger. Since Kant, who warned against a despotic world state – 'For the laws progressively lose their impact as the government increases its range, and a soulless despotism, after crushing the germs of goodness, will finally lapse into anarchy' (Kant 1991: 113) – political theorists are 'afraid of a global state' (Nili 2015), expressing doubts about the feasibility, desirability and necessity of uniting all humankind under one common political authority. Rawls, considered the canonical political philosopher of the twentieth century, understood himself as following Kant's thinking that a world government 'would either be a global despotism or else would rule over a fragile empire torn by frequent civil strife' (Rawls 1999: 36). In consequence, 'almost every theorist joins Rawls in accepting Kant's thesis that a global government would be either perpetually unstable or intolerably oppressive' (Wenar 2006: 108). The authors who extended Rawls's theory of justice to the world as a whole tend to avoid any consideration of a world state (Beitz 1979; Pogge 1989). The oxymoronic proposals such as 'statist cosmopolitanism' (Ypi 2011) try to eliminate the problem of the cosmopolitan institution by placing it in the existing institutions of nation-state. In this way, political theorists endorse a modified version of today's domestic state system that falls shy of the ideal moral theory they are proposing.[1]

Social and political movements express distrust both in local political institutions, including parties, parliaments and political representation, and in supranational and international institutions, such as the European

Union, World Bank, International Monetary Fund, World Trade Organization and others, that generated the anti-globalisation movement. I analysed most of these recent movements in my previous research, and I found them anti-institutional, until a sudden second look which had the force of a 'discovery': dissident and resistance movements advance institutional experimentation from the bottom up! This 'discovery' was possible only when I was trying to understand how to think about a cosmopolitan institution. Only then did I acknowledge that *Charta 77* – the very first case of cosmopolitanism of dissent that I analysed – inaugurated an institutional experimentation called *parallel polis*. The second look at the previously analysed cases revealed instantly that the Zapatistas' movement, the World Social Forum, and many other resistance movements experimented with alternative institutions. As Hardt and Negri (2017: 245) observed, even when they have lasted only briefly, the lived passion of all recent movements 'have produced an institutional desire and have set in motion a constituent machine that will be hard to stop'. So, it turns out that the institution is not only a problem but also a solution. The institution appears unavoidable. Even rejecting and criticising it, the very contestatory movements cannot but produce 'an institutional desire'. Then what is an institution, philosophically speaking? Sometimes, asking a philosophical question is the most efficient way of overcoming a fear. A look into what philosophy has to say about institution is liberating from fear, since both the analytic and the continental philosophy, in the last instance, consider institutions to be structures of meaning created through language, and pertaining to the imaginary dimension of society, necessary for humans to live together.

Analytical philosophy's perspective on institutions, especially John Searle's *The Construction of Social Reality* (1995) and 'What is an Institution?' (2005), defines institutions through a collective intentionality which assigns the 'status functions': X counts as Y. Rules of the form 'X counts as Y in C' are constitutive of institutional structures (Searle 2005: 5–10). Thus, an institution is any form of constitutive rule 'X counts as Y in C', for example the green paper counts as twenty dollars everywhere where the global monetary system of currency exchange is recognised. Institutions create deontic (expressing duties or obligations) powers (Searle 2005: 10–11): rights, duties, obligations, authorisations, permissions, empowerments and requirements based on the desire-independent reasons for actions. The creation of the deontic power and of the institutions themselves are an exercise of representation and imagination: 'A status function must be represented as existing in order to exist at all, and language or symbolism of some kind provides the means of representation' (Searle 2005: 7). In the last instance, the institutions exist and are unavoidable since there is language: 'No language, no status function; no status function, no institutional deontology' (Searle 2005: 12).

For the continental philosophy, the institutions are 'meaning producing events':

> Thus, what we understand by the concept of institution are those events in the experience which endow it with durable dimensions, in relation to which a whole series of other experience will acquire meaning, will form an intelligible series or a history – or again those events that will sediment in me a meaning, not just as survivals or residues, but as the invitation to a sequel, the necessity of a future. (Merleau-Ponty 1970: 40–1)

The pattern of thinking of institutions as meaning–structure events was provided by Husserl's phenomenological analysis of the institution of geometry. In 'The Origin of Geometry', Husserl points out that geometry consists in its content which is not physical – it exists in mental space, but at the same time it is not personal or psychological: the content of geometry is objective for 'everyone', actual or possible geometers. Nevertheless, geometry has an origin and a history of development and discoveries up to the time of non-Euclidean geometry. How is it possible to have an origin and a history of an ideal objective content? Husserl argues that persons 'living wakefully' (Husserl 1970: 358) are conscious of the 'world-horizons' and language belongs to this world-horizon, which makes the world objective and communicable. Therefore, geometry, as other sciences – and all other institutions – originates in language. Language and especially written signs assure the 'persistent existence of the "ideal objects" even during the period in which the inventor and his fellows are no longer wakefully so related' (1970: 360). The content of 'ideal objects' is sedimented in the scientific language created by means of the 'painstaking formation of the relevant words' (1970: 362) by inventors, and which are sedimented in the 'living tradition of meaning-formation' (1970: 366). Thus, the 'institution' of geometry has an instituting moment, which originates in language and which functions as a foundation of geometry. As well, it has an 'ideal content' before being material for the handbooks or guidance for different works. Also, a community of geometers is necessary in order to wakefully keep the content of geometry active to be taken further by the new generation of scientists.

The authors from the tradition of the continental philosophy that reflected on the institution in their works, such as Merleau-Ponty, Althusser, Castoriadis, Lefort, Laclau, Boltanski and others, have restated Husserl's line of thought. Thus, an institution is firstly an ideal content or a meaning–structure: the 'whatness of the what is' (Boltanski 2011: 56). Before being a set of laws or legal provisions, before being a tradition, a ritual or a building with offices, an institution is a set of meanings. The institution presupposes an instituting event, for example a revolution or a declaration of independence, when new meanings, or a new meaning–structure, have emerged or have been declared. The advent of an institution is its establishment or foundation, which does not happen *ex nihilo* but in the interaction with other existing institutions, usually by rejecting the meaning–structure that an institution stands for. After a meaning is configured or has emerged as a result of humans' permanent quest for meaning, the newly found meaning is 'a demand of a future', as Merleau-Ponty (1970: 41) said – it has to be recognised, protected, passed on further and even 'implemented'. Thus, institutions come to provide 'semantic security' (Boltanski 2011: 54–5) – or security of our meanings – not only in the present but also in the future: 'Institutions have the task of saying and confirming what matters. This operation assumes the establishment of types, which must be fixed and memorized in one way or another (memory of elders, written legal codes, narratives, tales, examples, images, rituals, etc.)' (Boltanski 2011: 75).

Institutions have some material support, but the institution itself is not definable by, or reducible to, this support, but rather by acts of intersubjective meaning-constitution that give stability to the institution. Institutions are more like a 'spirit' embodied in various 'apparatuses'. The 'spirit' is the crucial fact that keeps an institution working; the material support is fungible, and this was made visible by the current pandemic, when an institution like a university continued its functioning although its material support – mainly, the university buildings – could not be used. Institutions have to be differentiated from organisations and administration, but the institutions cannot be uncoupled from organisations and administrations because an instituted meaning has an immediate deontic character: this is the newly found meaning, therefore we have these new rights and these new obligations.

The meanings need to be reaffirmed and reconfirmed, thus institutions need to be continuously re-instituted, and so legitimated by acts of collective recognition and consent to their power. When meanings are not reaffirmed entirely, a change in institutions is required to acknowledge the change in the meaning, which is not necessarily accepted immediately by everyone (thus an adjustment of an institution can generate worries about the loss of meaning, like the lesbian, gay, bisexual and transgender (LGBT) marriage rights that are seen by the so called 'supporters of traditional family' as threatening to meanings and values).

The change of an institution is unavoidable: individual subjects create, maintain and ultimately destroy institutions and create new ones. Therefore, there is no society without institutions regardless of the development of individuals, the progress of technology or economic abundance because humans always will create meaning in or against the background of the received meanings. Every new set of meanings will look for its recognition and confirmation in a set of written or unwritten rules, similar to a new word that enters into the 'institution' of a dictionary: 'There is no dispassionate inquiry on human nature that does not carry along with it, as a sort of clandestine passenger, at least the sketch of a theory of political institutions' (Virno 2009: 95). Every vision, however utopian, has a need to institute itself as a 'triumph of reason over chaos' (Graeber 2015: 167). Every institutionalisation of a newly found meaning in the place of a previous set of 'outdated' meanings that no longer reflected the subjects' self-understandings, claim to be the 'triumph of reason over chaos', while 'reasons' and 'chaos' are different sets of meanings.

In the light of a minimal clarification on what an institution is, the distrust in and the fear of institution appear to come from the times when the institution was not man-made, but God-given. Now, once clarified that the institution is man-made, it follows that it can be un-made, the support and recognition could be withdrawn, and it is withdrawn, since there is a permanent process of institutional adjustment in current societies. However, the fear of institution might not disappear. Kafka's writings pointing to the perennial anxiety of the 'man before law' and the multiple insights of this parable that is the subject of perennial interpretations suggest that the fear of institutions, even of the man-made ones, is a shadow of the idea of institution itself.

Therefore, if every inquiry into human nature has as a 'clandestine passenger' a 'sketch of a political institution', as Virno noted, then cosmopolitanism – an inquiry into human nature par excellence – has its own sketch of a political institution. Perhaps, this sketch is more clandestine than others, since even the authors operating with sets of meanings that are cosmopolitan, avoid having a sketch of a political institution, stop halfway through their inquiry, and so their set of meanings appears as half a meaning. This chapter brings its clandestine passenger into visibility, by attempting to map firstly what the 'sketch of a political institution' was that was carried by the movements displaying a cosmopolitanism of dissent.

THE 'INSTITUTIONAL DESIRE' AND COSMOPOLITANISM OF DISSENT

I began my 'positioning' in political theory by advancing the concept of cosmopolitanism of dissent based on three interrelated notions inspired by Patočka's philosophy: permanent questioning, living in problematicity and solidarity of the shaken. This set of meanings was 'implemented' by the Eastern European dissident movement and confirmed further by different episodes of dissent and protest movements worldwide. At the 'second look', those episodes of dissent and protest movements revealed their 'institutional desire' (Hardt and Negri 2017: 245). Thus, the crucial question is how did these movements try to institute the meaning–structure constituted by permanent questioning, living in problematicity and solidarity of the shaken? How would the sketch of a cosmopolitan institution implementing permanent questioning, living in problematicity and solidarity of the shaken look like? So, once again in doing political theory of cosmopolitanism, I looked at the 'cases studies' – this time to map the new institutional ideas that emerged in these movements with the hope that I would detect a cosmopolitan dimension in these institutional experimentations. And the 'institutional desire' was indeed there, in the movement, appearing shortly after the manifesto or the declaration that expressed disagreement with the current meanings and institutions.

The declaration of *Charta 77* was issued on 6 January 1977. The *parallel polis* was described for the first time in May 1978:

> We join forces in creating, slowly but surely, parallel structures that are capable, to a limited degree at least, of supplementing the generally beneficial and necessary functions that are missing in the existing [state] structures and where possible, to use those existing structures, to humanise them. (Benda 1991: 35)

In October 1978, Havel in his famous text, 'The Power of the Powerless', argued that the parallel structures come from the existential need of the dissidents and their followers to live in truth:

> The parallel structures do not grow a priori out of a theoretical vision of systemic changes, but from the aims of life and the authentic needs of real people . . . Dissidents demonstrate that living within the truth is a human and social alternative and they struggle to expand the space available for that life. (Havel 1978)

Soon after, *parallel polis* included alternatives to all state structures: parallel or underground culture, parallel education and science, informational system (samizdat), economy, political structures and foreign policy (Benda et al. 1988). The parallel structures were described by Havel in terms of 'more meaningful' commitments, confirming that an institution firstly operates in the realm of meaning before having a body and an apparatus, while the apparatuses are created to preserve the meaning oriented to the future: 'Are not these informed, non-bureaucratic, dynamic, and open communities that comprise the "parallel polis" a kind of rudimentary prefiguration, a symbolic model of those more meaningful "post-democratic" political structures that might become the foundation of a better society?' (Havel 1978). Also, the parallel structures were for Havel (1978) alternative communities not only for the socialist states, but also for the Western democratic institutions caught in the consumerist society:

> There is no real evidence that Western democracy, that is, democracy of the traditional parliamentary type, can offer solutions that are any more profound. It would appear that the traditional parliamentary democracies can offer no fundamental opposition to the automatism of technological civilization and the industrial-consumer society, for they, too, are being dragged helplessly along by it.

Is it possible to identify in the *parallel polis* a sketch of a cosmopolitan institution? The *parallel polis* made a 'demand of a future', not only of the socialist regimes in Eastern Europe, but of a future for the entire technological civilisation and consumer society, or in other words, of the entire world. This is a hint to an institutional alternative for the whole world and, together with a 'prefiguration' of a society not oppressed by laws and decisions of representatives of authorities, it could 'qualify' as an idea for an institutional experimentation for the world as a whole, to the extent that the 'parallel' institution includes everyone, giving to all equal deontic powers. In other word, the 'parallel' cosmopolitan institution has to make everyone a citizen of the world, but one cannot be a parallel citizen of the world.

The Zapatistas' insurgence, although very local, was a case of cosmopolitanism of dissent by excellence, through their constant concern for 'brothers and sisters from five continents' and for the entire planet. The insurgence took place on 1 January 1994, and since then the Zapatistas have started to create alternative institutions as 'the material conditions for resistance'. The new institutions implied changes in all aspects of life: communally owned lands, 'solidarity economy', an ecological approach to agriculture, changes in production and reproduction of everyday life, such as health and education.[2] In December 1995, five autonomous regions, *Aguascalientes*, were created. In 2003, five political and cultural centres called *Caracoles* were created with their *Good Government Juntas*, and twenty-nine 'autonomous rebel municipalities', which marked the full separation of the Zapatista civil and military structures and authorities. The institutions, as 'the material conditions for resistance', are guided by the principles of government from below: 'To Propose, Not Impose; To Represent, Not Supplant; To Convince, Not Conquer; To Construct, Not

Destroy; To Serve Others, Not Serve Oneself; To Work From Below, Not Seek To Rise' (Enlace Zapatista 2005). All administrative structures have elected non-paid officials, each of whom work 15 days a month, and who 'govern by obeying' and through the rotation of administrative duties: 'now there are more *compañeros* and *compañeras* who are learning to govern' (Enlace Zapatista 2005). A Zapatista Rebel Autonomous Education System was also created – 300 schools and 1,000 educational 'promoters' chosen by the community: 'Education occurs among all of us. Nobody raises the awareness of another.'[3] Reportedly, 'the material conditions for resistance' brought real changes in production and reproduction of everyday life: 'Where once there was death, now life is beginning' (Enlace Zapatista 2005), with communally owned lands leading to a 'solidarity economy' and an ecological approach to agriculture. The crucial questions for this 'second look' at case studies – how do the institutional experiments 'implement' the meaning–structure configured by permanent questioning and living in problematicity, and how is it possible to identify a sketch of a cosmopolitan institution here – do not have straightforward answers. Although the Zapatistas continued to contest 'those from above who privatize the planet' (EZLN 1996), within the created institutions the community works to implement a coherent local set of meanings, as the principles of government display. 'The Other Campaign', launched in 2005, attempted to link different resistance groups throughout the country through institutional experimentation: 'We will engage in a struggle with everyone, with indigenous, workers, campesinos, students, teachers, employees, women, children, old ones, men, and with all of those of good heart' (Enlace Zapatista 2005). And the struggle is ready to be extended to the whole world, in solidarity with 'the brothers and sisters of Africa, Asia and Oceania':

> We cannot watch everything that is happening on our planet and just remain quiet . . . we want to tell all of those who are resisting and fighting in their own ways and in their own countries, that you are not alone, that we, the Zapatistas, even though we are very small, are supporting you, and we are going to look at how to help you in your struggles' (Enlace Zapatista 2005).

From all movements that 'instantiated' the cosmopolitanism of dissent, the World Social Forum was the closest to the institutionalisation of permanent questioning, concomitantly displaying features of a 'world parliament in exile' (Monbiot 2003: 79). WSF encouraged its participant organisations and movements 'to situate their actions as issues of planetary citizenship, and to introduce onto the global agenda the change-inducing practices that they are experimenting in building a new world in solidarity' (WSF 2001). The institutional novelty of WSF is the idea of 'open space':

> An open meeting space for reflective thinking, democratic debate of ideas, formulation of proposals, free exchange of experiences and inter-linking for effective action, by groups and movements of civil society that are opposed to neoliberalism and to domination of the world by capital and any form of imperialism and are committed to building a planetary society directed towards fruitful relationships among Humankind and between it and the Earth. (WSF 2001)

'Open space' was instantiated at each WSF event: a space for discussing alternative forms of action, no prevalence of a single political stance, inclusive, participatory, horizontal, decentralised, coercion-free and non-hierarchical.[4] Also, WSF passed no resolutions and organises no political activities.[5] And while the WSF consolidated itself as an open space of horizontal and plural encounters for the democratic debate of ideas, the open space showed some unexpected side effects, such as incompatibility among groups in the name of 'open space', a widespread impression of a top-down organisation, and the inevitability of leadership/hierarchy.[6] The achievements of WSF are still a matter of debate and interpretation (Wallerstein 2004; De Sousa Santos 2005).[7] This movement remains the closest to the performance of institutionalising the meaning–structure of permanent questioning from below, while reminding us that 'Another World Is Possible'. The spirit, if not the sketch of a cosmopolitan insti-tution, was in all WSF activities, and seeing WSF as 'prefiguration' is a salvatory perspective, protecting its legacy.[8] However, this prefiguration has to be doubled by a sketch of cosmopolitan institution 'from above', one in which the WSF activists will not need visas in order to participate at the WSF meetings everywhere in the world.

The institutional experimentations of social movements have been described through a new thinking of assembly, often inspired by the Deleuzian assemblage, and going beyond the provision of the freedom to assemble without government interference, consecrated in the Universal Declaration of Human Rights. The 'assembly' as form, usually networked, is a point of convergence for a variety of tendencies – those who opt for horizontality, and those who prefer some degree of vertical organisation, but mainly the assembly is defined as a politics of the common: something shared between people, not mediated by the state or capital (Thorburn 2012; Butler 2015). For Hardt and Negri, the assembly is the 'New Prince of multitude' defined as 'something like the centre of gravity of a dancing body' (2017: 228) who can initiate a process of constituent power (2017: 325) and 'invent new, non-sovereign institutions' (2017: 39).

While assemblages are seen as having a potential 'to make radical social change – the coming of the common – a true possibility' (Thorburn 2012: 275), without further elaboration it is not clear if this assembly will be a cosmopolitan one or not. The assemblages, as assumed in this thinking of assembly, are necessarily plural; however, currently people live as well in assemblages, different and plural ones, but none is a cosmopolitan institution that will give to everyone the minimal semantic security and deontic powers as would living in One World.

The re-examination of different cases studies, from which the three above are presented as representative examples, generates further questions. Should a cosmopolitan institution be conceived as 'open space', as a global confederation of *caracoles* or as a *parallel polis*? Can one construct autonomous or parallel cosmopolitan institutions, since a cosmopolitan institution, by definition, should include everyone? Could these institutional experiments develop and deliver justice, equality and 'semantic security' to all human beings as belonging to a single community? The answer to these questions is 'not really' – a cosmopolitan institution must give to everyone deontic powers and cannot function as a parallel structure. Thus, the examination of the institutional experimentation from below leads to a plausible conclusion which is at the same time a starting point to think further: a cosmopolitan institution cannot be only from below, it has equally to be from above. So, I arrived at a situation that I tried had to escape since my 'immersion' into cosmopolitanism studies. For a while, I managed to stay on the side of those doing cosmopolitanism from below. Now if I wanted to think further about the idea of a cosmopolitan institution, it was the time to move 'above'.

FROM THE CRITIQUE OF INSTITUTIONS TO THE INSTITUTION OF CRITIQUE

Why it is not possible, nevertheless, to remain 'from below' and to affirm a cosmopolitan institution? To expand a single institutional experimentation from below on the entire world is a way of proceeding that already has a legacy called 'imperialism'. To affirm the plurality of the institutional experimentations from below means to avoid giving to everyone the same 'deontic powers'. A cosmopolitan institution will always tend to be *one* assembly of different assemblages, otherwise if it is not one, then not everyone will have equal deontic powers as a citizen of the world. Moving to a 'from above' perspective does not mean joining some kind of elite cosmopolitanism or to join currently existing international institutions. The 'above' is a position from where, paraphrasing the motto, 'A cosmopolitan institution *for all* is possible.' The move I had to make was from the 'plurality' of institutional experimentations to a distilled 'essence' extracted from the plurality of experimentations. And in performing this move from the 'below' of plurality to the 'above' of 'for all', I had to avoid invoking theoretically – or, *horrible dictu*, to let in – the spectre of the global Leviathan.

The 'extract' that allows the move 'above' comes firstly in the form of a question: if all institutional experiments from below are possible as critiques of existing institutions, of what is unjust and intolerable in given institutions, then what exactly is the framework that enables this critique? Could this framework itself be an institution? Could it be plausibly called an 'institution of critique'?[9] And could this institution of critique be the very idea of a cosmopolitan institution? But concomitantly I was assaulted by other questions: how legitimate is it to 'capture' the critique of institutions in one cosmopolitan institution? Can and should critique be institutionalised? If critique is institutionalised, will it not be oppressive, obliging everyone to continuously critique and self-critique? Is it possible to institutionalise critique without exhausting it or making it irrelevant? How can an institution embody critique without undermining itself, without ceasing to be an institution? The rather unexpected consubstantiality of institution and critique allowed me to answer these questions and to ground the idea of the cosmopolitan institution in the very ability of being able to criticise the existing institutions.

The consubstantiality of critique and institution is not immediately visible, since the above-mentioned distrust in institutions is generated exactly because institutions are seen as irresponsive to critique, or, in some cases, even crushing all possible critique. However, the institution is a precondition of critique (Boltanski 2011: 97–9). As argued above, institutions are defined in different traditions of philosophy as meaning–structure and as 'status functions' assigned by collective intentionality through language. Since in language the 'semantic closure' of the meaning is impossible – this being the main lesson and legacy of post-structuralism – there will always be

> a distance between society as instituting and what is, at every moment, instituted. This distance is not something negative or deficient; it is one of the expressions of the creative nature of history, what prevents it from fixing itself once and for all into the 'finally found form' of social relations and of human activities. (Castoriadis 1987: 114)

Since there cannot be a definitive semantic closure, 'the formal genesis of institutions is inextricably a formal genesis of critique' (Boltanski 2011: 97). Institutions are always incomplete and beset with tensions, antinomies and contradictions, because institutions are only relatively stable meanings–structures. Critique works with the difference between the instituted sense of reality and the wider horizon of meanings and possibilities of the world.

The consubstantiality of critique and institution was made especially convincing by Boltanski (2011), whose sociological approach of the relation between critique and institution has an insightful philosophical relevance. According to him, in a pre-institutional situation we are in an 'original position' where a radical uncertainty prevails (2011: 57–61). This uncertainty is both semantic and deontic in kind; it concerns the 'whatness of what is' and what matters, what has value (2011: 56). The institutions bring a kind of 'sematic security', so although uncertainty cannot be eliminated entirely, at least it can be made bearable. To eliminate uncertainty, institutions apply 'semantic violence' (2011: 78–81). Violence is tacitly present in institutions because they struggle against the unmasking of their own tensions and contradictions, as law-preserving violence, in Walter Benjamin's sense. The tension between 'sematic security' and 'semantic violence', both produced by institutions, is a source of critique. The 'hermeneutic contradiction' (Boltanski 2011: 84–92) of institution, which is produced by the 'bodiless body of institution', its 'spirit' and the necessity of embodying the 'whatness of what is' in an apparatus, is another source of critique (2011: 74–8). The 'fragility of institutions' created by the representatives of the institutions, spokespersons who inevitably have certain points of view who 'betray' the 'spirit' of the institution, is another 'reserve' for critique, so during history there have been many rebellious movements directed in the first instance against the 'bad counsellors' of the 'good prince', and against the apparatuses of an institution, not against its 'spirit' (2011: 84–6).

Therefore, 'the formal genesis of institutions' cannot avoid being 'a formal genesis of critique' (Boltanski 2011: 97). Since the instituted meaning–structure cannot be fixed once and for all, institutions are a constant object of critique and have the task of incessantly re-saying what they mean and 'the whatness of what is' in order to try to protect certain meanings-structures and symbolic forms of collective imaginary. At the same time, since humans are in a permanent and creative quest for (new or more) meaning, institutions not only protect the established meaning but also attempt to incorporate new meanings or, more specifically, institutions adjust to critique. As Boltanski and Chiapello show (2005), critique played a substantial role in precipitating the reorganisation of capitalism, bringing a new 'spirit of capitalism' – an imaginary that justifies people's commitment to capitalism, and which renders this commitment attractive. The critique of capitalism made by the 1968 movements, both in the form of 'social criticism' that emphasised inequalities, misery, exploitation and the selfishness of a world that stimulates individualism, and the 'artistic criticism' that criticised oppression (market domination, factory discipline), the massification of society, standardisation and commodification, were incorporated by capitalism. The 'new spirit of capitalism' incorporated adaptability, flexibility, polyvalence, trustworthiness, abilities to communicate, variety of social connections, creativity and even the claims to 'make your life a work of art' if it is vendible, producing all the 'glory and misery' of the neoliberal individual. Capitalism's amazing ability to survive by incorporating some of the substantial criticisms it faced, helped to disarm the forces of anti-capitalism, giving way to a triumphant version of capitalism – neoliberalism. Not all institutions survive and incorporate critique though – the perestroika in the Soviet Union was a critique of the fossilised party system intended not to bring an end to it, but just to reconstruct the original meanings-structures and to animate the 'spirit', the founding values of the communist party and the Soviet Union. However, once the symbolic violence, protecting the fossilised meanings of the party with a wooden language, was diminished, the grounds and foundations collapsed.

Thus, institutions are the precondition of critique, and the possibility of critique is inscribed in the tensions contained in the very functioning of institutions. How does this consubstantiality of institution and critique allow the further rethinking of the idea of a cosmopolitan institution that will inscribe in it the very possibility of critique, in order to avoid producing and validating theoretically a global Leviathan? The most direct help is the theoretical possibility of conceiving an institution as perpetually contestable, contestation being inscribed in its very structure. Thus, the Leviathan, global or otherwise, cannot be born other than fragile, full of contradictions and tensions, perpetually forced to adjust to humans' creative powers and their quest for meaning. But the most rewarding finding was to realise that the possibility of critique inscribed at the core of each institution shows affinity with the definition of cosmopolitanism as permanent questions and living in problematicity.

The question of what the 'institutional desire' or the 'sketch of the institution' is that is carried out by the meaning–structure configured by permanent questioning, living in problematicity and solidarity of the shaken receives an answer – it is the institution of critique or, from the perspective of my definition of cosmopolitanism, it is the institution of permanent questioning. The difference between 'critique' and 'permanent questioning' is not one of substance but of temporal distance. Critique's origins are usually identified in Enlightenment, as emerging from Kant's two meanings of critique: critique as the determination of the limits of reason in *Critique of Pure Reason*, and in *What is Enlightenment* as the capacity to use your own understanding and to contest the authority: 'Enlightenment is the human being's emergence from his self-incurred minority . . . *Sapere aude*! Have courage to make use of your own understanding' (Kant 1991: 54). Perfected by Hegel, Marx and Nietzsche, critique as an idea and practice was enriched and expanded in the twentieth century by different authors, if not by all of them: Adorno, Foucault, Derrida, Bourdieu, Rancière and others (de Boer and Sonderegger 2012: 1–10).[10]

Cosmopolitanism was born through an act of a total contestation according to the Cynics' principle, 'Alter the currency!' (DL 6.20–1). The alteration of the value of the currency has all the features of radical critique. Foucault made the Cynics the heroes of *parrhesia*, speaking the truth fearlessly, and their *parrhesia* contains a critique of power and a critique of every aspect of society. The very fact that Cynics are readable from the perspective of critique of power is an indication that a very potent critique was already there, in the Cynics' way of life. The consubstantiality of critique and the first cosmopolitan stance[11] is revealed by the fact that all elements of a critical stance are already present in the Cynics' alteration of values. Thus, when we express critique, usually we: (1) make judgements, especially moral judgements of good and evil, discriminating and rational judgments (evaluative and mainly negative) of an object/state of affairs in the light of some standard for a practical aim or purpose; (2) stand back, as if it were possible to remove ourselves from the circumstances criticised; and (3) attempt to change things, persons, the world and so on, in a forward-looking attitude concerned with shifts in self-understanding and other transformations, according to the judgements made (de Boer and Sonderegger 2012: 1–10). The Cynics exhibit these elements: (1) the Cynic dog-like life is a life of a guard which barks at enemies, which knows how to distinguish the good from the bad and the true from the false, that is, to make a genuine discriminating rational judgement; (2) the Cynics stand back from the circumstances criticised through a series of tests of endurance and destitution in order to be recognised as a Cynic; (3) the principle, 'Alter the currency!' (*parakharaxon to nomisma*, DL 6.20–1), attempts to change things and persons, since *nomisma* means not only 'currency' but also law and custom; the principle implies changing the custom, rules, habits, conventions, laws and the polis itself, as the ultimate convention.

Critique, therefore, turns consubstantial both with cosmopolitanism and with institution. If the two consubstantiality theses are correct, that is, (a) critique and institution are consubstantial, (b) critique and cosmopolitanism are consubstantial, then (c) the idea of a cosmopolitan institution acquires a plausible consistency: institutionalising cosmopolitanism means concomitantly to institutionalise critique. To differentiate the cosmopolitan critique's precedence over the modern critique, the cosmopolitan institution of critique will be called the 'institution of permanent questioning', in this way integrating the initial minimal framework of defining cosmopolitanism: permanent questioning, living in problematicity and solidarity of the shaken. The cosmopolitan institution as the institution of permanent questioning confirms once more the post-foundational cosmopolitanism and it is a post-foundational approach of the idea of institution. The reflection on the idea of a cosmopolitan institution is not a concrete sketch of an institution with its apparatuses – which is a topic to be explored separately – but only an attempt to think about the grounds of the idea of a cosmopolitan institution in a new way.

But what is so 'new' here? Any group of warriors can constitute itself in 'spirit' as an 'institution of critique' and even in apparatuses of 'permanent contestation' through a more or less terrorist organisation. What is new, when critique itself is 'a machine that run out of steam?' (Latour 2004: 225), when 'critical barbarism' proliferates since 'mad scientists . . . let the virus of critique out of the confines of their laboratories and cannot do anything now to limit its deleterious effects' (Latour 2004: 225–6). What is new, when critique devoured its very condition of possibility, moving from philosophical deconstruction of the opposition between truth and appearance to 'no facts' or 'alternative facts' and 'post-truth'? The 'critical barbarism' is neither a permanent questioning nor a life in problematicity; on the contrary, it is the effect of the attempts to posit our 'absolute', 'final' and 'true' meaning, it is a refusal of life in problematicity. And thinking in a new way about the idea of a cosmopolitan institution as an institution of permanent questioning is not done *ex nihilo* – it is an attempt to rethink the very idea of a World Republic.

A WORLD REPUBLIC OF AN OPEN HUMANITY

If my proposed ground is new, then what were the previous grounds on which the idea of a cosmopolitan institution was advanced? What were the meanings–structures, the 'institutional desire' and eventually the 'sketches' of institution that the proposals for a World Republic advanced? Were there different meanings-structures or just one for two millennia?

The idea of a World Republic was born at the same time as the first cosmopolitan stance of the Cynics for whom 'the only true commonwealth is as wide as the universe' (DL 6.72), a 'commonwealth' grounded in the 'Alter the currency!' principle. Zeno, in his lost *Republic*, appears to ground the commonwealth in the idea of common humanity, given his metaphoric image of a 'herd that feeds together and shares the pasturage of a common field' (Plutarch quoted in Heater 1996: 13). Taking up Zeno's idea of a true republic 'as wide as the universe' this chapter argues for the idea of a cosmopolitan institution as a republic and not as a state, acknowledging that in some texts these are synonymous.[12] Since Zeno, the idea of one world and one human community has been restated periodically. In the religious visions of a World Republic, the ground was obviously in divinity, for example Dante, in *De Monarchia* (*c.*1310), argued that universal peace requires universal government, and the universal monarch 'will most closely resemble God, by mirroring the principle of oneness or unity of which he is the supreme example' (Dante 1995: 1.8); grounded in divinity as well were the incredible ideas of a World Republic advanced by monks and other luminaries (Heater 1996: 55–7, 62–70). The next uncompromising proposal for a World Republic, made by Anacharsis Cloots (1755–94) during the French Revolution, advocated the abolition of all existing states and the establishment of a 'republic of united individuals' that find themselves in the state of nature vis-à-vis each other. Sovereignty should reside within the people, and because it involves indivisibility, it implies that there can be but one sovereign body in the world, namely, the human race as a whole.[13]

During the rise of the nation-state, the idea of a world republic was forgotten, until the first half of the twentieth century, when it found its most prominent advocate in the novelist and social critic H. G. Wells (1866–1946), who from 1901 to his death in 1946 wrote prolifically about a world state, grounding it in the necessity to avoid war.[14] Wells outlined several cosmopolitan models aimed at accommodating different cultures at different stages of economic and social development, but keeping his original intention of unifying humankind in a sovereign world state of peace and prosperity (Partington 2003).

The first two decades after the Second World War were the heyday of the actions to implement the idea of a world government grounded in the idea of peace. Convinced that mankind could not survive another world war, scientists, activists and ordinary people were creating movements for a World Federal Government,[15] drafting World Constitutions,[16] organising thousands of discussion groups about peace, establishing registries of World Citizens[17] and issuing World Passports.[18] For example, a book, *The Anatomy of Peace*, published in 1945, had 500,000 copies printed in English, and was translated into twenty languages, declared that 'The modern Bastille is the nation-state, no matter whether the jailers are conservative, liberal or socialists' (Reves 1945: 270). Leading physicists wrote reports on 'the full meaning of the atomic bomb' entitled *One World or None* (Masters and Way 1946), and organised an Emergency Committee of Atomic Scientists (1945–55) and a Crusade for

World Government: 'World Government is possible now. We require a world government which has both the authority and the power to make laws applicable to individuals' (Usborne 1947). The initiatives attracted different strata of the population, and political and religious leaders,[19] but, paradoxically enough, philosophers and political philosophers are not among them, with some exceptions, such as Karl Jaspers (see Chapter 5). These activities diminished as the Cold War became the dominant framework of understanding reality and the idea of world government seemed forgotten.

After the end of Cold World, there was a rise in non-governmental organisations and institutions of global governance (International Monetary Fund, World Trade Organization etc.), all of which are different or even contrary to the idea of a World Republic, although a Campaign for a United Nations Parliamentary Assembly, has been active since 2007, which brings together different efforts that advocate for a democratic representation of the world's citizens at the United Nations,[20] given global interdependency of life, global threats and challenges. The challenges and the threats brought by technology prompted some visionaries to advance proposals for a global institution formulated from the perspective of digital technology, for example blockchain technology is seen as providing infrastructure for a trustworthy global digital ID for everyone, 'With a digital ID, embrace the Earth as your home'.[21] The 'accidental megastructure of planetary scale computation' has allowed other authors to see a 'megastructure as a single meta-technology that deformed the political geography of the Westphalian state system' and requires rethinking sovereignty (Bratton 2016), while 'the internet of things', regarded as 'the most powerful political tool ever created', requires a *pax technica* which is 'an empire of people and devices' (Howard 2015: 228).

The proposal for a world government formulated in recent decades within the field of International Relations invoke global justice, human rights and global security (Cabrera 2004; Tännsjö 2008; Falk and Strauss 2001; Scheuerman 2014; Leinen and Bummel 2018), to which some pragmatic reasons were added (Nili 2015; Ulaş 2017), and some arguments formulated from the perspective of the post-Anthropocene.[22] The most famous International Relations argument remains the Hegelian inspired one based on the logic of recognition: individuals and domestic social groups demand from one another the recognition of their own equal worth. As recognition is extended, they gradually come to identify with one another as equals in a common identity, forming a cohesive whole, 200 years from now (Wendt 2003).

Although this brief examination of the grounds on which the idea of world government was advanced is not a history of the idea, it is nevertheless visible that the ideas are not advanced by philosophers of the political: there is no such idea in Plato, Aristotle, Augustine, St. Thomas, Hobbes, Locke, Rousseau, Kant, Hegel, Rawls or in other more recent canonical philosophers. In most cases, the political imagination of a world without border thrives outside political philosophy, in science, literature, arts or accidentally in International Relations. However, there is an exception that 'saves the honour' of the last decades of political philosophy – the innovative account of a World Republic, advanced by Kojin Karatani (2003: 265–307; 2014). Karatani arrived at the idea of a World Republic by developing his philosophical account of various modes of exchange. The exchange of gifts and reciprocity which is the basis of clan society is called 'mode of exchange A'. The formation of the state in terms of voluntary surrender and protection, taxation and redistribution, is mode of exchange B, while the sphere of ordinary commodity exchange is mode of exchange C. To these three, Karatani added the mode of exchange D, a 'pure gift' which attempts to sublate the others, like the power of God, which is manifested in the form of universal religion in the age of the ancient empires, and which in modernity appeared as the Kingdom of Ends and communism. The Kingdom of Ends and communism itself, as Marx said and Karatani reminds us, could never exist within a single country:

> Even if one country should manage to realize a perfect civil constitution within, it would still be based on treating other countries solely as means (i.e., exploitation) and therefore could not qualify as the Kingdom of Ends. The Kingdom of Ends cannot be thought of in terms of a single country; it can only be realized as a World Republic. (2014: 297)

The realisation of a world system grounded in mode of exchange D – a World Republic – will not be easy, admits Karatani. Modes of exchange A, B, and C will remain stubborn presences:

> The nation, state, and capital will all persist. No matter how highly developed the forces of production (the relation of humans and nature) become, it will be impossible to completely eliminate the forms of existence produced by these modes of exchange – in other words, by relations between humans. Yet so long as they exist, so too will mode of exchange D. No matter how it is denied or repressed, it will always return. (2014: 307)

The analysis of Karatani's proposal cannot be done at length here, but it has to be noted that this mode of exchange is not called cosmopolitan, and Karatani never uses this word; however, we have in his work one of the most compelling philosophical arguments for a cosmopolitan World Republic.

This brief examination reveals once again that the final grounding of all proposals of a World Republic is that common humanity should be protected by an institution. What differs is the pre-final grounding that positively invokes peace, justice and equality, or negatively invokes the imminence of war, threat of climate change, destruction of humanity through technology and so on. The 'final' grounding for the idea of a cosmopolitan institution – common humanity – cannot be eliminated, it appears as the 'final' hidden ground of each approach. This chapter attempts to ground the idea of a World Republic in critique and permanent questioning, so does it eliminate 'common humanity'? The answer is simply 'No'. The attempt to rethink the idea of a cosmopolitan institution was determined by the motto 'No One Is Illegal', that is, to think about an institution that will be up to the motto which reiterates common humanity. But humanity itself, as is well known, is a troubled concept. The thinking anew of the idea of a cosmopolitan institution reiterates common humanity and through permanent questioning it opens the existing notions of humanity and keeps them open.

The trouble with the concept of humanity are well-known and rehearsed, and as usual those who want to summarise the troubles refer to the famous quote, 'whoever invokes humanity wants to cheat' (Schmitt 2007: 54). Humanity, a cornerstone concept of the Enlightenment, presupposed a universal moral core of humankind and viewed all persons as inherently free and equal, guided by the universal laws of reason towards a total emancipation from any kind of tyranny. However, the philosophy from the last century, starting with Nietzsche through Heidegger to Foucault and post-structuralism, had an anti-humanist stance since it questioned 'human nature', 'man' and 'humanity' both as historically relative and as abstract metaphysical constructions. Under these auspices, the criticism of the concepts of humanity and humanism proliferated in different subfields within humanities and social sciences. The concept of humanity itself was considered an instrument of imperialist expansion, its ethical-humanitarian form just a vehicle of economic imperialism, while intervention in the name of humanity was seen as denying others the quality of being human. Human rights based on the presupposition of the universal moral core of all human beings were also criticised as an instrument of imperialist expansion and the normalising of the structure of power. The critique of humanity goes hand in hand with the critique of cosmopolitanism, so affirming once again the common humanity does not seem a very felicitous way of grounding the idea of the cosmopolitan institution.

However, reaffirming humanity through permanent questioning makes a significant difference compared to all other affirmations of humanity. And this reaffirmation of humanity through permanent questioning was performed by the Cynics themselves. In *The Courage of the Truth*, Foucault declared the Cynic a 'functionary of humanity in general' and a 'functionary of ethical universality' (2011: 301). But how can the Cynics who live on the fringe of society, who harshly critique every institution, law and custom, who criticise the normal everyday ways of living a life, end up caring for all humankind and be functionaries of ethical universality? The Cynic leads a battle against customs, conventions, institutions and laws, and 'an explicit, intentional, and constant aggression directed at humanity in general, at humanity in its real life, and whose horizon or objective is to change its moral attitude' (2011: 280). To the idea of the guard dog who accosts enemies and bites them, Foucault adds the theme of the combatant who fights against the evils of the world in order to change it. The Cynic battle is for Foucault close to the modern notion of militancy: 'an overt, universal, aggressive militancy; militancy in the world and against the world' (2011: 285). The aims of the militant Cynic are twofold: to shake people up by attacking their vices and faults, and to 'convert them, abruptly' (2011: 285) in order to change them and the world. For this purpose, the Cynic combatant acts as the 'scout of humanity' (2011: 300), the man 'who roams, who runs ahead of humanity' (2011: 167), who reveals in advance the dangers and possibilities prefiguring the future world. Thus, the true life is 'a life of combat for a changed world' (2011: 303). The Cynic, declared a 'functionary of humanity in general' and a 'functionary of ethical universality' (2011: 301), ends up governing the universe, as gods. In the evening after a heavy day's work, the Cynic is 'restored, beyond his hidden monarchy, in true sovereignty, which is that of the gods over the whole of humankind' (2011: 303).

Assuming with Foucault that the Cynics care for humankind by being its functionary, the question is nevertheless: Why such a detour? Why should they contest humanity, criticise humans and their meanings so harshly and radically and only after that come to care for them? Why not care for humans directly, as they are, with all their imperfections and limits, why such a reversal and a detour? The answer that this chapter advances is that the Cynics could not embrace humans and their humanity as they are. There is a dissent and resistance in the Cynics' stance exactly against this immediate 'submission' to humanity *as it is now*. The Cynics in their attack on the conventions of life in the polis refuse to accept the current meanings of humanity and concomitantly attempt to open it and free the potential that is imprisoned in the given notion of humanity. The Cynics, in a manner similar to Havel's description of dissidents' action, 'struggle to expand the space available for that life' (Havel 1978). The Cynics contest the current world, interrupt it and point to a new world and a new humanity. However, the opening of humanity cannot be a single gesture, it cannot be done once and for all, it is a gesture of a permanent opening or, in other words, of keeping it open.

Foucault's Cynics open humanity through their scandal of living in truth and speaking it fearlessly. Through a harsh critique of the polis and all its conventions, the Cynics point to another life and to the horizon of another world. The humanism that Foucault attributes to the Cynics does not foreclose the possibilities of being human, it is a permanent opening to alterity and experimentation within the horizon of another world which structures the Cynics' true life. Cynics care for all men in order to make possible another life and another world, but without specifying the content and fixing the limits of the other life and the other world, and therefore without a limit to the human.

If the Cynics had elaborated their sketch of 'the only true commonwealth' which is as wide as the universe (DL 6.72), what would it look like? Well, it would be a World Republic with 'functionaries of humanity' that keep humanity open. The Cynics' World Republic with 'functionaries of humanity' do not foreclose the possibilities of being human; on the contrary, it is a permanent opening to alterity and experimentation within the horizon of another world which structures the Cynics' true life. The Cynics are functionaries of humanity through the very gesture of pointing to another life and another world, but without specifying their content. And while the function of the functionaries of humanity is precisely to keep humanity open, all other citizens of a World Republic will have the same function – to keep humanity open – by engaging in permanent questioning as radical cosmopolitan democracy. A World Republic that will keep humanity open cannot be otherwise than an institution of radical democracy, but elaboration of its 'apparatuses' requires a separate book.

However, it has to be mentioned that instituting a World Republic as the institution of critique is not one single moment, but a process involving several instituting stages. Using Claude Lefort's terminology, these stages could be called *mise-en-sens*, *mise-en-scene*, *mise-en-forme* (Lefort 1988). So, the process of instituting a World Republic as an institution of critique starts with the stage of *mise-en-sens* when a symbolic mutation, similar to the change that emerges in the relationship between the symbolic order of the ancient regime and modern democracy, will make the world intelligible to us as One World. The fact that the world could be organised as one, despite its multiple divisions, implies a reference to a place from which it can be seen, read and named, which is a symbolic representation that rises above conflict and division, and gives the image of unity of all human beings as an 'open humanity' that lives in problematicity and in a shaken solidarity – the only possible unity of humanity. As well, during the *mise-en-sens* stage, the 'citizens of the world' arrive at the image of themselves not as taking part in a universal consent or a global semantic security, but at an image of themselves as sharing a semantic insecurity and vulnerability, being in a shaken solidarity and living in problematicity. This symbolic mutation from a global universal consent to a perpetual questioning leads to the next stage of instituting a World Republic – *mise-en-scene* where this unity-in-conflict or shaken solidarity is staged and the scene is the world as a whole. The next stage will be *mise-en-forme* which concerns the very embodiment of the meanings acknowledged earlier, and here the concrete procedures of organising a World Republic have to be elaborated with 'technical' details, such as who should represent whom, will this be a parliament of humans only or also a 'parliament of things'.[23]

A concern that could be expressed here is how this institution will confront questions of resources and power. The answer is that in conceiving a World Republic as an institution of critique, during the *mise-en-sense* stage, the very notion of power changes. Lefort's theory of democracy is a rich resource for rethinking power in the cosmopolitan condition. Lefort (1988) famously argued that democracy emerges after the 'dissolution of the markers of certainty' that happened in the West. Because in modern democracy the division of power does not refer to an outside that can be assigned to the Gods or holy ground, the power is an 'empty place', it belongs to no one and those who exercise power do not possess or embody it. The exercise of power requires a periodic and repeated contest; the authority of those vested with power is created and recreated as a result of the manifestation of the will of the people in elections, which highlight the impossibility of a general and final perspective. Lefort's account of democracy offers the tools for theorising democracy beyond the borders of the nation-state without the risk of creating a global Leviathan, and theorists of cosmopolitanism must consider all possibilities opened by a place of power which is rendered empty for a democracy involving the world as a whole. Another crucial fact is that when imagining and thinking about a World Republic during the *mise-en-sense* stage, as an institution of critique and radical democracy, it has to be imagined going beyond the forms of power as currently entangled in the knot created by nation-state-capital. Karatani's World Republic is not political in the present sense of the world; it is based on gift and reciprocity, and signifies the disappearance of the political state qua organising form and separate realm, confirming the critiques of the idea of a world institution as an end of the political: 'Were a world state to embrace the entire globe and humanity, then it would be no political entity and could only loosely be called a state . . . and would altogether lose its political character' (Schmitt 2007: 57). Thus, the idea of a World Republic as an institution of critique has to be imagined beyond the current configuration of power and the current fight for resources.

The elaboration of the apparatus of a World Republic is a secondary task compared with the process of arriving at a cosmopolitan meaning–structure that will make 'a demand of a future' (Merleau-Ponty 1970: 41) by requiring an institution to protect it. The would-be cosmopolitan citizens might be still afraid of a World Republic and may laugh at the idea. The next chapter tries to clarify who fears and why, whose laughter is louder and who laughs at the end.

NOTES

1. On the current divide of cosmopolitan political theorists on the institutional implications of their position, see Cabrera (2018).
2. This brief overview of the Zapatistas' institutional experimentation is from the Sixth Declaration of the Selva Lacandona, which summarises the activities carried out in the previous two decades (see Enlace Zapista 2005).
3. Available at <https://schoolsforchiapas.org/> (last accessed 5 December 2021).
4. On the WSF as open space, see Patomäki and Teivainen (2004).
5. With some exceptions, such as the Porto Alegre Manifesto, written by the Group of 19, which resulted in controversy over whether or not the Forum should have a manifesto. Available at <https://www.opendemocracy.net/en/porto-alegre-manifesto-in-english/> (last accessed 5 December 2021).
6. For a critical view of the WSF as a hierarchal organisation, see Worth and Buckley (2009).
7. For the latest discussion on the legacy of the WSF, see the special issue of *Globalizations*, 2020, 17(2) 'Transformative Responses to Authoritarian Capitalism: Learning with the World Social Forum'.
8. The WSF's declaration on its twentieth anniversary. Available at <https://criticallegalthinking.com/2020/08/11/a-second-manifesto-for-the-world-social-forum-from-an-open-space-to-a-space-for-action/> (last accessed 5 December 2021).
9. For the idea of critique as an institution see Frase (2005) and Steyerl (2009).
10. This chapter does not engage with critical theory tradition, since it is still immersed in methodological nationalism, without yet elaborating a global critical theory, and many contemporary inheritances of critical theory are still bound to localised or closed normative structures, recently under the guise of 'forms of life', for example Jaeggi (2018).

11. On cosmopolitanism as a critical approach largely compatible with critical social theory, but without acknowledging the Cynic origins of cosmopolitan critique, see Delanty (2009, 2012).

12. Three expressions are currently in use in the scholarly approaches to this idea: world state, world government and world republic, and are used interchangeably, although the expression 'World Republic' is used mainly to refer to the historical accounts of this idea, from the pre-Weberian understanding of the state (see Lu 2021). The use of the word 'republic' instead of 'state' does not mean for this text that I subscribe to the republican tradition of thinking in political theory or in current international relations.

13. The idea of a World Republic is elaborated in Clootz (1792, 1793). Anacharsis Clootz joined the French Revolution at its beginning, and was active in the Jacobin Club. On 19 June 1790, he presented to the National Assembly a 'mission of mankind' made up of thirty-six foreigners, proclaiming that the world supported the Declaration of the Rights of Man and Citizen. On the 'strangeness' of Clootz's proposal, see Kristeva (1991: 161–4).

14. Wells described his concept of a world state firstly in *Anticipations of the Reaction of Mechanical and Scientific Progress upon Human Life and Thought* (1901) and then in *A Modern Utopia* (1905). After the First World War he returned to the issue in *Men Like Gods* (1923), *The Open Conspiracy* (1928), *The Shape of Things To Come* (1933) and others.

15. 'We, world federalists, affirm that mankind can free itself forever from war only through the establishment of a world federal government; human race will cease to exist unless a world government capable of enforcing world law is established by peaceful means . . . The choice is indeed between one world or none' (Declaration 1947, available at <http://www.wfm-igp.org/> (last accessed 5 December 2021). Established in 1947, the World Federalist Movement still exists. Available at <http://www.wfm-igp.org/about/overview/> (last accessed 5 December 2021).

16. A Preliminary Draft of a World Constitution was originally published in 1948 under the auspices of the University of Chicago. An All-Party Parliamentary Group for World Government was created in the UK and among the members were more than 200 UK Members of Parliament. A conference held in London in 1951 had the support of leaders around the world (see Heater 1996: 159–63).

17. In 1945, in France, Robert Sarrazac founded the *Front Humain des Citoyens du Monde* – a scheme for individuals to register themselves as world citizens, according to the maxim: 'I think I am a world citizen, therefore I am'; the organisation still exists. Available at <https://www.citoyensdumonde.net/> (last accessed 9 January 2022).

18. World Passports still can be requested. Available at <https://worldservice.org/> (last accessed 5 December 2021). This is the initiative of Garry Davis (1921–2013), who in 1948 gave up US citizenship, declared himself a citizen of the world and claimed world citizenship on 'UN soil' in France. The 'Garry Davis Council of Solidarity' was founded in France by Camus,

Sartre and Gide. In 1949 a World Citizens' Registry was created. By the end of the year, the register had 800,000 members from seventy countries.

19. John XXIII issued *Pacem in Terris* in 1963, which proposed a World Order Model Project in three phases: consciousness-raising, mobilisation of pressure and the achievement of incremental transformation. Available at <http://www.vatican.va/content/john-xxiii/en/encyclicals/documents/hf_j-xxiii_enc_11041963_pacem.html> (last accessed 5 December 2021).

20. Available at <https://en.unpacampaign.org/> (last accessed 5 December 2021). The campaign has the support of more than 1,400 parliamentarians worldwide and represents one of the most important current movements for democratic global political integration. Its site is available in English, German, French and Spanish. Apart from year-round activities, the campaign organises World Parliament Now – a 'Global Week of Action for a World Parliament', an annual event, taking place in October.

21. Available at <https://tse.bitnation.co/> (last accessed 5 December 2021).

22. A post-Anthropocene perspective is available at <https://greattransition.org/> (last accessed 5 December 2021).

23. Latour deploys Stengers's notion of cosmopolitics to articulate cosmopolitically his own account of the 'parliament of things' in *We Have Never Been Modern* (1991), which brings together human and non-human perspectives. Stengers's and Latour's works inspired a post-humanist anthropology, with allusion to cosmopolitics (de la Cadena 2010; Blaser 2016) – an approach that is incompatible with this book. Stengers's notion of cosmopolitics as 'applied' in post-humanist anthropology risks leading to oxymoronic cosmopolitanisms. The presence of the non-human being in the situation is not direct but mediated by the humans who must bear witness and be disturbed by the beings that cannot have their own say in the situation, therefore pointing to the capacity of the human to open themselves to the non-human.

Chapter 5

LAUGHTER, FEAR AND 'CONVERSION'

═══════

In all my years of studying cosmopolitanism, I have heard only one joke about it – or apparently about it, since the joke was told within an event exploring the topic of cosmopolitanism – and it was a grim joke. In the 1930s, a German Jew is looking desperately for a country of exile. He enters a shop and asks for a globe. After having searched on the globe without success, he asks the shopkeeper: 'Do you have another globe?' According to the scholar who included the joke in his talk, this joke gives expression to the nightmare of a world without alternatives and cautions against the notion of a global state, since in a global state no place of exile would exist anymore, and there would be no salesperson to ask for another globe. The joke reiterates the 'despotism' and 'no exit' criticisms formulated by innumerable theorists rejecting the idea of a world state. The fact that I happened to hear only one joke about cosmopolitanism – and that a grim one – may point to the fact that cosmopolitanism is a very serious topic. However, quite frequently, when the idea of a World Republic is advanced, there is laughter: theorists laugh at the naivety and idealism of those advancing it. Then laughter is replaced by fear since, in their naivety, these authors do not see the threats that their theoretical endeavours are allegedly posing, and the laughing–fearing theorist feels responsible to point to the dangers and to prevent them. But who exactly laughs at the idea of a World Republic, who is afraid of it and why?

'DO YOU HAVE ANOTHER GLOBE?'

Therefore, who laughs and why? Under the auspices of the joke about another globe, let's see what is laughable about the idea of a World Republic. Cosmopolitan theorists can be self-critical and they can laugh (at) themselves. Obviously, there is no choir of theorists laughing perennially in unison at those advancing a World Republic and which the self-critical cosmopolitan theorist could join. These theorists deride the idea in several lines, and then move further by expressing fears concerning the dangers that these theoretical endeavours pose. Some of them derided the idea using the entire authority of political philosophers and their legacy legitimates others to laugh. Among the authors, Hannah Arendt is a legitimator of those laughing at the idea of a world citizen and a World Republic. Thus, those who attempted to think about a world institution that would make the human rights belong to the human and not only to the citizens – as her famous paradox discovers – are for Arendt 'marginal figures', 'jurists without political experience', 'professional philanthropists', 'professional idealists', with a language that reminds her that of 'societies for the prevention of cruelty to animals':

> All attempts to arrive at a new bill of human rights were sponsored by marginal figures – by a few international jurists without political experience or professional philanthropists supported by the uncertain sentiments of professional idealists. The groups they formed, the declarations they issued, showed an uncanny similarity in language and composition to that of societies for the prevention of cruelty to animals. No statesman, no political figure of any importance could possibly take them seriously; and none of the liberal or radical parties in Europe thought it necessary to incorporate into their program a new declaration of human rights. (Arendt 1973: 292)

But how can a 'statesman' or a 'political figure of any importance' literally 'take them seriously', when philosophers do not? But if a 'statesman' or a 'political figure' does not take the idea seriously, this is not an impediment for a political theorist to take the idea seriously and to think about it further. If here is something laughable in the statement above, then it is the figure of the philosopher who looks for the approval of a 'statesman' or a 'political figure of any importance' in order to think. However, there is nothing amusing in a philosopher who limits the rights of citizens and surrounds them with fences, as Arendt does when she doubts the fact that someone can be a citizen of the world:

> A citizen is by definition a citizen among citizens of a country among countries. His *rights and duties must be defined and limited*, not only by those of his fellow citizens, but also by the boundaries of a territory. Philosophy may conceive of the earth as the homeland of mankind and of one unwritten law, eternal and 'Valid for all'. Politics deals with men, nationals of many countries and heirs to many pasts; its laws are the positively established *fences* which hedge in, protect, and limit the space in which freedom is not a concept, but a living, political reality. (Arendt 1968: 81–2, emphasis added)[1]

If the state already does all these manoeuvres – limits rights and duties, establishes fences, both in forms of laws and physical walls – then what is political philosophy for? For approving the fences and limitation of rights? Again, if there is something hilarious in the idea of 'the earth as the home-land of mankind and of one unwritten law', it should be the philosopher's rejection of it, content to lay under a 'fences which hedge' where freedom is a 'living . . . reality'. But this is a saddening image in its hilarity.

And laughter of a charismatic theoretical authority legitimises others' laughter at the 'naïveté . . . and lunacy' of those taking into consider-ation the idea of an institution for the whole world:

> Most analysts of global governance see world government as atavistic idealism that is beyond the pale. To investigate or support such a policy is seen as naïveté at best, and lunacy at worst. And certainly, no younger scholar would wish to cut short her career by exploring such a thought for a dissertation. (Weiss 2009: 262)

There is nothing wrong with satire and parody of the idea of a World Republic. The main aim of this chapter is to clarify what exactly is hilari-ous in it and if hilarity is an impediment for affirming it further. Kant him-self admitted the satire of the perpetual peace: 'We shall not trouble to ask where this applies to men in general, or particularly to head of states (who can never have enough war), or only to philosophers who blissfully dream of perpetual peace' (Kant 1991:93). Perpetual peace could be achieved only in a graveyard; however, this does not impede Kant thinking about it for the living world. He assumes the laughter and takes the naivety as a *clausula salvatoria* to protect himself from any 'malicious' interpreta-tion: 'The practical politician tends to look down with great complacency upon political theorist as a mere academic. The theorist's abstract ideas, the practitioner believes, cannot endanger the state' (1991: 93). Then, in the case of a conflict with the theorist, the statesman should 'not scent any danger to the state in the opinion which the theorist has randomly uttered in public' (1991: 93). However, the *clausula salvatoria* did not help Kant to himself advance the idea of a World Republic; he stopped on the way to it, although all his work, as Karatani has shown, leads to the mode of exchange D or the very idea of a World Republic (Karatani 2003, 2014).

The laugher is not directed only at political theorists, but at everyone advancing an idea of a world institution. For example, H. G. Wells wrote relentlessly from different perspectives about the necessity to institute a world state, and his work was incessantly ridiculed (Heater 1996: 127–33). Aldous Huxley's *Brave New World* portrayal of the world state was written as an anti-Wellsian satire: 'A squat grey building of only thirty-four storeys. Over the main entrance the words, Central London Hatchery And Conditioning Centre, and, in a shield, the World State's motto, Community, Identity, Stability' (Huxley 2006). Huxley noted that he was writing on 'the horrors of the Wellsian utopia and a revolt against it' and reiterated that *Brave New World* 'started out as a parody of H. G. Wells'.[2] George Orwell called *Brave New World* a caricature of 'the by now familiar Wellsian Utopia'. For Orwell, Wells was just a sensible man: 'What is the use of pointing out that a world state is desirable? All sensible men for decades past have been substantially in agreement with what Mr. Wells says; but the sensible men have no power' (Orwell 1941). But, again, everyone is open to criticism no matter the topic on what he writes: inconsistency, shallowness, contradictions – and Wells's texts had all these flaws[3] – have to be exposed. But to deride someone for 'being a sensible man with no power' and at the same time to express fear on 'the horrors of the Wellsian utopia' is equally contradictory and shallow.

It is rather interesting that both political theorists and writers of fiction deride the same feature – lack of power of 'sensible men', 'marginal figures', 'jurists without political experience', 'professional idealists' and so on. Why is lack of power and marginality laughable? What exactly is the laughing mechanism here? In the theory of humour, many authors emphasised the fact that the comical always seems to involve a certain encounter of two different (often directly opposed) levels or experiences turned on their head at a certain moment. In a joke there is always a horizon of expectation: we do not know the point of the joke until our horizon of expectation is turned on its head – an unexpected result that produces laughter.[4]

In laughing at those advancing the idea of a World Republic, the mechanism is the same: there are two levels of experience to which the laughing theorists keep pointing – the lack of power of those who advance the idea, and the very idea of a World Republic, which in these theorists' view would be an immense power and threat. There is an incongruence and opposition here, but only if one isolates some 'sensible individuals' and 'marginal groups' and contrasts them with the idea of a World Republic, which is considered too powerful. But why are not 'men without power' able to advance all kinds of ideas? And why are they laughable if they advance an idea? Referring to postmodernists who laugh at the idea of history and who

> in the core of global capitalism have continued to scorn the very idea of Idea, while religious fundamentalism has rapidly gained ground in the periphery and semi-periphery because in both intent and practice it at least aims to supersede capitalism and the state

Karatani asks, 'But what right do intellectuals in advanced capitalist countries have to laugh at this?' (Karatani 2014: 234). Paraphrasing Karatani, one has to ask: what right do those theorists have to laugh at 'sensible men', 'marginal figures' and 'men without power' having an idea of a World Republic?

This examination of the mechanism of laughing at the idea of a World Republic does not aim – *horrible dictu* – to ban the right to laugh at this idea or at any other ideas. On the contrary, in this section I have shown that the idealists wanted to laugh with the realists, but this could not happen because what is funny for realists is not funny for idealists, and vice versa, and perhaps it is an impossibility to the extent that Quixote himself cannot stop from his wanderings and start laughing with others at his own actions. But political theorists advancing the idea of a World Republic are not Quixotes; the laugh caused by them is short and nervous, since they are considered more dangerous than Quixote.

WHO IS AFRAID OF A WORLD REPUBLIC?

If cosmopolitans fail to laugh with critics of cosmopolitanism, maybe they can fear together? Therefore, who fears and why? Well, Kant himself, who saw in a world state a 'fearful despotism'. Although Kant is the only philosopher who expresses a clear cosmopolitan position, and a cluster of contemporary approaches, among which global justice and global democracy, are called Kantian cosmopolitanisms, he is also the philosophical authority who legitimated the fear of the world state:

> Such a state of universal peace is in turn even more dangerous for freedom, for it may lead to fearful despotism, distress must force men to form a state which is not a cosmopolitan commonwealth under a single ruler, but a lawful federation under a commonly accepted international right. (Kant 1991: 90)

In the same context, Kant added: 'For the laws progressively lose their impact as the government increases its range, and a soulless despotism, after crushing the germs of goodness, will finally lapse into anarchy" (Kant 1991: 113). Rawls reiterated Kant's fear:

> I follow Kant's lead in *Perpetual Peace* in thinking that a world government – by which I mean a unified political regime with the legal powers normally exercised by central governments – would either be a global despotism or else would rule over a fragile empire torn by frequent civil strife as various regions and peoples tried to gain their political freedom and autonomy. (Rawls 1999: 36)[5]

Arendt laughs but she also is afraid of a World Republic, and her fear is provoked by the naivety of those advancing the idea, since their idealism is seen as dangerous when put in practice:

> Such a world government is indeed within the realm of possibility, but one may suspect that in reality it might differ considerably from the

version promoted by idealistic-minded organizations . . . For it is quite conceivable, and even within the realm of practical political possibilities, that one fine day a highly organized and mechanized humanity will conclude quite democratically – namely by majority decision – that for humanity as a whole it would be better to liquidate certain parts thereof. (Arendt 1973: 299)

Carl Schmitt worried about a world state in terms similar to Arendt's, since

To confiscate the word humanity, to invoke and monopolize such a term probably has certain incalculable effects, such as denying the enemy the quality of being human and declaring him to be an outlaw of humanity; and a war can thereby be driven to the most extreme inhumanity. (Schmitt 2007: 54)

Schmitt also expressed the fear of totalitarianism:

As long as a state exists, there will always be in the world more than just one state. A world state which embraces the entire globe and all of humanity cannot exist. The political world is a pluriverse, not a universe. (Schmitt 2007: 53)

This worry presupposes that a world state should have one language, one set of political principles and one set of cultural traditions, which will eliminate different cultural groups: 'the survival of these groups would be at risk; under the rules of the global state, they would not be able to sustain and pass on their way of life' (Walzer 2004: 176). Worries are related as well to instability: 'the prospect of world government would be an invitation to prepare for world civil war' (Waltz 2010: 112), and to solidification of the existing global hierarchy. A frequently expressed fear is the fear of the impossibility of being able to exercise the right to exit: unlike the citizens of the nation-states who can make a meaningfully decisive choice against an oppressive regime under which they do not wish to live, the citizens of the world state will have nowhere to go once it becomes oppressive.[6] Some theorists fear that the process of creating a world government may cause more harm than good since it seems reachable only in the wake of a global catastrophe (Pogge 1992; Nagel 2005), and this catastrophe will happen since thinking about a world institution 'involves us in the construction of visions we do not understand well enough to comprehend what their realisation would look like' (Risse 2012: 80).

A long list of fears! Now, who still dare to affirm further the idea of a World Republic? Well, those who do not fear, because those who do fear it do not advance it. The answer is almost comic, but this is the pattern of interaction between those who advance an idea of a world institution and those who reject it: there is no common ground. This lack of common ground is manifested mainly in the lack of a common theoretical framework in advancing and rejecting an idea of a world institution. But the most puzzling aspect is that critics of a World Republic use one theory (and world view) when criticising it and other set of theories for affirming existing institutions. For example, at the level of the nation-state, the political power is conceptualised, under Lefort's auspices, as an 'empty place of power', while at the global level the place of power is regarded as 'full' with ineliminable despots and tyrants. Or at the level of the nation-state, politics is the place of contest of the agonistic but respectful adversaries, while at the global level the adversaries turn into 'friends' and 'enemies', with 'enemies' producing a totalising world hegemony (Mouffe 2005). Why do some concepts and theoretical frameworks cease to be valid at the border of the nation-state, and even worse, their opposites become valid?

In the normative tradition of doing political theory, the difference is evident through the distinction between ideal theory, which assumes that all agents comply with the demands of justice, and non-ideal theory, which assumes partial compliance with the demands of justice. As it was observed (Scheuerman 2014; Ulaş 2017), statist authors conceive their theories in ideal terms, and criticise the world state in non-ideal terms. If a coherence is to be maintained both in advancing a statist theory and in criticising the world state, then the objections dissolve, but also the need of a nation-state dissolves, or if the objections are kept, the nation-state becomes the target of the same criticisms. As well, there is a peculiar non-interference of arguments and counterarguments, since the arguments for are formulated within methodological cosmopolitanism while the arguments against are formulated within methodological nationalism. Thus, it is impossible for cosmopolitan theorists to incorporate the premises of non-cosmopolitan arguments into their approaches and continue to advance cosmopolitan approaches, and vice versa: it is impossible for the critics to adopt methodological cosmopolitanism and continuing to criticise the idea of a World Republic in the same way.

The criticism of the impossibility of the right to exit the world state, which is part of the tyranny objection (DuFord 2017), is an illustration of the theoretical incoherence of the criticisms enumerated above. This criticism is very easy to reject: one needs just to look around at tyrannical rule in the domestic state system and to ask how many people are able to exit and escape it. Only a lucky few, usually in life-threatening conditions. When the Jew from the grim joke above was looking for another globe, there was no world state instituted; the world was then, as it is now, composed of nation-states. Millions of Jews managed to find, if not another globe, at least another country, but the millions that were victims of the Holocaust did not manage to go into exile. Is the risk-taking individual solution of exit the only solution that political theory can offer against an oppressive rule? Obviously not. It advances count-less arguments on how to make the state non-oppressive and respect the freedom of its citizens. So why is this main concern of political theory dropped when thinking about a world state? Why not think further about a non-oppressive and freedom-respecting world institution, as is done in the case of the domestic states? What makes one theorist willing to think about 'another globe' and another to dismiss the idea as naive and dangerous? Is this a matter of how one argues or of how one fears?

When campaigning relentlessly for a world government, Einstein admitted that he had fears as well: 'Do I fear the tyranny of a world government? Of course, I do. But I fear still more the coming of another war' (Einstein 1947). To be sure, those advancing proposals of a World Republic may display a 'cosmopolitanism of fear' (Shklar 1989: 36). The Cynics' 'true commonwealth in the cosmos', Zeno's *Republic* or Dante's universal monarchy were advanced 'free of fear' in the name of common humanity or divine reason. The proposals for a world state advanced in the last hundred years have made use of fear, subsequently underlining a Hobbesian argument from *Leviathan* (1996): to escape perpetual war and misery humans must be in a political community with a firm, authoritative ruler. Starting with H. G. Wells who wrote that a world state is needed to prevent nation-states from destroying the entire world, fear became *the* 'ground' for the idea of a world state. Currently, fears are multiple: climate change, technology, terrorism, reprogenetics, transhumanism and artificial intelligence, autonomous weapons systems, bioterrorism, nanobots and new pathogens, the fra-gility of the global food supply and water security as a global concern (Leinen and Bummel 2018).[7]

Thus, in the discussions of world government, fear appears inescap-able: if a world state is not instituted, apocalypse will follow; if insti-tuted, a global Leviathan will result, otherwise if the world government is not law-enforcing and efficient, why institute it? In this generalised use of fear, political theorists appear as having to go through a 'leap of faith' and to choose between two monsters, as Einstein has chosen the 'monster' of the world state. However, has the political philosopher the right to feel fear in the same way as 'lay people'? Let's imagine that the interwar Jew or the current 'illegal' people go to a political philosopher and ask: 'Do you have another globe?' According to the default position in political philosophy, the political philosopher will say: 'We do not have another globe, it is naive and dangerous, it will be a universe not a pluriverse, a "fearful despotism", it will liquidate certain parts of itself, it will not give to you the right to exit.' Then the 'illegal' people will have to say: 'Indeed, we do not need another globe, we are already in it.' The bookkeeper does not need to have 'another globe', but is the political philosopher exempt from the unwritten rule to have 'another globe'? It may be dangerous, but it does not yet exist and political philosophers may prevent it from growing up into a fearful global Leviathan by thinking it otherwise. However, choosing the non-existent monster appears to be a very difficult option, both for 'lay people' and for political philosophers, but why?

CHANGES, METAMORPHOSES AND 'CONVERSIONS'

Acting as a cosmopolitan citizen was always considered a demanding activity and a complicated virtue. A common critique of cosmopolitanism is that human motivational drives, such as empathy or a sense of fairness, cannot be extended to anonymous strangers or to large groups (Miller 2002), thus the cosmopolitan motivation can never arise or cannot arise without moral costs. What exactly is demanding, and why does 'Another World' seem nevertheless possible? The 'secret' is that theories of cosmopolitanism, along with a vision of a better world, presuppose a self-transformation after which individuals will emerge fully motivated to care for the world and distant others. In the normative political theory, the difficulty is acknowledged as a 'motivation gap' (Lichtenberg 2014; Hobbs 2020), and different strategies have been suggested to address it. Philosophers operating in a broadly Kantian tradition have suggested that reason can do the necessary work, with rational moral judgements serving to motivate action (O'Neill 2000). As well, normativity 'cancels' the problem of motivation: 'Agents of transformations are those who benefit from present injustice (rulers, imperialists, powerful states) . . . Why would rulers give up the advantages they enjoy under the current system in order to create a new, more rightful one? Because they should' (Ingram 2013: 114).

The problem of motivation was taken further by 'sentimental cosmopolitanism' (Woods 2012) which argues that encouraging greater sentimental engagement with individuals beyond national borders can motivate greater compliance with duties of justice. Authors make a catalogue of outrageous instances of global wrongs that have to induce a moral restructuring of the world view: 'A child born in Sweden today has a life expectancy at birth of 79.9 years. A child born in Sierra Leone has a life expectancy at birth of 34.5 years' (Nussbaum 2006: 224).

In this sentimental cosmopolitanism, the suffering of the other acquires a normative function (Woods 2012).[8] Suffering must prompt empathy and compassion, to call forth our moral attention and to make us ask ourselves what we can and should do to alleviate the suffering. The suffering of the others might equally inspire feelings of anger, shame and disgust – 'How Many Skinny Babies Can You Show Me?' revolts someone at the proliferation of images called 'starvation pornography' (Woods 2012: 41). Thus, disgust, anger and shame become a source of cosmopolitan sentiments which ought to fill the motivational gap (Hobbs 2020).

The oxymoronic or adjectival cosmopolitanisms,[9] such as 'rooted' or 'statist' versions, also aim to redress the motivational gap by reconciling local attachments and global obligations but failing completely in the transformation process since these rooted cosmopolitanisms only reproduce the status quo. In the context of such hyphenated cosmopolitanism produced within political theory, the 2030 Agenda for Sustainable Development, adopted by all United Nations Member States in 2015, sounds radical. Starting from the title 'Transforming our world: the 2030 Agenda for Sustainable Development' until the last target, the 2030 Agenda stresses its 'universal and transformative Goals', its 'supremely ambitious and transformational vision' and its determination to take 'bold and transformative steps'.[10] The 2030 Agenda envisages radical transformations in all fields and it affirms clearly what some political theories fail to recognise – that a better world requires a radical shift and a bold transformation of the existing one.

For sociological accounts of cosmopolitanism, self-transformation is envisaged as a process that already takes place in the encounter with others in the context of global concerns (Delanty 2014), and which reiterates the Enlightenment cosmopolitanism of transcending local allegiances through intellectual pursuits, but also the main motive of the encounter with the other as a 'stranger' that creates perplexities caused by the clashes of beliefs and habits seen as opportunities for developing an awareness of our interdependence and a critical consciousness of the limitations of our perspective (Kristeva 1991; Honig 2001; see Chapter 7). While in most sociological approaches, the transformation just happens in the globalised world through different interactions, for Ulrich Beck the transformation is a 'metamorphosis' happening as a hidden emancipatory side effect of global risks:

> There is a double process unfolding. First, there is the process of modernization, which is about progress. It is targeted at innovation and the production and distribution of goods. Second, there is the process of the production and the distribution of bads. Both processes unfold and push in opposite directions. Yet, they are interlocked. This interlinkage

is not produced through the failure of the process of modernization or through crises but through its very success. The more successful it is, the more bads are produced. The more the production of bads is overlooked and dismissed as collateral damage of the process of modernization, the greater and more powerful the bads become. (Beck 2015: 78)

Unlike the political theory of Thomas Hobbes that declares that 'man is a wolf to man', the cosmopolitan theory of Beck states that 'civilization is a wolf to civilization' (Beck et al. 2013: 5). Through different theses, processes and steps, Beck attempted to move from 'civilization is a wolf to civilization' to a cosmopolitan vision:

First thesis: There are hidden emancipatory side effects of global risk. Second thesis: normative horizons of global justice are being globalized. Third thesis: Global risks produce compasses for the 21st-century world. Fourth thesis: Global risks *enforce* a categorical metamorphosis of generation. (Beck 2015: 78, emphasis added)

Thus, global risks cannot just let us remain unchanged – these enforce the change or the metamorphosis, and this enforcement is called 'emancipatory catastrophism', which Beck described by using three conceptual lenses: first, the anticipation of global catastrophe violates sacred (unwritten) norms of human existence and civilization; second, it causes an anthropological shock; and, third, a social catharsis (Beck 2015, 2016).

Global catastrophe and anthropological shock could be considered as happening already, while the social catharsis is less detectable, and if it happens, where is the assurance that it will be a cosmopolitical one, and not a nationalist–populist catharsis of 'taking our country back' from the global catastrophe? There is no assurance, and Beck admits it (2015: 77); however, there are some features of Beck's theoretical framework that show that social catharsis cannot be otherwise than cosmopolitan. The social catharsis cannot happen by clinging to the old familiar ways of doing things, since this will not be a way of action caused by catastrophe: 'The catastrophe cannot act otherwise than by a compulsion to react' and the compulsion to react 'releases a cosmopolitical force' (Beck et al. 2013: 5). Acting or reacting collectively to the catastrophe will lead to 'cosmopolitan imagined communities of risk', as Beck argued in his last works (Beck 2011, 2015, 2016). The compulsion to react calls as well for a scientific revolution from 'methodological nationalism' to 'methodological cosmopolitanism' (Beck and Szneider 2006). Thus, Beck's theory brings the transformation implicit in different other theories of cosmopolitanism to the fore, dissects it and, in particular, makes clear that the metamorphosis is not an easy transformation, but a forced one. The 'compulsion to react' released by global catastrophes and anthropological shocks produces a 'cosmopolitical force' of transformation.

Before the climate catastrophe, the 'compulsion to react' was determined by the imminent catastrophe of the atomic bomb, which released a 'cosmopolitical force' of transformation in the first two decades after the Second World War, marked by a powerful cosmopolitan revival (presented in Chapter 4). Analysing philosophically the 'paradigm' of the atomic bomb, Karl Jaspers, in *The Future of Mankind* (1961) presented a choice between two 'fantasies' – 'either all mankind will physically perish or there will be a change in the moral-political condition of man' (Jaspers 1961: 4). Jaspers calls this change 'conversion', not in terms of a religious conversion, but as a radical philosophical transformation of human existence. The needed 'conversion' has several facets: it entails turning from abstract thinking to a 'new' mode of thinking, turning from individual and collective bondage to existential and political freedom, and turning from narrowly dogmatic 'faiths', whether political ideologies, positivism, scientific Marxism or Christianity, to the appropriation of 'philosophical faith'. Conversion goes beyond understanding by the intellect and happens 'at a depth of human existence which man achieves by no special knowledge, by no special activity, [but] only by himself' (1961: 10), that is, in his inner transformation (Walters 1988).[11] In its inscrutable logic, 'conversion' completes the whole picture of the modalities of self-transformation assumed by different theories of cosmopolitanism.

This chapter started with the self-critical intention of laughing and worrying with the critics of the idea of a World Republic, and both laughter and fear failed. The theorists advancing the idea and those rejecting it are amused by different comedies and worried by different nightmares. A move from one position to another is not made possible by a reasoned principle, but through a 'forced choice' which sometimes sounds like a 'leap of faith', or a 'conversion'. Now, once the (self-) transformation inherent in cosmopolitanism is revealed and dissected, it reconnects with the radicality of the first cosmopolitical stance.

A 'FORCED' CHOICE OR WHY COSMOPOLITANISM IS DIFFICULT

All calls to change, metamorphosis and 'conversion' restate the Cynics' founding principle 'Alter the currency!', which for the Cynics meant to change everything: customs, rules, habits, conventions, laws, the polis and the life itself, as it was understood and lived by men. The change of all truths accepted and revered by men was attempted against the Socratic and Platonic vison of true life, envisaged as a sovereign life, enduring without change or alteration (Foucault 2011: 264–8). So, we have in the Cynics' true life a reversal of what the true life in Socrates and Plato's philosophy was:

> The Cynics reversed the idea of the unconcealed life by dramatizing it in the practice of nakedness and shamelessness; they reversed the theme of the independent life by dramatizing it in the form of poverty; and they reversed the theme of the straight life by dramatizing it in the form of animality; they reverse and invert the theme of the sovereign life (tranquil and beneficial: tranquil for oneself, enjoyment of self, and beneficial for others) by dramatizing it in the form of what could be called the militant life, the life of battle and struggle against and for self, against and for others. (Foucault 2011: 283)

This logic of reversal is at the heart of the entire Cynic movement and philosophy. Because it breaks totally and on every point with the traditional forms of existence, with their habits and conventions, the reversal points to something radically other – 'to *an other life* and *an other world*' (2011: 245; emphasis and orthography in original). Through these reversals and breaks, the Cynics raised 'a very grave problem' concerning the true life: 'for life truly to be the life of truth, must it not be *an other* life, a life which is radically and paradoxically other?' (2011: 245). The alteration of the currency and the change of its value mean that the forms and habits of existence must be replaced, that 'life led by men in general and by philosophers in particular should be *an other* life' (2011: 244). Further, the principle of *an other life* becomes an 'aspiration for *an other world*' (2011: 278). The *an other* life brings the horizon of *an other* world as the objective of this Cynic practice:

> The Cynic addresses all men. He shows all men that they are leading a life other than the one they should be leading. And thereby it is a whole other world which has to emerge, or at any rate be on the horizon, be the objective of this Cynic practice. (2011: 315)

Thus, the final aim of the Cynics' life in truth is to show that the world will be able to reach the truth only at the price of change.

The declaration, 'I am a citizen of the world', could be made only after negating everything that was accepted as true life by the entire polis. Only by negating the given was the statement that 'the true commonwealth is the one in the cosmos' possible. The acknowledgement of the possibility of this 'true commonwealth' required work to negate the existing polis and a way of negating it, which was the Cynics' dog life, a chosen life of endurance, humility and destitution. The Cynics had to negate with their own life because they – or, more exactly, their polis – did not have the atomic bomb, or the risks and side effects of civilisation described by Beck. However, without doubt, the Cynics were the first to say that 'civilization is a wolf to civilization'. The Cynics set off the force of negativity at work in each cosmopolitan stance, and their principle 'Alter the currency!' is restated in every call to change, to transform, to convert ourselves, to which many variations can be added, and especially the call to think in a new way.

For the Cynics, the alteration of the value of the currency was not an easy action. The job of the Cynic is a hard mission, and there is no self-appointment. Instead, there are a series of tests and experiences one has to conduct on oneself in order to recognise oneself as a Cynic in the practice of *askesis*, endurance, poverty, destitution and exile. As well, the Cynic imposes hardships on himself, he has no clothes, shelter or hearth, he has to accept the insults and the blows, and then to appear stronger than the others. The first cosmopolitan stance makes it clear that it is difficult to be a citizen of the world. And all other affirmations of cosmopolitanism should not deny that it is a difficult stance, and will always need one more effort, as in Derrida's address, *Cosmopolites de tout de pays, encore un effort*.[12] Obviously, to become cosmopolitan one does not need to practice *askesis*, poverty and destitution, or to renounce shelter, clothes or family's ties, but the stance does not become easier. There are some 'structural difficulties' in becoming a cosmopolitan, and an example of a call to think in a new way in the face of the catastrophe can help in mapping these difficulties.

In July 1955, Bertrand Russell and Albert Einstein issued a statement called the Russell-Einstein Manifesto, which was signed by the world's leading scientists, calling for citizens of all nations to suspend their particular interests and to think of themselves simply as human beings. Thus, the manifesto declares:

> We are speaking on this occasion, not as members of this or that nation, continent, or creed, but as human beings, members of the species Man, whose continued existence is in doubt. The world is full of conflicts; and, overshadowing all minor conflicts, the titanic struggle between Communism and anti-Communism. Almost everybody who is politically conscious has strong feelings about one or more of these issues; but we want you, if you can, to set aside such feelings and consider yourselves only as members of a biological species which has had a remarkable history, and whose disappearance none of us can desire. We have to learn to think in a new way. (Russell and Einstein 1955)

The manifesto reiterates that nuclear war will destroy not only individual cities, but all life on the earth, for some suddenly, but for most only through long and painful suffering. The choice is not between saving the human species or letting it disappear, since a collective universal apocalyptic disappearance may appear preferable to individual disappearance, when the others and the world go on as before, unaffected by your disappearance: 'there will be universal death, sudden only for a minority, but for the majority a slow torture of disease and disintegration'. Only the lucky few on which the bomb will fall directly will have the chance of instant death, so one has to consider that he can be among those dying through 'a slow torture of disease and disintegration'. Emphasising the stark likelihood that this will happen if nothing is changed, the authors of the manifesto offer an alternative: 'Shall we put an end to the human race; or shall mankind renounce war?' They admit that

> what perhaps impedes understanding of the situation more than anything else is that the term 'mankind' feels vague and abstract. People scarcely realize in imagination that the danger is to themselves and their children and their grandchildren, and not only to a dimly apprehended humanity. They can scarcely bring themselves to grasp that they, individually, and those whom they love are in imminent danger of perishing agonizingly. (Russell and Einstein 1955)

The manifesto points to a situation that contains the elements of a 'cosmopolitan conversion' in general. There is a threat, the atomic bomb, that risks destroying the 'biological species' with a 'remarkable history' called the species of man. Part of the picture are some minor and major conflicts, such as that between Communism and anti-Communism, which produce some creeds and strong feelings. The creeds and the strong feelings are our local attachments, allegiances or belonging, which every account of cosmopolitanism, even the oxymoronic ones, ask to moderate. Another crucial element of the situation is the 'vague, dimly apprehended' humanity. Humanity is presented as being at risk of disappearance; however, people do not realise that this is also a danger to themselves, their children and their grandchildren. What the manifesto tries to achieve is to start 'remembering humanity': 'We appeal, as human beings, to human beings: Remember your humanity, and forget the rest.' 'Remember your humanity, and forget the rest' is what every picture of starving African children does, as well as the data about global poverty and global risks. These are the elements of a situation that has to lead the human species to a new way of thinking, or in the terms of this chapter, it has to lead to a cosmopolitan 'conversion'.

Given these elements of the situation and their interdependency, the 'conversion' cannot be otherwise than a 'forced choice', and this 'forced' choice explains the difficulty of becoming cosmopolitan. First, the transformation implied here, but also in many other calls for a cosmopolitan transformation, is a forced choice since it is presented as unavoidable. Humans cannot choose destruction and disappearance through an atomic apocalypse since, as the manifesto warns, only the lucky few will have the chance of an instant death, while the majority will die through 'a slow torture of disease and disintegration' and thus it forces one to react to avoid slow torture. As Beck (2015: 77) noticed, global risks *enforce* a metamorphosis.

Second, the choice is 'forced' and a difficult one because all certainties, creeds and strong feelings have to be set aside. The call does not offer another creed or some new feelings. All certainties and received meanings that structure everyday life have to be renounced but there is no set of shining new meanings awaiting someone after 'conversion', as in the 'classical' religious conversion. Thinking in a new way envisaged by the call and a cosmopolitan 'conversion' cannot be otherwise than a shift to a life in problematicity and permanent questioning – the 'foundation stones' with which I started the construction of my cosmopolitan theory are reconfirmed once more.

Third, the choice is 'forced' since it requires choosing a 'vague, dim humanity' in order to make it exist. The humanity is dim and vague not only in this case, but in all other cases when it is invoked, and the very invocation of it is an attempt to make it exist. In most of the calls to become aware of the global risks, people are bound together only by their common disappearance, and not by any real form of global community. The accounts of cosmopolitanism speaking of the suffering of the distant others also point to a humanity which does not exist yet, since there are such inequalities and injustice around. The numerous criticisms of cosmopolitanism as being impossible since it vehiculates an 'abstract' humanity paradoxically confirm the situation, but in an inverse way: indeed, humanity exists as something vague, dim and abstract, and each cosmopolitan stance calls to make humanity real, less abstract and less vague.

Fourth, the call addresses individuals asking them to consider themselves 'only as members of a biological species', which is a crucial element of every cosmopolitan 'conversion'. It points to the fact that a cosmopolitan stance – or a stance trying to save humanity from destruction – cannot be an individual one, but only an intersubjective or transindividual one.[13] Becoming cosmopolitan is difficult and cannot be otherwise since it requires moving from our 'closed' individual selves to an 'extended self': belonging to 'species Man' as the manifesto says. In becoming cosmopolitan, individual subjectivity undergoes a shift to transindividuality, which is not a diminishing of the self or a rejection of the individual. On the contrary, it is an intensification of the individual as 'species being' and a 'citizen of the world', freed from the local constraints and limitations. It is exactly this intersubjectivity or transindividuality as an extended self that is presupposed every time cosmopolitanism is associated with a demanding responsibility towards the others.

And finally, the 'conversion' is a 'forced' choice since it requires acknowledging that the negative force that risks destroying the planet is not an external threat but the effect of our own creations. It requires acknowledging that the inhuman is not only in others but also in us, that in our clinging to our creeds and strong feelings we are also producing the evils that come back in a boomerang-like move to destroy us. Recognising the 'evil in us' is almost an impossible task, but nevertheless achievable (as Chapter 7 argues) through a difficult 'forced choice'.

If this 'conversion' is so difficult and 'forced', then why should one aim for it? Why not continue to find a 'solution' with the means that we currently have, as critics of cosmopolitanism say, in an attempt to protect individuals from unnecessary difficulties and efforts? Critics of cosmopolitanism view humans merely clinging to their lives, and hence sustaining the status quo, and ignore that humans are never content with what they have or know, and that they may question what is considered 'given'. They may question everything, including their creeds and strong feelings. Although questioning appears more difficult than mere survival in the given circumstances, it is nevertheless an expression of freedom, and the choice of actual freedom is not easy, but a 'forced' choice. Understanding that there is not another globe, that this is the only globe that we have, and it is our responsibility to make it liveable for everyone equally, is not an imposed duty but an act of a difficult freedom.

NOTES

1. Paradoxically, while Arendt derides cosmopolitanism, her 'life and work' is considered cosmopolitan (see Sznaider 2007, 2015).
2. Quoted in Beauchamp (1989).
3. Despite Wells's condemnation of Nazism, Orwell stated that 'Much of what Wells has imagined and worked for is physically there in Nazi Germany' (Orwell 1941). Wells subordinated every other purpose in his life, unrelentingly, for half a century, to the idea of a world government and died an embittered man because his message seemed to fall on deaf ears: 'in his last moments, cried bitterly that he – and mankind – had failed' (Heater 1996:128).
4. The incongruity theory is the dominant theory of humour, and was affirmed by Aristotle, Kant, Schopenhauer, Bergson and others (see Morreall 2020).

5. For a critique of those who use Kant, as Rawls does, to justify sidestepping a discussion of the ideal of a federal world government, and for a clarification of how Kant rejects the idea of a world state but advocates a voluntary league or a World Federation without being inconsistent, see Kleingeld (2004).

6. For a review of the argument see DuFord (2017).

7. Leinen and Bummel (2018) enumerate a whole panoply of fears/threats, which structures the content of their book. All aspects of life are presented from the perspective of threat to make more convincing the necessity of a World Parliament.

8. The archetypical image of the suffering in normative political philosophy that has to motivate action is the drowning child, used first by Peter Singer, in his 1972 article on the famine in East Bengal.

9. See Introduction, the section entitled 'Cosmopolitics'.

10. <https://sdgs.un.org/> (last accessed 9 December 2021).

11. Critiques of Jaspers hope for the 'conversion' of humanity were numerous: the concept of a moral–political 'conversion' was considered indeterminate with respect to its content – one can convert to whatever, and the transformation itself is not valuable; conversion makes politics and legal order overly dependent upon individual morality; 'conversion' is part of the Western tradition of existential thinking, thus it is not available to all humanity which it has to save. Also, part of the criticism was of the 'Better dead than red' stance, because since the beginning of the Cold War, Jasper had expressed concern about the advance of totalitarianism in the socialist regimes, a fact that weakened his argument on the 'conversion' to unconditional political and existential freedom (see Walters 1988).

12. *Cosmopolites de tout de pays, encore un effort* is the title of Derrida's book published in French in 1997, and translated in English as *On Cosmopolitanism and Forgiveness* (2001).

13. Transindividuality is an attempt to overcome the binary in which the individual is posed against the collective in a kind of zero-sum game, putting in its place an examination of the constitution of individuality and collectivity. It is an approach initiated and advanced by Gilbert Simondon in most of his works, but which Balibar argues ultimately can be found at work in Spinoza's *avant la letter* (see Balibar 2018).

Chapter 6

SEX&DRINK: THE TROUBLE WITH COSMOPOLITAN DESIRE

In the autumn of 2015, I was invited to give a lecture to a cohort of undergraduate students from politics-related fields, at a university in South-Eastern Europe. Before starting my talk, entitled 'Cosmopolitanism: A political theory for the world as a whole', I decided to ask them what they knew about cosmopolitanism: 'What is cosmopolitanism? What does it mean to be a cosmopolitan?' Silence. Asking again. Encouraging not to hesitate. Finally, the first answer: '*Cosmopolitan* is a magazine about sex.' And the second: '*Cosmopolitan* is a drink.' After some breathless long seconds, I found my voice: Yes, the word 'cosmopolitan' is used in the title of a magazine and in the name of a drink. There are such expressions as 'cosmopolitan style', 'cosmopolitan fashion', 'cosmopolitan cities' and so on. All these expressions point to us how desirable is for people the state of being called 'cosmopolitan'. Thus, we need to imagine the world from a cosmopolitan perspective where everyone could be a cosmopolitan. Therefore let see how we can think, imagine and eventually do this.

I continued the lecture expecting the imminent questions that were in the air: 'But is sex cosmopolitan?' 'Is cosmopolitanism achievable through sex?' 'If sex is cosmopolitan, why do we need these abstract theories?' No one asked them during the discussion that followed, perhaps because the convener who invited me to give the lecture warned the audience to ask 'serious' questions. Immediately after the lecture, I rushed to clarify why the magazine about sex is called 'cosmopolitan'.

The history of the *Cosmopolitan* magazine shows that the title and the content were associated contingently. When in 1965 the author of a bestseller, *Sex and the Single Girl* (Gurley Brown 1962), bought the magazine to tell the truth about sex – 'that sex is one of the three best things out there, and I don't even know what the other two are'[1] – the

131

magazine was already called *Cosmopolitan*, as it was named in 1886 by its initial founders who, in the spirit of Enlightenment, intended to make their readers familiar with science, culture and world literature.[2] Once bought, the magazine already 'had a name', and under this name the magazine claims that it changed the world by empowering women to 'take charge of their own sexual pleasure' and presents its legacy in terms of 'sexual liberation'.[3] In the same search, I discovered that without any link to the magazine, different scholars were writing about 'cosmopolitan sex'. Does it mean that cosmopolitanism is nevertheless achievable through sex? I asked, and slipped into researching it myself. However, after months of intermittent research, I still did not have an answer to the question 'Is sex cosmopolitan?'

FROM ENLIGHTENMENT COSMOPOLITANISM TO COSMOPOLITAN SEX

The academic topic called 'cosmopolitan sex' exists. Scholars from different subdisciplines within humanities and social sciences identify 'cosmopolitan desire', classify 'cosmopolitan sexualities', document 'cosmopolitan sex' mediated by different dating apps, interview respondents about their 'cosmopolitan transformation' after a one-night stand with a person of other nationality than their own and so on (see Siskind 2014; Young-Bruehl 2010). The starting premise of these approaches is that globalisation in the last three decades has facilitated all kind of intercourses, including sexual ones. For example, a fully fledged book follows 'cosmopolitan sex workers' claiming to refer not to women trafficked for sex, but to women who, in 'the process of migration for sex work, exhibit qualities that have been associated exclusively with elite travellers' (Chin 2013: 21) and who migrate as a way to realise neoliberal globalisation's promise of a free market in which people are the authors of their own destinies (Chin 2013: 21). Facilitated by globalisation, 'cosmopolitan sex' shapes the so-called 'cosmo-sexual cities',[4] where those involved in sex instantiate a 'cosmopolitan sexual citizenship' defined as 'a broad set of practices and modes of consumption that produce and govern a type of sexual subject whose lifestyle, political and consumer choices qualify as suitably "cosmopolitan"'.[5] And 'cosmopolitan sex' is considered a sufficiently generous umbrella to include sex that happens at global events (for example, World Cups), in sex tourism or in different urban gayborhoods viewed as a 'cosmopolitan spectacle' (Connor and Okamura 2021). The dating apps facilitate further the cosmopolitan sexual intercourse made possible by globalisation: 'Overnight, my Grindr literally became the United Nations. Before Haiyan all we had on Grindr was mehhh – four or five people. After Haiyan, boom – white men!', exclaims an app user, and the researcher explains: 'Filipino gay one-night stand with the French-Canadian aid worker is his first sexual encounter with a white man: "It wasn't my best, but it was perhaps my most memorable"' (Ong 2017: 667). The dating apps and other forms of sexual encounters facilitated by the internet allow scholars to map 'cosmopolitan digital intimacies' (Lambert 2019).

The list of examples could continue, but it is already sufficient to point out what exactly qualifies sex as 'cosmopolitan': (a) sexual encounters between people who identify differently from the perspective of ethnicity, race and nationality, and (b) a plurality of such experiences, eventually facilitated by travelling worldwide. Who could imagine a more enjoyable means of becoming a citizen of the world? However, I could not subscribe to these academic approaches since they involuntarily revealed a comic dimension to their subject of inquiry. Obviously, these academic texts are elaborated with legitimate methodologies from applied social sciences; however, the comic effect appeared inevitable. In the light of these scholarly approaches, Don Juan is the ideal cosmo-sexual citizen of the world, as the famous *Mille e tre* aria reveals:

> In Italy, six hundred and forty;
> In Germany, two hundred and thirty-one;
> A hundred in France; in Turkey, ninety-one;
> But in Spain already one thousand and three'.[6]

The legend of Don Juan was rewritten by different authors in the genre of comedy and alluding to cosmopolitanism. Thus, Molière's *Don Juan* expresses his world view in cosmopolitan terms, and we should observe its imperial tone of loving the whole world:

> All beautiful women have a right to our love, and the accident of being the first comer shouldn 't [*sic*] rob others of a fair share in our hearts . . . the fact that I am in love with one person shall never make me unjust to the others. I keep an eye for the merits of all of them and render each one the homage, pay each one the tribute that nature enjoins . . . I feel it is in me to love the whole world, and like Alexander still wish for new worlds to conquer. (Moliere 1966: 202)

Byron's *Don Juan* poem (written between 1819 and 1824) is considered a quintessence of the philosophical tales of the Enlightenment such as Montesquieu's *Lettres Persanes* (1721), Swift's *Gulliver's Travels* (1726), Voltaire's *Candide* (1759) and Goldsmith's *Citizen of the World* (1762),[7] but parodying them. The Enlightened philosophers through their intellectual pursuits attempted 'to transcend chauvinistic national loyalties or parochial prejudices' and to 'modify their attachment to their geographical region or sphere of activity with a more expansive, albeit abstract, attitude toward the whole world' (Schlereth 1977: XI). Byron's *Don Juan* achieves the Enlightenment dream through engagement with cultural difference as instantiated by women characters structured by national-sexual peculiarities: the idyllic seduction by the Greek women, the near-castration experience with the Turkish one, the passionate Russian demands, the half-concealed desires of the English ones and many others.[8]

Molière's *Don Juan*'s imperial tone of loving the whole world and Byron's *Don Juan*'s attempt to overcome national differences through sexual exchange are conceivable in the genre of comedy. The comic effect comes from Don Juan's distortion of the universal language of the moral law: 'The distortion consists in the fact that what he proposes as an object of universal distribution is the one thing which is exclusive by its very definition: the "gift of love"' (Zupančič 2000: 128), while Don Juan feels in himself the power to literally 'love the whole world', right and left. If Don Juan instantiates the cosmo-sexual citizen of the world, and this hypostasis cannot avoid a comical dimension, then the alleged cosmopolitan sex cannot be otherwise than a parody. The intellectuals of Enlightenment attempted to overcome national differences through the exchange of ideas; nowadays this power of transformation is prescribed to sexual exchange – apparently a laughable progress. But in a society which sees sexuality as a means of self-discovery and self-expression is it still possible to laugh at Don Juans and at a 'cosmopolitan sex'? In a society where consent, harassment, rape, orgasm gap, bad sex, sexual dysfunctions, sexual pleasure and so on, are sensible topics, is it still possible to see sex in a register of parody? What if indeed sexual exchange overcomes national differences in the way the knowledge of world literatures and languages allegedly did in previous epochs? One could fail in becoming cosmopolitan through sexual exchange, but so did some Enlightenment intellectuals in attempting to overcome national belonging through exchange of ideas.

The question of 'cosmopolitan sex' may turn serious, but I preferred the comic register and was ready to abandon 'sex research' but not before concluding that, in both its comic and serious dimensions, 'cosmopolitan sex' is a direct heir of Enlightenment cosmopolitanism. The Enlightenment cosmopolitanism was 'more symbolic and theoretical than actual and practical' (Schlereth 1977: XII) and referred to the exchange of ideas and world literature. Two centuries later it turned into a cosmopolitanism of sexual exchange. The *Cosmopolitan* magazine illustrates unintentionally this transformation from the Enlightenment cosmopolitanism to a 'cosmopolitan sex': from the attempt of the founders in 1886 to educate the readers in a cosmopolitan spirit through familiarisation with world literature, culture and science, to the imperative to explore their sexuality starting from 1960s under the same label: 'cosmopolitanism'.

In the Enlightenment spirit, scholars see a transformative process in cosmopolitan sex, and the move is from sex to cosmopolitanism, that is, sex with ethnic or racial others allegedly makes us cosmopolitan, in a manner reminding us of the intellectuals becoming cosmopolitan through acquiring knowledge and experiences of other cultures. But my next 'revelation', which brought me back to 'sex research', was rather surprising: it is not sex that makes people cosmopolitan but, on the contrary, cosmopolitanism makes sex possible.

'A BETTER SEXUAL WORLD FOR ALL'

Cosmopolitanism makes possible 'A Better Sexual World for All', which means that for a diversity of sexual expressions to be possible some apparently unexpected preconditions are necessary at the global level, as the book *Cosmopolitan Sexualities* (Plummer 2015) argues from a sociological perspective. This book is full of classificatory lists on sexual diversities, some unexpected, such as pauperised sexualities, sickness sexualities, homeless sexualities, exiled sexualities and so on. The aim of this classificatory guide is to show that sexuality is everywhere, and that classification itself is impossible: new sexualities are around the corner waiting to be included, for example a new entry would be 'pandemic sexualities'.[9] The main question of the book is 'How should we live in the Sexual Labyrinth?' and the answer is by cultivating critical cosmopolitan sexualities, as 'Common Grounds to work for in a Better Sexual World for All': 'Cosmopolitan sexualities are those sexualities that live convivially and reciprocally with a variety of the diverse genders and sexualities of others, both within and across cultures' (Plummer 2015). The conviviality and reciprocity require an imagination of 'openness' and 'tolerance' towards sexual differences. But, above all, two things are crucial in order to have cosmopolitan sexualities: democracy and human rights. This does not mean that without democracy there are no sexualities, but that in non-democratic regimes sexualities are impoverished and partial:

> Cosmopolitan sexualities depend on the development of social structures – call them 'democracies' – that allow for diversities, autonomy and freedom to flourish. Certain kinds of social order – those that are authoritarian,

closed, dictatorial, ruled by despots and religious absolutisms – are not easily conducive to cosmopolitan sexualities. (Plummer 2015)

To be sure, in democratic regimes, sexualities are regulated as well, permanently, although in different ways, as the author observes: when sexualities are expressed by the poor, they require instruction and containment, whereas those of the rich need liberating.

The framework of human rights, their implementation and supervision by different institutions of transnational governance and global civil culture is another crucial condition for cosmopolitan sexualities. Given the implementation of human rights and democracy in the last half century in different countries, 'the growth of cosmopolitan sexualities has been a partial success story: there have been real changes in gender and sexualities on the ground that only the most fanciful utopians could ever have dreamed about in the past' (Plummer 2015). Therefore, the sexual diversity today is a result of the cosmopolitan framework of human rights applied globally through different conventions and treaties. The acceleration in human sexual variety in the early decades of the twenty-first century shows to the author that a 'grounded utopia' of cosmopolitan sexualities is possible. However, the list of the things to be done is still long and it includes, among others, establishing agendas for the international public debate on cosmopolitan sexualities, developing international law and cosmopolitan legal systems that frame the cosmopolitan sexualities project, creating the monitoring apparatus for cosmopolitan sexualities and so on.

This approach to cosmopolitan sexuality reiterates a 'cosmopolitanism from above' and is the object of innumerable criticisms. This book acknowledges that it advances an approach that puts together two set of problems: those of cosmopolitanism and those of sexuality. Thus, it admits that cosmopolitanism of democracy and human rights, in the Western style, is viewed as a threat of 'colonizing universalisms that are insensitive to difference' (Plummer 2015). Cosmopolitanism of democracy and human rights applied to sexualities belongs to the liberal humanist project and it risks being considered a Western hegemonic import and an act of imperialism by apparently giving to the entire world human sexual rights. Acknowledging all these risks, the book nevertheless embraces this cosmopolitanism and its humanist tradition, since there is no other providing a framework for sexualities to flourish.

The problems of sexuality are more thrilling than those of cosmopolitanism. The dangers from sex come from many directions:

> it reaches deeply into interpersonal relationships, making them full of potential joy, but also of pain and hate; it is a source of great human pleasure, but also so close to great human rage and violence; it is a source of

disease and illness; it links into some of the basest fears of what it means to be animal-like and human at the same time. It can be psychologically frightening, physically disturbing and socially disruptive. For some, it provokes disgust, shame, dishonour. (Plummer 2015)

However, the solution to the disarray of sex problems is in 'more cosmopolitanism', that is, more rights and more democracy worldwide. Cosmopolitanism is, for this author, a 'flawed concept' but it is the best we have in order to achieve 'A Better Sexual World for All'.

Paradoxically, cosmopolitanism of democracy and human rights appears more potent here than sex. Sex and the plurality of sexual expressions can be crushed under an authoritarian regime that regulates sexual behaviour, and where some behaviours risk heavy punishment. The achievement of sexual diversity is not an effect of a separate set of rights or provisions, different from the general framework of universal human rights declarations: it is the effect of the creation of a global human rights regime that has at its heart the idea of dignity, crucial for human sexuality, as the book argues (Plummer 2015). Thus, by protecting basic – and universal, however controversial this universality may be – human rights, a regime creates the conditions for a variety of sexual expressions. However, there is nothing 'sexual' in this cosmopolitanism, and sex that will follow once the framework of human rights is implemented may be 'cosmopolitan', but it can be only 'local' or 'national'. Democracy and human rights are just a precondition but not a guarantee for becoming cosmo-sexual citizens of the world.

But this guarantee is not necessary anymore. Once we have a global framework in which no one is illegal and where everyone can live with dignity, sex loses its relevance as a means to a better world. The alleged cosmopolitan transformative power of sex is lost and sex is made dependent on a legal framework implemented from above. What a disappointment, but also what a relief! So, the discussion of cosmopolitan sex has to be abandoned and I have to go back to the idea of a World Republic that will give everyone equal entitlements and duties. At this point I was ready to abandon once again my research on 'cosmopolitan sex', when I realised that the idea of a World Republic is not free from a certain 'sexual' risk, and I have to be ready to answer a potential question about sex in a World Republic.

Paradoxically, 'A Better Sexual World for All' achievable, as the argument goes, in a World Republic does not necessarily mean better sex for everyone, and it does not mean equal sharing of sex. The argument on cosmopolitan sexualities from above should stop at the general human rights framework, otherwise if it goes further to the individual subject and formulates claims to equal share of sex and sexual justice, it would be a move to a kind of authoritarian regime, subverting the very framework of rights that it was implementing.[10] No one is entitled to have sex with someone else, no matter how much suffering this may produce in the 'desiring' citizens, and the democratic state cannot adopt policies that would encourage citizens to 'share' sex equally. In de Sade's *Philosophie dans le boudoir*, the libertine Dolmancé reads the manifesto *Français, encore un effort si vous voulez être républicains* which declares the right of every citizen to freely use any other person's body. The argument does not lack coherence or logic: if the sovereign subject is first of all sovereign over his or her own body, it means that each individual has the right to share his or her own body. As a juridical constitutional contract, founded on republican reciprocity, the proposal moves the state to the boudoir, or, the boudoir becomes the state. Sex becomes the very substance of politics in the boudoir–state, and there will be no opposition since this organisation of the state will be in accordance with Nature. In the *120 Days of Sodom*, this vision becomes a source of total domination and unconditioned violence, an absolute control on the part of the masters of the intimacy of their slaves (de Sade 1990a, 1990b).

The claim to equal sharing of sex is put in a parodic register in Aldous Huxley's *Brave New World*, where the citizens of the world state along with the motto 'Community, Identity, Stability' have endorsed, from an early age, another crucial one 'Everyone belongs to everyone else.' In this world state dystopia, the only function of sex is for pleasure; biological reproduction is provided for by technological means. Adults are expected to be engaging in an endless series of sexual relationships with everyone else. The meeting of six men and six women once a week to hold an 'Orgy-Porgy' is the religious ceremony of this community. The state eradicated the emotions of love and jealousy to make sure that the motto 'Everyone belongs to everyone else' is respected and fully implemented. The vision of a 'cosmopolitan sex' in a world state cannot be formulated otherwise than in a register of parody (of H. G. Well's writings on the world state, see Chapter 5). Again, the comic and the parody turn out to be the only adequate genre for the topic of 'cosmopolitan sex'. It was time to abandon 'sex research' once again, but perhaps I still had an unacknowledged hope to harvest the power of sex for my approach to cosmopolitanism, which moved me further to other tempting theories.

THE UTOPIA OF PAST PLEASURES

The tempting theories were those 'detecting' in sex the power of negativity, and which start with Freud's discovery that something about sexuality is constitutively unconscious, that is, constitutively problematic, irreducible to any kind of truth about itself, a constant threat of collapse into nonsense, and with the allusion from *Three Essays on the Theory of Sexuality* that sexual pleasure occurs whenever a certain threshold of intensity is reached, and the organisation of the self is momentarily disturbed.[11] The approach continued with Lacan's discovery that 'there's no such thing as a sexual relationship' (*il n'y a pas de rapport sexuel*) since according to another famous formula of Lacan, 'desire is always the desire of the Other',[12] which means that our desire and the *rapport sexuel* itself are always mediated by language, and supported by an imaginary/phantasmatic dimension. For the authors that elaborated on the philosophical implications of Freudian and Lacanian psychoanalysis (and which of course cannot even be approximated here), ontologically speaking sex is a lack, a void, less than nothing, minus one, while epistemologically speaking sex is a 'non-knowledge' (Zupančič 2017; Žižek 2019). The 'minus one' that is in the structure of sex as a form not as a content is the ground for the theory of desire and its irreducibility to need. Thus, the negativity inherent in sex points relentlessly beyond the normal daily life, sex being 'the first and most basic experience of a properly meta-physical experience. Sexual passion introduces a violent cut into the flow of our daily life: another dimension intervenes into it and makes us neglect our daily interests and obligations' (Žižek 2019: 115). In different terms, George Bataille wrote that the key function of eroticism is to 'destroy the self-contained character of the participators as they are in their normal lives', in their 'continual spending and repeatedly exposes himself to danger' (Bataille 1997: 259). Through negation of normal life, eroticism is the *via negativa* towards a mystical dimension:

> the totality of what is (the universe) swallows me (physically), and if it swallows me, or since it swallows me, I can't distinguish myself from it; nothing remains, except this or that, which are less meaningful than this nothing. In a sense it is unbearable. (Bataille 1997: 276)

'Sex as unbearable' (Berlant and Edelman 2014) is experienced as a site of an 'intensified encounter with what disorganizes accustomed ways of being' (2014: 64), and which leads to a non-sovereign status of the subjects. Thus, sex disorients and induces a 'loosening of the subject that puts fear, pleasure, awkwardness, and above all experimentality in a scene that forces its participants to disturb what it has meant to be a person and to "have" a world' (2014: 117). Negativity cannot be eliminated from the structure of sex; sex 'keeps coming back to the unbearable' (2014: 121).

But what happens after 'world destruction' or 'after sex'? Does the world reconstitute itself as it was, and the subject recompose its pre-sex sovereign subjectivity? Asking these questions, I encountered the most 'tempting' approach, envisaging transformative potentialities of sex to be harvested for a radical cosmopolitics. Sex has not only world-destroying potentiality but also world-making potentialities, argues Muñoz in *Cruising Utopia: The Then and There of Queer Futurity*, a book that, in its theoretical vindications of the negativity and radicality of sex, does not give up on 'potentiality or concrete possibility for another world' (Muñoz 2009: 1). Not giving up the hope of the transformative force of Eros and its implicit relationship to political desire, *Cruising Utopia* intends to 'distil some real theoretical energy from historical accounts of fucking and utopia' (2009: 18), by going back to authors that allow reimagining a utopia, mainly Ernst Bloch's *Principle of Hope*. In not giving up the hope of the possibility of another world, *Cruising Utopia* differentiates itself from the queer theory which rejects the universal politics of 'reproductive futurism' and embraces the force of a negativity linked with irony, jouissance and, ultimately, the death drive itself.[13] *Cruising Utopia* argues that while queer rejects reproductive futurity, it does not need to give up on concepts such as politics, hope and future.

Cruising Utopia presents itself as 'a resource for political imagination' meant to serve 'as something of a flight plan for a collective political becoming' (Muñoz 2009: 189), without specifying that political imagination has to be confined to a certain space or another. The building blocks of this utopia are 'queer utopian memories' – remembrances and their ritualised telling through film, video, performance, writing – as having 'world-making potentialities' (2009: 35). Thus, the subject is not only condemned to an endless repetition of sex as disturbing of what it means to be a person and to have a world, the subject is also endowed with the memories of what happened. These memories, embodied in works called 'public-sex mimetic cultural production', re-enact 'a culture of sexual possibility' (2009: 35) and a space for 'actual, living sexual citizenship' (2009: 35). The 'queer utopian memories' are the link between the present of the pleasure which is passing into the no-longer-conscious (or the past) and which invests in the not-yet-here (the future). Saving the present of pleasure is a crucial element of this view of Utopia:

> Some will say that all we have are the pleasures of this moment, but we must never settle for that minimal transport; we must dream and enact new and better pleasures, other ways of being in the world, and ultimately new worlds. (2009: 1)

To dream better pleasures one has to find 'The Not-Vanishing Point' (Muñoz 2009: 81) of the present pleasure, which *Cruising Utopia* compares with dance – an art which disappears in the very act of materialising, a perpetual vanishing point. Although the dancers and the audiences have been aware of this ephemerality, they engage in it since every vanishing point signals a return and continuation: 'Rather than dematerialize, dance rematerializes. Dance, like energy, never disappears; it is simply transformed . . . It is more nearly about another understanding of what matters' (2009: 81). Like activists and social movements that, after the event of protest is gone and radicalism seems to vanish, evoke the configuration of prefigurative politics, *Cruising Utopia* asks not 'to let failed revolutions be merely finite moments. Instead, we should consider them to be the blueprints to a better world' (2009: 146). A better world has to be achieved through the work of desire that rematerialises past pleasures: 'the no-longer-conscious, the rich resonance of remembrance, distinct pleasures felt in the past' (2009: 26). The book, which is both a theory and a manifesto, issues a call 'to take ecstasy with you', to take ecstasy 'with one another, in as many ways as possible' (2009: 187).

I took *Cruising Utopia* literally as a resource for political imagination in my 'secret hope' to harvest the radicality of sex for an idea of radical cosmopolitan sex, but the resource turns out to be a problematic one. Can there be a universalising political imagination of remembering and catching the non-vanishing points of pleasures felt by others in different historical contexts, or does one need to feel his own pleasures in order to take the ecstasy with him? How do we move from the rich remembrance of the past pleasure, which is individual even if sex was public, to a collective world-making and political becoming? Could one start imagining a collective political becoming from the ecstasy of others? In other words, does everyone require his/her own reserves of memories of past pleasures in order to desire, imagine (and construct) a better new world for all or can this 'better world for all' be imagined from the 'historical accounts of fucking' (Muñoz 2009: 18) described in this book? Any other local experiences proposed as building blocks of a universal vision are immediately and rightly accused of imperialism and ethnocentrism, and sex is not an exception. For example, using LGBT+ rights, the US government legitimises war and imperialism through the discursive association of the West with modernity-progress-LGBT-friendliness and of the rest of the world with homophobia and backwardness, as the concept of 'homonationalism' (Puar 2007) captures. Homonationalism is evident in pinkwashing campaigns in the Western countries that use LGBT rights to justify, for example, anti-immigration policies claiming that immigrants come to 'spoil their values'. While homonationalism is an 'analytics of power' (Puar 2013: 337) which allows the conditions of possibility for national and transnational politics to be examined, this analytics does not presuppose a methodological cosmopolitanism. It is an overwhelmingly inward gaze of its own American academic context, ignoring the perspective of a possible queer cosmopolitics to which this critique of homonationalism was so close, although otherwise 'there is nothing inherently or intrinsically anti-nation or antinationalist about queerness' (Puar 2007: 77). Queer activism and queer studies prefer to frame their activity in terms of 'Queer nation' and 'Queer nationality,'[14] and the radical promise of queer 'alternative erotic cosmopolitanisms' (Pérez 2015: 3) is still to be imagined.[15]

If the proposed resource for political imagination is derived from 'the rich resonance of remembrance of distinct pleasures felt in the past' that generated ecstasy 'then and there' to be taken further as an act of the fidelity to the event of queer (usually public and radical) sex, then the concrete 'then and there' – New York and the USA in the last decades of the twentieth century – weakens the radicality of sex which was supposed to be reclaimed for cosmopolitan purposes. The rich resonance of distinct pleasures felt in the past presupposes once again the 'banality' of democracy and human rights. Only in a political regime where democracy and human rights allow the expression of all kinds of sexualities is such a resource of 'queer utopian memories' possible. When the queer theory refers to 'sexual avant-gardist acts whose ideological projects are both antinormative and critical of the state' (Muñoz 2009: 56), it envisages a state that allows this critique and allows 'sexual avant-gardist acts' to take place. In a non-democratic state, ignoring or mimicking rights, the memories of past pleasures could not be so rich, and thus offer less ways of 'taking ecstasy with one another'. So, once again the power of sex, its negativity and radicality depends on some 'banal' preconditions such as democracy, human rights, respect for human dignity, tolerance and so on. My attempt was to co-opt the power of sex as a means of achieving an equal and just world for all, but it turns out that sex depends on the existing political power that allows it to be rich, avant-gardist and radical.

Obviously, all these impossibilities are not the fault of *Cruising Utopia*, which is just 'pure utopia' for no place, while I was trying to formulate a cosmopolitan political theory for the world as whole. This book emanates an engaging beauty, and in its intellectual generosity it instilled the hope that the transformative force of Eros could be appropriated for the idea of radical cosmopolitics. But my hope to harvest the power of sex for cosmopolitan purposes failed, and it had to fail: the failure is in the negativity inherent to sex. The lack and void of sex as a concept also means the impossibility of speaking about sexual experience, or as the Lacanian scholars put it, of transcribing the real of sex into the order of the signifier, thus sexuality cannot be directly harvested for whatever politics. I abandoned 'sex research' once again but came back for a 'final clarification', made possible, paradoxically, by the first cosmopolitical stance – that of the Ancient Cynics. I had to come back because I was doing 'sex research' at the 'request' of the others who 'interpellated' me to answer how sex and drink are 'cosmopolitan'.

THE TROUBLE WITH 'COSMOPOLITAN DESIRE'

The Cynic way of life was a critique of pleasure and desire viewed not as natural needs but shaped by the conventions of the polis. Notoriously, it is said that the Cynics turned to genuine sexual urges, arguing that one can learn this from animals' simple remedies. 'Fish wisely rub themselves on rough surfaces when in need' (Dio Chrysostom 6.18), and so Diogenes 'uses his hand', performing 'the works of Aphrodite' (DL 6.69) in public: 'If only, he exclaimed, one could relieve a hungry belly also just by rubbing it' (6.46). He joked that Aphrodite was present for him everywhere and for free, while others would pay many talents to have 'that one' member scratched again and again. For some Cynics, masturbation and 'free love' was natural, wise and god-like all at once, but there was disapproval of 'Greek love'. According to legend, Diogenes warned a good-looking young man who was sleeping unguarded, 'Up, man, up, lest some foe thrust a dart into thy back!' (DL 6.53), and warned another good-looking young man going off to a symposium that he will return 'worse' (6.59). Cynics did not go to the gymnasia, palaestra and baths of the Greek cities to exercises or bathe, but to 'bark' at vice: baths, with their homosexuality and self-indulgence, were incompatible with physical toughness, temperance and sexual integrity (Desmond 2008: 91). Diogenes scowled at adulterers (DL 6.68), not because of respect for the marital vow but because serial adultery only stokes sexual appetite, endlessly and unnecessarily. According to sources and legends, the Cynics advocated free love and community of men and women, while their view on raising children included communal raising but also the view that the extinction of mankind would be no worse than that of wasps or flies (Desmond 2008: 95). Thus, the Cynics differentiated between some natural, animal-like needs and unnatural desires that were generated by the convention of life in the polis, as though illustrating, again *avant la lettre*, the psychoanalysis' discovery that while needs are natural, sexuality – that is, desire and pleasure – is a break from 'natural life'. However, the Cynics' turning to animal dog-like life was not a turn towards nature, but a way of criticising the conventions of the polis, and in the case of sexuality, a way of criticising desire as shaped by conventions. Diogenes' critique of certain sexual behaviours displays that desire is not natural but induced by the conventions of the polis and shows that one does not need to follow it blindly, otherwise one can easily become 'a slave to needless sexual pleasure' (Desmond 2008: 89). The dog barks at the convention-like desire to change desire's currency. Their barking points to a critique of desire – a difficult task, then and now, but it turns out to be the only plausible approach to the link between sex and cosmopolitanism.

Critique of desire is a difficult task since desire is privileged as a realm of freedom and transgression and is considered an immutable quality outside history. So can a critique of desire be performed and where is the cosmopolitan potential of such a critique? Paraphrasing Foucault who in an interview said that the best part of homosexual sex is 'when the lover leaves in the taxi',[16] that is, in the move from the act itself to its remembering, it could be assumed that the cosmopolitan part of sex is when the one-night stand partner of a different ethic, national or racial origin leaves, and one starts the process of remembering it and achieving an improbable 'cosmopolitan subjectivity', as those reporting 'United Nation experiences' found after their sexual encounters with an ethnic and racial other. However, there is no guarantee that such an 'after sex' cosmopolitan subjectivity will ever be achieved. If there is an infinitesimal cosmopolitan potential in this situation, then it is not in the 'after sex', but paradoxically in what could happen 'before sex' if the subject could ask some almost impossible questions: Why do I desire a Latino lover or a Black man? Why do I desire an East Asian woman and how do I know that I desire this? However, the critique of 'cosmopolitan desire' cannot be a self-critique of the individual trembling with desire for 'brown bodies' or for 'hot blonde' girls. The critique of desire should not be directed at its manifestation in a concrete individual encounter, but at the structures producing that desire and the phantasies that sustain it. This dismantling of structure producing (incommensurable) racialised desires started with Frantz Fanon and Edward Said's discussions of the erotic of racial and colonial oppression and continued within subfields such as Black queer studies (Holland 2012) and Marxist materialist feminist studies (Hennessey 2000) that showed the necessity of viewing desire as historically produced. Thus, a radical cosmopolitics that reclaims the Cynics' legacy cannot proceed otherwise than exposing the troubles with 'cosmopolitan desire', as it is produced and sustained by current economic and political structures.

A significant trouble of cosmopolitan desire comes from the fact that the erotic of ethnic and racial others does not exist in a vacuum and bears the traces of systemic racism. For some authors, the ethnic and racial differences are the very substance of the erotic imaginaries: 'there is no "raceless" course of desire' (Holland 2012: 43) and 'Is it even imaginable to think the erotic . . . without contemplating its intercourse with race?' (Pérez 2015: 1). For other authors, since 'desire is always desire of the Other', the fact that it comes with a preference that in other registers is called 'racist' is just a 'benign variation' which 'might thus give rise to a vitalizing experience of engagement and curiosity rather than encouraging a fearful retreat to normativity's fortified bunkers' (Berlant and Edelman 2014: 64–5). Admitting that racial difference can be and often is erotic and fetishised, some other scholars maintain that this racial fetishism is not symptom of racial bias, and that the ways people of colour are devalued matter in a much more socially damaging manner, while racial bias can and does coexist with the erotics of racial fetishism (Muñoz 2009: 193–207). It is beyond the aim of this chapter to clarify how refusal of reciprocity or equivalence in the sexually eroticised practices shapes so many people's erotic imaginaries and sexual life. But a critique of 'cosmopolitan desire' has to emphasise that while we may count some sexual encounters as transgressions, it may be just a conformation of the structures of power that dictated to us the desire for the racialised other.

Another equally troubling aspect of cosmopolitan desire is that it presupposes that the identities of participants in 'cosmopolitan sex' have to manifest themselves in the way these were reified by the current and the previous forms of power. For example, the 'cosmopolitan' effects of encounters mediated by dating apps comes from the fact that users identify differently according to 'ethnicity' following dominant US labels such as 'white/Caucasian', 'Asian', 'Black', 'Middle Eastern' and 'mixed', and which the dating apps provide to users to denote their racial difference. Although 'cosmopolitan' sex is understood as a way of transcending existing differences, in fact it reifies them, since it subscribes to the existing racial imaginaries. Differences are necessary in order to have a 'cosmopolitan desire', and so the very 'cosmopolitan desire' is not working towards a cosmopolitan subjectivity but to a perpetuation of differences and a continuous mixture of them. A cosmopolitan desire is a contradiction in terms, and it displays the wrong that is embodied in the dominant understanding of cosmopolitanism as a mixture of differences.

An almost insurmountable problem of cosmopolitanism comes from the fact that this desire of mixing differences is shaped by the market and capitalism. 'Cosmopolitan sex' appears as part of the economy that depends on the 'fetishisation and consumption of the Other', as Beck observed: 'Images of an in-between world, of the black body, exotic beauty, exotic music, exotic food and so on, are globally cannibalised, re-staged and consumed as produce for mass markets' (Beck 2004: 150–1). The desire to be 'cosmopolitan', to acquire the quality of 'being worldly' is about making a number of consumer choices – travelling to certain 'exotic' places, buying certain types of consumer products, eating in certain 'ethnic' suburbs – that overlook the operations of power and give to majoritarian cultures 'permission to consume minoritarian Others' (2004: 151). The cosmopolitan desire falls short of any emancipatory power and reveals itself to be just a 'consumption of the exotic other'. A radical cosmopolitics has to be critical of the erotic economies of capitalism and of a neoliberal consumer society obsessed with pleasure and desire, dictating how the individual must desire and enjoy, including the desire of the exotic others, which apparently 'qualifies' as 'my cosmopolitan desire'.

A further trouble with cosmopolitan desire comes from the fact that although globalisation from the last three decades generated conditions for diverse sexual encounters through travelling around the world, the travel experiences are not accessible in the same degree to all individuals, given the lack of freedom of movement for all. For example, travelling is an experience more accessible to the members of an international non-governmental organisation providing know-how to the Filipino specific communities, than vice versa. The neoliberal cosmopolitan sex workers are described as the elite of sex workers, free to make their choice for a 'cosmopolitan' way of life. Similarly, 'sexual citizens' pursue certain modes of consumption and lifestyle and so acquire the 'cosmopolitan sexual citizenship'. The trouble with 'cosmopolitan sex&drink' is that it risks undermining every approach of cosmopolitanism, by making it complicit with an elitist lifestyle and consumption. The 'mystery' of the drink called 'cosmopolitan' – a cocktail made with vodka, triple sec, cranberry juice and freshly squeezed or sweetened lime juice – illustrates this complicity. The first person who tasted the mixture proposed by a bartender declared, 'How cosmopolitan!'– and this event supposedly led to the naming of the new beverage.[17] Perhaps the mixture reminded the customer of the taste of drinks or food he had had in different part of the world in his interactions with the 'exotic others' – an experience not available to everyone. The adjective 'cosmopolitan' added to fashion, architecture, style of life, urban places, persons, sex and so on makes cosmopolitanism sound like a luxury or a caprice whose satisfaction is not accessible to everyone, but only to 'sexy cosmopolitans'.

Summarising the troubles with cosmopolitan desire, it has to be reiterated that our erotic selves, before being a realm of freedom and transgression, were shaped by nation, state, community and race, and are dictated by the mechanisms of the market and capitalism. Thus, the critique of 'cosmopolitan' desire structured by capitalist economies and by political power is a difficult task, since it requires concomitantly the critique of power and of capitalism. This critique is a task yet to be undertaken in the 'spirit' of permanent questioning to understand what we do when trembling with desire for 'exotic others'. Concomitantly, the 'very idea of a cosmopolitan desire' has to be dismantled. From the troubles enumerated above, cosmopolitan desire displays a complicity of three spheres: cosmopolitanism, capitalism and sex, all being driven by similar longing for the other(s). The same desire cuts across the three spheres, uniting them in a baffling knot, and the knot has to be unknotted. But how did the knot happen? Sex/sexuality presupposes an undeniable desire for the other(s), and this is the minimal certainty about sex. Capitalism is an economic system based on the private ownership of the means of production, whose central characteristics include capital accumulation, competitive markets, voluntary exchange and wage labour, and allegedly, as the founders of economic theory discovered, the invisible hand of the free market or *laissez-faire*. Cosmopolitanism is the idea that all human beings are members of a single community or 'citizens of the world'. These are the meanings of the three words by which we differentiate them for a minimal intelligibility. So why do these words slide into a whirlpool of confusion producing combinations and, apparently, realities called 'cosmopolitan sex', 'cosmopolitan drink', 'cosmo-sexual cities' and so on? The plausible way of proceeding here is to notice that all three concepts have an inherent logic of going beyond the given. As examined above, sex pushes beyond the physical towards the spiritual and metaphysical, and sexual desire as 'the desire of the others' is irreducible to need and moves us towards the ultimate, although 'failed absolute' (Žižek 2019) promised by sex. Capitalism, through its incessant exchanging of commodities, competition and works of the 'invisible hand' of the market, displays a logic of perpetual expansion, both spatially all over the world but also through inventing new products and new needs. These two clarifications are sufficient for grasping the confluence of the logic of sexual desire with the logic of capitalism expansion. Capitalism, as many authors have already argued, mimics the structure of our desire, making us enjoy what capitalism produces but keeping our satisfaction incomplete, compelling us to want something new, better and more.[18] Since the invention of the science of political economy, capitalism has been described as corresponding to natural impulses, such as greed, while unashamed self-interest was considered the mechanism that keep the system going for the benefit of all.

Cosmopolitanism as the idea that all human beings are 'citizens of the world' is not part of this picture since it does not emerge neither from an individual's desire for the others nor from self-interest. The Cynics, in their assumed poverty and destitution, lived in common on the streets, pointing that 'The only true commonwealth is as wide as the universe' (DL 6.72). Zeno's *Republic* portrayed humankind as a 'herd that feeds together and shares the pasturage of a common field', and there is no direct self-interest in having more of the pasture and grazing more (or putting a fence around it and making it a commodity to sell access to grazing to others for their survival). If there is a desire in this image, then it is a desire for a world where all could feed together and share the pasturage of a common field. Since its beginning, cosmopolitanism may have not been free from a desire – a desire for another life and another world. Then the 'second birth' of cosmopolitanism happened, taming and forgetting the Cynics' radical stance, as argued in Chapter 2, in which cosmopolitanism was tangled with the self-interest of 'great glory' and with the imperial intent. 'Those, then, whose office it is to look after the interests of the state . . . must strive, too, by whatever means they can, in peace or in war, to advance the state in power, in territory, and in revenues', (Cicero 1913: II.85), and all this has to be done for 'popularity and glory for themselves' by those who 'render eminent service to the state' (II. 85). So, when the invisible hand of the market arrived on the stage of world history, it came up with a 'bourgeois cosmopolitanism' that, more efficiently than the young Romans administrating the empire, managed to augment the capital by empire, farmlands and revenues from the entire world: 'The bourgeoisie has through its exploitation of the world market given a cosmopolitan character to production and consumption in every country' (Marx and Engles 1978: 476). In cosmopolitanism of consumption and indulgence of 'new needs for the products from new lands and climes' (1978: 476), the knot of desire for exotic others, capitalism and cosmopolitanism was cemented. The critique of cosmopolitan desire must work hard to untie the knot.

Cosmopolitics is not free from desire, but this is a militant desire for another life and another world. Thus, the task of emancipatory radical cosmopolitics is to reorient the desire for the 'exotic others', their bodies and drinks, towards the horizon of another world that is possible.

NOTES

1. <https://www.cosmopolitan.com/lifestyle/a1746/about-us-how-cosmo-changed-the-world/> (last accessed 10 December 2021).
2. <https://www.britannica.com/topic/Cosmopolitan-magazine> (last accessed 10 December 2021).
3. <https://www.cosmopolitan.com/lifestyle/a1746/about-us-how-cosmo-changed-the-world/> (last accessed 10 December 2021)
4. For the concept of a cosmo-sexual city, see Maggin and Steinmetz (2015: 19–43).

5. For 'cosmopolitan sexual citizenship' see Burns and Davies (2009); Burns (2012).
6. Different translations of the *Mille e tre* aria are available on the internet.
7. For the sources that are parodied see Wohlgemut (2009).
8. For Byron's *Don Juan* as a 'borderline engagement of cultural difference' see Daly (1998).
9. <https://www.forbes.com/sites/kimelsesser/2020/10/07/how-the-pandemic-has-changed-our-sexuality/?sh=59262e1417fc> (last accessed 10 December 2021).
10. For a discussion on the 'right to sex' see Srinivasan (2021).
11. Freud develops these contentions in Freud (1953–74: 125–248).
12. 'There's No Such Thing as a Sexual Relationship' (*Il n'y a pas de rapport sexuel*), the enigmatic utterance that can be taken as the motto of Lacan's later thinking, appears for the first time, in five occurrences, in 'L'Etourdit' in 1972. See Lacan (2009).
13. See Edelman (2004). It is beyond the aims of this section and this chapter to engage with queer theory as such, while the explorations of the cosmopolitan potential of queer is still to be elaborated by queer theorists; see Pérez (2015) for an incipient approach.
14. See Walker (1997); Berlant and Freeman (1993: 193–229).
15. The very few attempts at an incipient queer cosmopolitanism proceed through a critique of the gay neoliberal cosmopolitanism, considered a product of the nineteenth-century *fin de siècle*, an agent of capitalism and colonialism, whose desires are animated by capitalism with is cultures of leisure time and consumption (Pérez 2015: 1–25). The queer critique acknowledges the need for 'alternative erotic cosmopolitanisms' (2015: 3), and looks at the proletarian queer, including 'the unexpectedly queer, proletarian cosmopolitanism of sailors, soldiers, and cowboys' (2015: 9).
16. For a 'deciphering' of this affirmation, see Bersani (1987), especially pp. 219–20.
17. The different histories of the cocktail called the 'cosmopolitan', and which can be found on different web pages, agree in their mention of this detail.
18. See, for example, McGowan (2016).

Chapter 7

A RADICAL LOVE OF HUMANITY

The troubles of cosmopolitanism outside political theory do not end with 'cosmopolitan pleasures'. From outside theory, a scholar of cosmopolitanism is seen as floating in exaltations such as 'love of humanity', 'brotherhood of men', 'responsibility towards the Other (with capital O)', 'love thy neighbour', 'philanthropy', 'peace' and other notions whose meaning have been almost lost due to their excessive use. These exaltations were attributed to me more often than the connections to an enjoyable 'cosmopolitan sex&drink'. Even if I was not writing or speaking about these notions, but about migration or about a World Republic, the very fact that I was trying to advance a cosmopolitan theory was considered an expression of these effusions, but mainly an expression of the most paradigmatic 'exaltation' associated with cosmopolitanism – 'love of humanity'. So, at a certain moment I caught myself asking, 'Do I love humanity?' An arresting question. Does the theorist of cosmopolitanism feel more love for humanity than the non-cosmopolitan author? Whatever love of humanity means, perhaps theorists of cosmopolitanism do not have a monopoly on it, but it is attributed to them more often than to others. But is it only attributed, or indeed is a theory of cosmopolitanism a 'symptom' of the love of humanity? As in the previous apparently dead-end situations, the insight came from the Cynics' legacy: the Cynics loved humanity with an impossible radical love, and perhaps all love of humanity cannot be otherwise than impossible and radical. And the radical love of humanity starts with the Cynic dog loving his neighbour and his enemy as himself.

THE IMPOSSIBLE COMMAND: 'LOVE THY NEIGHBOUR!'

'Do not seek revenge or bear a grudge against anyone among your people, but love your neighbour as yourself', says the Old Testament (Lev 19: 18), to which the New Testament adds, through the words of Saint Paul: 'You shall love your neighbour as yourself! Love does no wrong to a neighbour;

therefore love is the fulfilling of the law' (Rom. 13: 8–10), while the Gospel according to Matthew extends the call asking you to love your enemy: 'I say to you, love your enemies and pray for those who persecute you' (Matt. 5: 43–6). This is the command and its variations, and the tradition of deciphering it is rich and intermittently covers two millennia.[1] However, with Freud,

> Let us adopt a naive attitude towards it, as though we were hearing it for the first time; we shall be unable then to suppress a feeling of surprise and bewilderment. Why should we do it? What good will it do us? But, above all, how shall we achieve it? How can it be possible?(Freud 1961: 109)[2]

For Freud, the command is a demand of civilisation, as he argues in *Civilization and its Discontents*; however, he 'naively' explains why the command is impossible. Thus, unconditionally loving the neighbour bestows on them an 'undeserved love':

> My love is something valuable to me which I ought not to throw away without reflection. It imposes duties on me for whose fulfilment I must be ready to make sacrifices. If I love someone he must deserve it in some way . . . He deserves it if he is so like me in important ways that I can love myself in him; and he deserves it if he is so much more perfect than myself that I can love my ideal of my own self in him. (1961: 109)

If the neighbour does not provide such an image, if he is a stranger with no merit of his own or no importance in our emotional life, it becomes hard to love him.

Further, the command seems impossible since love is a matter of preference: 'my love is valued by all my own people as a sign of my preferring them, and it is an injustice to them if I put a stranger on a par with them' (1961: 109). For the neighbour is left only the 'universal love – just because he is a creature of this earth, like an insect, an earthworm or a grass-snake' (1961: 110), but in this case the neighbour receives 'only a modicum of love' which is 'not as much as the judgement of my reason entitles me to reserve for myself', since one apparently cannot love oneself with a modicum of love. Thus, 'What is the point of a precept enunciated with so much solemnity if its fulfilment cannot be recommended as reasonable?' (1961: 110). This neighbour is not only unlovable, but he is also the object of my hate, as Freud admits frankly:

> I must honestly confess that he has more claim to my hostility and even my hatred. He seems not to have the least trace of love for me and shows me not the slightest consideration. If it will do him any good, he has no

hesitation in injuring me, nor does he ask himself whether the amount of advantage he gains bears any proportion to the extent of the harm he does to me. (1961: 110)

The neighbour looks only to 'mocking, insulting or slandering me, or using me as a foil to show off his power' (1961: 110), so that the neighbour's security means my own insecurity and helplessness. 'If this grandiose commandment had run: "Love thy neighbour as thy neighbour loves thee", I should not take exception to it' (1961: 110). The command extended to love the enemy is 'even more unintelligible', although essentially it is no different as 'at the bottom it is the same thing' (1961: 110). Hence,

> The element of truth behind all this, which people are so ready to dis-avow is that men are not gentle creatures who want to be loved, and who at the most can defend themselves if they are attacked; they are, on the contrary, creatures among whose instinctual endowments is to be reckoned a powerful share of aggressiveness. As a result, their neighbor is for them not only a potential helper or sexual object, but also someone who tempts them to satisfy their aggressiveness on him, to exploit his capacity for work without compensation, to use him sexually without his consent, to seize his possessions, to humiliate him, to cause him pain, to torture and kill him *Homo homini lupus*. (1961: 111)

Freud's reflection on loving the neighbour concludes:

> The command to love our neighbours as ourselves is the strongest defence there is against human aggressiveness and it is a superlative example of the unpsychological attitude of the cultural super-ego. The command is impossible to fulfil; such an enormous inflation of love can only lower its value and not remedy the evil. (1961: 143)

In *The Ethics of Psychoanalysis*, Lacan affirms that Freud's aversion to his neighbour comes from his belonging to the horizon of Aristotelian ethics, with its conception of the good and happiness: 'The whole Aristotelian conception of the Good is alive in this man who is a true man; he tells us the most sensitive and reasonable things about what it is worth sharing the good that is our love with. But what escapes him is perhaps the fact that precisely because we take that path, we miss the opening on to jouissance' (Lacan 1992: 186). Here is the expression of the difference between the pleasure principle, postulated by Freud, and jouissance, postulated by Lacan. The 'pleasure principle' is not about hedonism or actively striving for pleasure, it is about regulating and diminishing tension and any kind of excess experienced as unpleasurable. The traditional

Aristotelian morality is precisely the link between pleasure and the good: 'The first formulation of the pleasure principle as an unpleasure principle, or least-suffering principle, naturally embodies a beyond, but that it is, in effect, calculated to keep us on this side of it rather than beyond it' (Lacan 1992: 185). Lacan considers that Freud was not able to properly go 'beyond the pleasure principle', although he tried by linking it to a destructive 'death drive' as opposed to the pleasure principle, and later by postulating the coexistence of two competing principles (Eros and Thanatos, or life and death drives) in any human being. The 'beyond' against which the pleasure principle is supposed to protect us constitutes its own 'impossible' excluded kernel in which Lacan situates his concept of jouissance as distinctive from pleasure. Thus, the concept of jouissance or enjoyment is the structural effect produced by going beyond, 'traversing' a certain limit. If the pleasure principle as a defence formation or a protective barrier keeps us within the Aristotelian good, then jouissance or enjoyment, as the structural effect of this very breaking of the barrier, appears as the evil: 'If we continue to follow Freud in a text such as *Civilization and Its Discontents*, we cannot avoid the formula that *jouissance* is evil' (1992: 184).

Thus, the whole Freudian and Lacanian discussion of the command 'Love thy neighbour' will revolve around the problem of Evil – on how to 'rethink the problem of evil once one acknowledges that it is radically altered by the absence of God' (Lacan 1992: 185). In the commandment 'Love thy neighbour', love is required to break the protective barrier of the pleasure principle as the fence separating us from 'the beyond' which appears as evil. Love leads us into the terrain of the evil. And the evil 'dwells in the neighbour' since the neighbour points to or even instantiates this 'beyond' pleasure. But if evil inhabits the neighbour and since we are neighbours to someone else – the evil is in me:

> Every time that Freud stops short in horror at the consequences of the commandment to love one's neighbour, we see evoked the presence of that fundamental evil which dwells within this neighbour. But if that is the case, then it also dwells within me. And what is more of a neighbour to me than this heart within which is that of my jouissance and which I don't dare go near? For as soon as I go near it, as *Civilization and Its Discontents* makes clear, there rises up the unfathomable aggressivity from which I flee, that I turn against me, and which in the very place of the vanished Law adds its weight to that which prevents me from crossing a certain frontier at the limit of the Thing. (1992: 186)

The concept of the neighbour points to an inevitable hostility, an aggression that springs up in us every time we come too close to our neighbour, so it is linked to a structure called *extimité* or extimacy (*ex* from 'exterior' and '*intimité*'/intimacy), and which problematises the opposition between inside and outside, between container and contained: 'A coincidence of something most intimate, intrinsic to me, with something most external and foreign; something that belongs to me, yet at the same time strikes me as utterly foreign, disgusting even' (Zupančič 2019: 90), or explained with an insightful example: if someone spits into a clean glass of water, it turns very hard to drink the water containing the saliva. So, something that was part of yourself a moment ago becomes something foreign and even an object of disgust.[3] Similarly, the neighbour – and to the extent that we are all neighbours – is 'something strange to me, although it is at the heart of me' (Lacan 1992: 71) or 'that most neighborly of neighbors who is inside me' (1992: 187).

So, if there an 'unfathomable aggressivity' and an object of disgust in the neighbour and in me, is love of the neighbour still possible? The crucial aspect here is that love of the neighbour is not Good, altruism or philanthropy:

> As long as it's a question of the good, there's no problem; our own and our neighbor's are of the same material. Saint Martin shares his cloak, and a great deal is made of it. Yet it is after all a simple question of training; material is by its very nature made to be disposed of – it belongs to the other as much as it belongs to me. We are no doubt touching a primitive requirement in the need to be satisfied there, for the beggar is naked. But perhaps over and above that need to be clothed, he was begging for something else, namely, that Saint Martin either kill him or fuck him. In any encounter there's a big difference in meaning between the response of philanthropy and that of love (Lacan 1992: 186)

The alleged surplus need of the beggar has to point to incommensurability of the altruism and love: 'It is in the nature of the good to be altruistic. But that's not the love of thy neighbour' (1992: 186). Being altruistic stands within the confines of the good, of a reciprocal good, which is the way the ordinary relations between humans work in everyday life. Altruism is fully compatible with the good, but love is situated beyond a certain limit of the calculus of the good, pleasure and reciprocity:

> My egoism is quite content with a certain altruism, altruism of the kind that is situated on the level of the useful. And it even becomes the pretext by means of which I can avoid taking up the problem of the evil I desire, and that my neighbour desires also. That is how I spend my life, by cashing in my time in a dollar zone, rubble zone or any other zone, in my neighbour's time, while all the neighbours are maintained equally at the marginal level of reality of my own existence. Under these

conditions it is hardly surprising that everyone is sick, that civilization has its discontents. (1992: 187)

The Cold War context, alluded to in this quote, stands as the paradigm of all relations between neighbours: everyone desires evil, my neighbour and I, but no one admit this, attributing the evil only to those from the 'other zone', as those from dollar zone attribute the evil to those from rubble zone. Every neighbour on the margins of their existence desire evil, but attributes it only to the other neighbours, so indeed it is no surprise that everyone and civilisation itself are sick. This understanding was already implicit in Freud's 'naive' questioning: the love of the other appears as undeserved, beyond preference, incommensurable, asymmetrical. Lacan 'moved further' in loving the neighbour by giving some examples of saints and mystics, such as Angelica de Frolino who washed the legs of a man with leprosy, drank the water and had a piece of skin stuck in her throat, or of another saint eating the excrement of a sick man (1992: 187–8). Although these examples display excess and lack of reciprocity, going beyond good and altruism, these manifestations of love of the neighbour are nevertheless 'puerile' (1992: 187).

THE NEIGHBOUR, OR THE 'EVIL IN US'

Approaching the command 'naively' with Freud and Lacan, its difficulties have been displayed, and the piece of skin that stuck in the saint's throat is like a symbol of the impossibility to love thy neighbour in such an excessive and incommensurable way. How then to love thy neighbour, and through love of the neighbour to move to love of humanity, which will be also a way of giving birth to radical cosmopolitics, as this chapter contends? The conceptual link between the aggressivity in my neighbour and in me and cosmopolitanism has already been made. Julia Kristeva, in her history of the foreigner, *Strangers to Ourselves* (1991), building on the insight from psychoanalysis and on her own work on abjection, made an invitation to a 'cosmopolitanism of a new sort':

as an invitation (a utopic or very modern one?) not to reify the foreigner, not to petrify him as such, not to petrify us as such. But to analyze it by analyzing us. To discover our disturbing otherness, for that indeed is what bursts in to confront that 'demon,' that threat, that apprehension generated by the projective apparition of the other at the heart of what we persist in maintaining as a proper, solid 'us'. By recognizing our uncanny strangeness we shall neither suffer from it nor enjoy it from the outside. The foreigner is within me, hence we are all foreigners. If I am a foreigner, there are no foreigners . . . The ethics of psychoanalysis implies a politics: it would involve a cosmopolitanism of a new sort that, cutting across governments, economies, and markets, might work for a mankind whose solidarity is founded on the consciousness of its unconscious-desiring, destructive, fearful, empty, impossible. (Kristeva 1991: 191)

In this and other works, Kristeva alluded to a cosmopolitanism placed in the individual psyche: 'The foreigner lives within us: he is the hidden face of our identity . . . By recognizing him within ourselves, we are spared detesting him in himself' (1991: 1). Arriving at a cosmopolitanism of a new sort needs work to be done in the individual subject's psyche in the very fact of meeting and confronting strangers through travel or immigration 'as a journey into the strangeness of the other and of oneself' (1991: 182). The meeting with the strangers presumably leads to a shattering of the subject: 'confronting the foreigner whom I reject and with whom at the same time I identify, I lose my boundaries' (1991: 187). The work of confronting the stranger is almost endless: 'As test of our astonishment, source of depersonalization, we cannot suppress the symptom that the foreigner provokes; but we simply must come back to it' (1991: 190). With a Freudian echo, Kristeva states that the recognition of the foreigner in us happens in the 'process of *Kulturarbeit*, the task of civilization' (1991: 189).

The invitation to acknowledge the evil in us is formulated by Kristeva in the context of confronting the foreigner as the ethnic, national and racial other. And this invitation is different from the commandment to love thy neighbour which does not specify characteristics other than being a neighbour, that is, close to oneself. As the next section will argue, a cosmopolitan stance is possible without emphasising ethnic, national and racial differences, since the Cynics were the first to express a cosmopolitan position, but without confronting the ethnic other, but just the neighbour or *Nebenmensch* (the 'next-person'). However, what is common in 'loving the neighbour as yourself' and confronting the 'foreigner in us' is not at all an exaltation or emotional effusion but a perpetual questioning for what is human and inhuman, in the other and in us. As Žižek remarks, love for the neighbour always involves a relation with an 'inhuman partner', and inhuman is not the same as non-human:

'He is not human' means simply that he is external to humanity, animal or divine, while 'he is inhuman' means something thoroughly different, namely, that he is neither simply human nor simply inhuman, but marked by a terrifying excess which, although it negates what we understand as 'humanity', is inherent to being-human. (Žižek 2005: 160)

Inhuman, the terrifying excess that negates what we understand as 'humanity', is inherent to being-human, and a terrifying experience to confront. As Chapter 5 has shown, the 'conversion' invoked in the context of the threat posed by the atomic bomb presupposed a change in understanding that humanity itself produced the bomb, similar to other atrocities produced by humans. Inhuman acts during history were not committed by a separate non-human species, but by ordinary human beings: 'it is all too easy to dismiss the Nazis as inhuman and bestial – what if the problem with the Nazis was precisely that they remained "human, all too human"?' (Žižek 2012: 762). All these horror events are an invitation to have the traumatic experience of locating the Evil, or the 'inhuman', not only in the other, in the neighbour, but also in us: 'this self-relating, this inclusion of oneself in the picture, is the only true "infinite justice"' (Žižek 2007: 287).

It should be specified that the invitation to locate the inhuman/the evil in us is not identical to the call for an infinite responsibility for the Other as envisaged by Emmanuel Levinas for whom the unconditional responsibility for the neighbour is the true terrain of ethics. Assessing Levinas's contribution to the discussions concerning the love of the neighbour is beyond the aims of this chapter. However, the chapter makes it clear that neighbourly love is not a Levinasian worshiping of the Other; it should be viewed as a critical approach to the other and ourselves. Love of the neighbour presupposes a perpetual questioning of what it means to be human, a questioning that is inherent in the Cynics' *philanthropia* or love of humanity.

THE FIRST COSMOPOLITAN LOVE

Cosmopolitanism was (also) born as an act of neighbourly love through encountering the monstrous and the inhuman in the neighbour and in us. It was born through an act of radical love since the Cynics' loved humanity, as their *philanthropia* shows. However, they didn't love it directly or unconditionally, but in a roundabout way. Two contradictory features have been attributed to the Cynics: *philanthropia* and *mizanthropia*, or love and hate of humanity. Diogenes was famous for insulting his contemporaries in terms that verged on the misanthropic (Shea 2010: 17). Some commentators deny any vision of mankind or philanthropy, claiming that the Cynics showed contempt for the mob. Although the Cynics, in advance of most fourth-century thought, ignored the traditional barriers that make female inferior to male, slave to master, foreigner to Greek, they allegedly drew a single great dividing line separating 'the few wise men from the many fools' (Baldry 1965: 110). For other commentators, the Cynics showed benevolence towards their fellowmen (Moles 1996: 119). But how could the Cynics love and hate humanity simultaneously? These are not separate and contradictory features, but part of the 'logic' of the Cynics loving their neighbour, which contains several elements: changing the currency of humanity, becoming animal in order to become human, detection of the inhuman in us and in the neighbour, and militant love.

Changing the Currency of Being Human

The principle 'Alter the currency!' is regarded as the most fundamental Cynic principle. *Nomisma* means not only 'currency', but also nomos, law and custom, so the principle implies changing the custom, rules, habits, conventions, laws and the polis itself as the ultimate convention. Since all these are made by humans for humans to conduct their life, the principle is as well a call to alter the currency of being human. Many of Diogenes' famous sayings refer exactly to his ways of searching for men and not finding any, which are his many attempts to define what is human, the most paradigmatic being, 'He lit a lamp in broad daylight and said, as he went about, "I am looking for a man"' (DL 6.41).

The critique of what it is to be human is done in the Cynic style, as an attack, often aggressive. One well-known anecdote is from when Diogenes was in the marketplace in Athens, calling out loudly, 'Men, gather round, I am looking for men!' When a crowd gathered, he hit them with his stick, reproaching, 'It was men I called for, not scoundrels' (DL 6.32). Or sometimes, the critique is more humorous: 'Leaving the public baths, somebody inquired if many men were bathing. He said, No. But to another who asked if there was a great crowd of bathers, he said, Yes' (DL 6.40).

The Cynic's lack of respect for his fellow human beings is part of his method (Shea 2010: 18), and the attributed misanthropy is an effect of this method. The alteration of the currency of humanity indeed presupposes that the human species is currently worthy of hatred, but the very fact of intending to change it is the core of the peculiar Cynic love. Most of the critiques, as legend and anecdotes point out, were dismantling the link between the fact of being human and of being good: 'When he was asked where in Greece he found good men, he replied, "Good men, nowhere; but good boys in Sparta"' (DL 6.27). Being human does not mean being inherently good as a species, and this lack of good is multiplied by the convention of the polis: 'He would speak of rhetoricians, orators, and those seeking to become celebrities, as "three times human", meaning by this, "three times wretched"'(DL 6. 47). Attempting to dismantle and change all customs, rules, habits, conventions, laws and the polis itself, the Cynics attempted in the last instance to change the humans and mankind. This cannot be done smoothly, thus Diogenes shocked his contemporaries to make them see that what they considered to be human or humane was worthy of the name and had to be changed.

Becoming Animal in Order To Become Human

The Cynics shock by becoming animal. The Cynics animal dog-like life is considered an option for a life according to nature rather than to nomos and has been described as simplicity of natural desire, the bounty of the natural world and man's natural fitness for his environment (Desmond 2008; Allen 2020). However, becoming animal is an experiment and part of the broader method of altering the currency of everything. The animality is a perfect touchstone for questioning accepted definitions of what it means to be human (Shea 2010: 17–19). The chosen animal is not an arbitrary one, but an 'attire' that allows several performances. First, a dog (*kynikos*) does in public, in front of everyone, what only dogs and animals dare to do, and which men usually hide. Thus, dogs perform private activities, assigned to the household, like eating, sleeping, urinating and so on, in the public space and under the eyes of the others, challenging the social norms and the order of society. The dog experiment allows the Cynics to perform shameless acts of social provocation, discrediting everything that is associated with human goodness and dignity: 'They trample on all laws that can be identified with honour and justice, and more than this, [they] trample on those laws which have been as it were engraved on our souls by the gods' (Shea 2010: 18–19), complained the emperor Julian about the Cynic gangs of his day. The animal experiment allows the overthrow of hierarchies and disregards all conventional dignity of humans as grounded in religion, sociability, respectability and political allegiance.

Second, the option for the dog as an animal is a strategic one, since the dog is a discerning animal: 'When some boys gathered around him and said, "Let's be careful, lest he may bite us," Diogenes answered, "Don't be afraid, boys, dogs don't eat garbage"' (DL 45). It is this animal that symbolically allows aggressive dog-like judgement and discrimination. The Cynic's dog life is a life of a guard which barks at enemies, which knows how to distinguish the good from the bad and the true from the false. Crucial for the argument in this section is the fact that the dog is the animal that stands near the man, thus the Cynic dog-like presence is always his *prochain or Nebenmensch*. The Cynic dog embodies the neighbour, the unlovable and irritable neighbour, but who is there, and his presence unavoidable. Through barks and bites, the Cynic dog performs what all the neighbours intend to do but refrain since they try to follow through on the Good of a promised reciprocity: you do not bark at me, I do not bark at you, although all we want is to bark and bite each other. The Cynic dog barks and bites, and so he breaks the defence barrier that keeps us within the Aristotelian Good or the fence separating us from 'the beyond'. If there is an enjoyment in being a Cynic, it is exactly in this going beyond, 'traversing' a certain limit, and this aspect of the Cynic life still induces fascination (Allen 2020). The Cynic dog's presence on the streets of the city is thus the spatial instantiation of the neighbour as the person close to you, and concomitantly an instantiation of the neighbour as the source of aggressivity and discomfort.

The third performance allowed by the choice of a dog for the Cynics 'unique philosophical experiment' (Shea 2010: 18) is that of a faithfulness to human. The dog is considered man's most faithful animal; for centuries, dogs have been labelled as 'man's best friend'. In Homer's *Odyssey*, when Odysseus returns incognito after twenty years, his beloved dog Argos is the only one who recognises him. To avoid betraying himself by greeting the dog, Odysseus nevertheless sheds a tear, and Argos dies now since he has fulfilled his destiny and shown his faith, his incommensurable faith for his master. The choice of the dog for the experiment points to the Cynic's faithfulness to the human, but to the human that he will recognise when walking with a lamp in broad daylight looking for men.

The Detection of the Inhuman in the Neighbour and in Us

Long ago the Cynics proffered an invitation to discover our 'our disturbing otherness' (Kristeva 1991: 191), or the 'inhuman or a terrifying excess' (Žižek 2005: 160), or 'unfathomable aggressivity' of the neighbour (Lacan 1992: 186). As Freud 'honestly confesses', the neighbour looks only to 'mocking, insulting or slandering me, or using me as a foil to show off his power' (Freud 1961: 110). As though instantiating this quote, the Cynic is the object of insult and mockery, and he insults and mocks back. 'When someone struck him with his fist, Diogenes exclaimed, "By Hercules! How could I have forgotten to put on a helmet when I walked out?"' (DL 6. 41), or in other words, how could he have forgotten what neighbours/humans can do to neighbours/humans just to satisfy some desire by acting in this way.

> One day he made his way with head half shaven into a party of young revellers and was roughly handled by them. Afterwards he entered on a tablet the names of those who had struck him and went about with the tablet hung round his neck, till he had covered them with ridicule and brought universal blame and discredit upon them. (DL 6.33)

The Cynics show that I desire evil and *mon semblant* desires evil as well. 'Seeing some women hanged from an olive-tree, he said, "Would that every tree bore similar fruit"!' (DL 6.52). However problematic this 'wit' may appear, especially because the 'fruits' were women, one can say that it displays what we desire for the neighbour, but we never admit it. I cash in the rubble zone, my neighbour cashes in the dollar zone, we both project the evil only in the other and civilisation is sick.

The neighbour as a structure of *extemite*, of what is most disgusting and foreign in us, is incessantly performed by the Cynics. The disgusting element in the neighbour is staged by exposing the disgusting parts of oneself in public. The unconcealed life of the Cynics, its absolute vis-ibility, may induce the idea that there is nothing bad in what nature implanted in man, thus there is nothing to hide, a view affirmed by Fou-cault as well, for whom the Cynics' unconcealment 'must bring to light what is natural in the human being, and therefore what is good' (Fou-cault 2011: 254). However, the unconcealment does not bring to light only what is good, but also what is evil, disgusting and abject. The Cynic does all activities in the public space – eating, sleeping, urinating, mas-turbating and so on – and this provokes disgust in the neighbours, and the Cynic in the public space is literally the neighbour of all the others. By displaying the disgusting and inhuman in himself, the Cynic displays the disgusting and the inhuman in the others: 'You eat like a dog' says the passer-by to Diogenes, 'But you too are dogs, since only dogs form a circle around a dog which is eating. I am a dog, but so too are you, no less than I am' (DL 6.61). 'At a feast, certain people kept throwing all the bones to him as they would have done to a dog. Thereupon he played a dog's trick and drenched them' (DL 6.46).

The life of the Cynic is full of humiliation, insults and dishonour, extreme poverty, destitution and dependency: 'When he was begging alms from a statue, someone asked him why he did so, to which he answered, "To get practice in being refused."' (DL 6. 49). The situation of being insulted, despised and humiliated by others did not have any positive value in Greek society in which honour, glory, good reputation and the record one leaves in men's memory were the desired forms of afterlife. Instead, the Cynics were actively looking for humiliation, as Foucault remarks: 'the Cynics actively look for humiliating situations which are valuable because they train the Cynic in resistance to everything to do with opinions, beliefs, and conventions' (Foucault 2011: 251). This is not an experience of humility similar to the Christian one, which is a mental attitude manifesting itself and testing itself in the humiliations one suffers, like that of the saint drinking the water after washing a sufferer of leprosy. The Cynic humiliation is a game with conventions of honour and dishonour, a test of endurance, that is necessary in order to become a Cynic. There are a series of tests and experiences one has to conduct on oneself in order to recognise oneself as Cynic in the practice of *askesis*, endurance, poverty and destitution. The Cynic imposes hardships on himself: he has no clothes, shelter or hearth, he has to accept the insults and the blows, in order to train his capacity to discern between what is good and what is bad. Paradoxically, by testing their self-resistance the Cynics display others' capacity for actively producing humiliation, but whom the Cynic nevertheless love, with a militant love.

The Militant Love

Towards the end of *The Courage of the Truth*, Foucault presents the Cynics as loving humanity in an asymmetrical excessive way, as detected in the command to love the neighbour by both Freud and Lacan:

> To the suffering and injustice, he suffers at the hands of someone else, the Cynic responds in a completely dissymmetrical way with the assertion that he, the Cynic, is linked by a bond of friendship, or anyway by a bond of philanthropy to the very people who do him harm. He will put up with the violence and injustice, not only so as to become resistant, and to prepare himself for all the misfortunes which may occur – which is the classical form – but as an exercise of friendship, of affection, or at any rate of the intense bond with the whole of humankind. (Foucault 2011: 300)

In the following paragraphs, quoting Epictetus, who says that the Cynic 'must be beaten like an ass and, being beaten, must love those who beat him as though he were the father and brother of all', Foucault specifies that we have here a reversal and means that 'the insult gives the Cynic the opportunity to establish a relationship of affection with the very people who do him harm and, through them, with the whole of humankind' (Foucault 2011: 300). Foucault does not use the word 'love' but uses expressions such as 'a relationship of affection', 'an intense bond', 'a bond of friendship' and 'a bond of philanthropy', all of which display an unexpectedly coherent picture of loving the neighbour. The neighbours are those committing the insult to which 'the Cynic responds in a completely dissymmetrical way' with a 'bond of philanthropy to the very people who do him harm'. The asymmetrical affection manifested by (Foucault's) Cynics performs exactly what Freud described as an impossible command: it is an 'undeserved love'. The neighbour does not display an ideal image of myself, he has no hesitation in harming me, therefore the neighbour is more entitled to my hatred. Despite all these insurmountable difficulties, the Cynic manifests a 'bond of philanthropy to the very people who do him harm'. However, this asymmetrical bond of philanthropy is radically different from the acts of the saints who drink the water used for washing the sufferers of leprosy, since the Cynics love the neighbour with a militant radical love, as Foucault's reading of the Cynics showed.

Thus, the Cynic leads a battle, and the fronts of the struggle are multiple: against his own desires and passions, against customs, conventions, institutions, laws and 'an explicit, intentional, and constant aggression directed at humanity in general, at humanity in its real life, and whose horizon or objective is to change its moral attitude' (2011: 280). To the idea of the guard dog which accosts enemies and bites them, Foucault adds the theme of the combatant who fights against the evils of the world in order to change it. For Foucault, the Cynic battle is close to the modern notion of militancy: 'an overt, universal, aggressive militancy; militancy in the world and against the world' (2011: 285). The aim of the militant Cynic is twofold: to shake people up by attacking their vices and faults, and to 'convert them, abruptly' (2011: 285) in order to change them and the world. The militant love is a love to change those who are the object of the 'affection'. The alteration of the currency and the change of its value mean that the forms and habits of existence must be replaced, that 'life led by men in general and by philosophers in particular should be *an other life*' (2011: 244). Further, the principle of an other life becomes an 'aspiration for *an other world*' (2011: 278).

Cynics cannot not love humanity, but their love is an act of intervention and interruption of humanity, of changing the currency of what is understood to be human. But why approach it in such a roundabout way? Why should they contest humanity, criticise humans and their meanings so harshly and radically and only after that create an intensive bond of philanthropy with them? Why not care for humans directly, as they are, with all their imperfections and limits? The Cynics have a clear answer to all these questions: accepting the humans as they are, without questioning their current values, implies a risk of dehumanisation of us all.

A RADICAL LOVE OF HUMANITY

Cosmopolitanism was born through a radical act of changing the values of the currency but mainly of changing the values and currency of being human. The Cynics cannot embrace and accept the humans and their humanity *as they are now*. They interrupt humanity incessantly, trying to free the potential that is imprisoned in its current understanding and to make possible another human, another life, another world. The interruption is made with their own way of living and interacting with others which go to the root of what it is understood to be human. By going to the root, the Cynics' *philanthropia* displays an unprecedented and unique way of having an affective relationship with humans, which cannot be otherwise than a radical love of humanity. This radical love of humanity emerges not from an abstract feeling towards some distinct and unknown others but from an excessive and shocking interaction with the humans around, in the space of the city which the Cynic inhabits without shelter or a home, or, in other words, from the interactions with the neighbour. Lacan considered saints' love of the neighbour 'puerile', without looking for the other examples. Perhaps the example par excellence is the Cynics' love of the neighbour. The whole *mise en scène* of the Cynic existence displays the evil, the disgusting, the inhuman both in the Cynic and in the other, *mon semblant*. What happens after the inhuman in us and in the other is displayed is what happens in all other love or falling in love: a change, or a flickering possibility that life, in order to be a true life, must be *an another life*, and the world must be *an another world*. The first cosmopolitan love alters the command, from 'Love your neighbour as yourself' into 'Shake your neighbour as you shake yourself'. Shake and get rid of the local attachments, particularities, traditions and customs, and see that there is a horizon of another life and another world that seem possible.

As argued in all previous chapters, cosmopolitanism could not be born otherwise than through the works of negativity, and this chapter adds that it could not be born otherwise than in a context of a radical evaluation of what it means to be human, re-evaluation performed with and through a radical love of humanity. But then, again, the inevitable question: if it was born through a radical love of humanity, where did radicalism disappear to, and why was cosmopolitanism left with exaltations, such as humanitarianism, charity and philanthropy, that sound like platitudes? A platitude is a statement often used as a thought-terminating cliché, aimed at quelling social, emotional or cognitive unease. The unease with the love of humanity is considerable, as Freud 'naively' pointed out. Cosmopolitanism ends with being conflated with the support of humanitarian actions across the world, and indeed with the organisations who fight cruelty against animals, as Arendt did, because it is almost impossible to love your neighbour as yourself:

> It is easy to love the idealized figure of a poor, helpless neighbour, the starving African or Indian, for example; in other words, it is easy to love one's neighbour as long as he stays far enough from us, as long as there is a proper distance separating us. The problem arises at the moment when

he comes too near us, when we start to feel his suffocating proximity – at this moment when the neighbour exposes himself to us too much, love can suddenly turn into hatred. (Žižek 1992: 8)

Thus, we have empty catchphrases and moralistic platitudes about charity, philanthropy, brotherhood, peace, responsibility for the Other, all vehiculated for avoiding the demandingness of radical love of the neighbour, which is a demandingness to acknowledge the evil and inhuman in us. To avoid encountering the neighbour both in the other and in ourselves, we have acts of charity and humanitarianism, often made by celebrities who allegedly should raise our awareness of the plight of those who suffer and starve, while transforming humanitarianism in one of her/his personal brands. Giving to charity or philanthropic causes, one can 'love' from a distance, without getting personally involved and avoiding the encounter with the neighbour within us. The radical love of humanity now presupposes to do what the Cynics would do – attack the roots of the system that makes charity part of the game and puts a humanitarian mask on the underlying exploitation of the whole economic system.

Delegated love at a distance reveals once again the difficulties of loving your neighbour as yourself, which mirrors the difficulties of being cosmopolitan. Neighbourly love cannot be claimed or expressed without the possibility of change, both in ourselves and in the others. That which cannot be loved – the abject and inhuman in us and in the others – cannot be rejected, ignored or simply accepted: it forces us to question our own and other's values, to realign and change them. If all true love produces 'works of love' that happen after falling in love, then the work of loving the neighbour is a continuous attempt at a realignment of our ethical and political values, through confronting the abject, the evil and the inhuman in others and in us.

Avoiding the traumatic experience of confronting the neighbour, we are exposing ourselves to a possibility of dehumanisation. The command 'Love your neighbour as yourself' keeps reminding us that we have to see the 'monster' in ourselves, but without cancelling ourselves in the face of the other, submitting to an infinity responsibility towards the other. The radically and reciprocally loving neighbours form the community of the shaken, as formulated by Patočka and which was one of the three elements taken as 'building blocks' for a minimal theory of cosmopolitanism: permanent questioning, live in problematicity and shaken solidarity.

The expression 'solidarity of the shaken' is formulated in the chapter 'The Wars of the Twentieth Century and the Twentieth Century as War' from *Heretical Essays in the Philosophy of History*, where Patočka writes that although 'peace', 'light' and 'day' are seen as virtuous aspirations, their implications are destructive (1996: 119–37). 'How do the day, life, peace govern all individuals, their bodies and soul? By means of death, by threatening life' (Patočka 1996: 129). In the longing for a final eschatological peace, conflicts and contingencies are considered barriers that should be eliminated. Battlefronts were a reality in both the First and the Second World Wars, to which Patočka refers in his text, and an expression of how everyday identities work, mobilising humans for action: 'Peace transformed into a will to war could objectify and externalize humans as long as they ruled by the day, by the hope of everydayness, of a profession, of a carrier, simple possibilities for which they must fear' (Patočka 1996: 130). War begins through the attempt to create an illusion of security by naturalising our identities and defining differences as deviant and dangerous: 'the most pleasing slogans of the day . . . in reality call to war, whether they invoke the nation, the state, classless society, world unity or whatever other appeal' (Patočka 1996: 136). The experience of mortality, contingency and finitude take place in a battlefront. Confronting their finitude on the battlefront and discovering the contingency of their certainties that brought them to war, the participants at the battlefront experience an unprecedented solidarity generated unexpectedly by love: 'Here we encounter the abysmal realm of the "payer for the enemy", the phenomenon of "loving those who hate us" – the solidarity of the shaken for all their contradictions and conflict' (Patočka 1996: 131).

Solidarity of the shaken is a community which is formed and lives constantly at the front, in the literal sense of the battleground, and in the sense of an ontological self-awareness of contingency: 'all the pillars of community . . . are shaken' (Patočka 1996: 39). What those on frontline understand is the contingency of every foundation, of every meaning and of their identities, the contingencies of the values that brought them to the frontline. Those in solidarity of the shaken understand that contingency makes the final resolution of the conflict over truth impossible, and this very understanding binds them together. Solidarity of the shaken does not mobilise identities for a new 'state of war'; on the contrary, it displaces the boundaries of identities constantly shaking and opening them. For keeping the problematicity of meaning away from solidification and stabilisation in one ideology or another, the solidarity of the shaken 'will say "No" to the measures of mobilisation that makes the state of war permanent' (Patočka 1996: 135). Shaking should be continuous for making visible the contingency of meaning and for avoiding positing solid/firm grounds: 'to find a firm shore, but then again to problematize that which emerges as a shore' (Patočka 2007: 57). The shaking should be continuous and the questioning permanent, assuring that the ground is in the searching itself, the meaning is in the quest for meaning: 'The effort to find new ground in searching itself, of problematizing that which is found' (2007: 57).

The solidarity of the shaken is not possible otherwise than through the 'abysmal' phenomenon of 'loving those who hate us', as Patočka writes, or through a radical love of humanity. Only a radical love of humanity can keep us away from solidification of our moral conviction and perceptions of seeing the evil in the others, and thus literally going to the battlefront. The same radical love of humanity that emanated from the figure of Diogenes who walked the streets of Athens in broad daylight, lantern in hand, looking for a human being, without ever specifying how such a human might look like.

NOTES

1. For a recent reading and interpretation of the tradition, see Žižek et al. (2005).
2. For complementing the *naive attitude* with the theological background, see Reinhard (1997).
3. An explanation offered by Žižek and reiterated by Zupančič (2019: 90). Žižek applies the Lacanian 'Borromean knot' to the case of the neighbour in the following way: 'First, there is the imaginary other – other people "like me," my fellow human beings with whom I am engaged in the mirror-like relationships of competition, mutual recognition, and so forth. Then, there is the symbolic "big Other" – the "substance" of our social existence, the impersonal set of rules that coordinate our coexistence. Finally, there is the Other qua Real, the impossible Thing, the "inhuman partner," the Other with whom no symmetrical dialogue, mediated by the symbolic Order, is possible. And it is crucial to perceive how these three dimensions are hooked up. The neighbour (*Nebenmensch*) as the Thing means that, beneath the neighbour as my semblant, my mirror image, there always lurks the unfathomable abyss of radical Otherness, of a monstrous Thing' (Žižek 2005).

Chapter 8

IF YOU ARE A POLITICAL PHILOSOPHER, WHY ARE YOU NOT A COSMOPOLITAN?

There were many moments in my odyssey towards a cosmopolitan political theory beyond all grand narratives when I had the impression that I arrived at something new – an impression to be replaced by the awareness that it is only a new complication in approaching cosmopolitanism. Thus, at the beginning, I was enthusiastically going through an exercise of detecting a 'hidden' cosmopolitanism in the work of different authors who did not express a cosmopolitan viewpoint – an exercise which was at risk of becoming a theoretical distortion. This bizarre exercise stopped when I finally asked some 'methodological' questions: if a reading reveals the cosmopolitan potential of a political philosophy, then where was cosmopolitanism 'hiding' before revealing it? Was cosmopolitanism an excess of theory which I was detecting, or was it a lack in the theory which I was filling with my 'reparative' reading? How can a political philosophy be non-cosmopolitan if all political philosophies postulate principles of universality and generality? These questions were leading invariably to more 'naive' questions: if you are a political philosopher, why are you not cosmopolitan? and 'what is political philosophy for?'

MORE OR LESS THAN UNIVERSAL?

In the year when I was studying national identity at one of the most enlightened places in the world (according to university rankings), a big attraction among not only students of political philosophy, but other students as well, was the lectures of G. A. Cohen – each lecture a stand-up philosophical performance, combining passionate commitment with intellectual rigour, and with an irreverence for everything, including himself. His lectures were wonderfully life-enhancing, disconcerting and somehow liberating. (From all his performances, one I remembered in every detail, and even tried to reproduce for some small audiences, was a pantomime showing the difference between analytical and continental philosophers.) One of G. A. Cohen's texts that I read at that time was entitled, 'If You're an Egalitarian, How Come You're So Rich?' (Cohen 2000), which starts from the evidence that many people, including many egalitarian political philosophers, profess a belief in equality while enjoying high incomes of which they devote very little to egalitarian purposes. The text advances an argument against the Rawlsian view that favouring an egalitarian society has no implications for the behaviour of individuals, since private action cannot ensure that others have good lives, and all the private action can achieve is a 'drop in the ocean'. Justice is a matter for the state to enforce, since private effort cannot remove the fundamental injustice, which is inequality of power; in addition, private effort involves an unreasonably large psychological burden. For Cohen, on the contrary, justice should also be a question of personal choice, within a just ethos, for a society to qualify as just.

During my decade of researching cosmopolitanism, Cohen's question was readjusting itself into one pertaining directly to my topic of research: if you are a political philosopher, why you are not a cosmopolitan? Similar to Cohen's egalitarians, political philosophers, as university professors, have the status of a global elite, with all the benefits of being at top-ranked universities, enjoying all troubled 'cosmopolitan' pleasures of consumption, and flying to different parts of the world to give keynote speeches on the importance of particular attachments, on the necessity of nation-states or on the criteria for admission of *im*migrants in Western countries, of 'strangers in our midst'. How can the question not be formulated when a political theorist waits for someone to give to him world citizenship in order to consider it a worthy object of his attention, as though world citizenship could arise and be implemented without political philosophers thinking about it:

> No one has ever offered me citizenship, or described the naturalisation process, or enlisted me in the world's institutional structures, or given me an account of its decision procedures (I hope they are democratic) or provided me with a list of the benefits and obligations of citizenship or shown me the world's calendar and the common celebrations and commemorations of its citizens. (Walzer 1996: 125)

Even if not asked directly of political philosophers, the question, 'if you are a political philosopher, why you are not a cosmopolitan?' was in the air, not only floating above all non-cosmopolitan keynote speakers but also above the works of all political philosophers, dead or alive.

The philosophers usually listed in the Western canon of political philosophy, which includes Plato, Aristotle, Augustine, St Thomas, Machiavelli,

Locke, Hobbes, Rousseau, Hegel, Mill, Tocqueville, Arendt, Foucault, Rawls and many others, are not 'cosmopolitans', just 'philosophers'. Being 'philosophers', some of them expressed clear anti-cosmopolitan positions, such as Rousseau, Hegel, Arendt and Rawls. The first and almost the only canonical philosopher who affirmed cosmopolitanism directly is obviously Kant. He used the word 'cosmopolitanism', he wrote two texts allegedly dedicated to this topic, *The Idea of History with a Cosmopolitan Purpose* and *Perpetual Peace*, and his cosmopolitanism was a source of inspiration for creating the League of Nations and the United Nations. But even Kant is invoked by the critics of cosmopolitanism in support of a non-cosmopolitan position (see Chapter 5). Canonical political philosophy keeps cosmopolitanism at the margins, and so does the trendy political philosophy of recent decades, as is exemplified by the political philosophy of Foucault, Deleuze, Badiou, Lefort, Laclau, Mouffe, Rancière, Žižek and others. There are a few authors who have written about how current theorising in humanities and social science impedes a cosmopolitan world view, and who argued that theory itself must undergo a shift to 'alternative geographies' (Harvey 2009), to 'a different epistemological performance' (Spivak 2012), to methodological cosmopolitanism (Beck 2015; Cole 2000) and to the epistemologies of the South (De Sousa Santos 2018). Science itself, captive in industrial and nation-state interests, was invited to undergo a shift to 'cosmopolitics' (Stengers 2018).

However, unlike other fields in humanities and social sciences, is not philosophy inherently cosmopolitan? Is it not always cosmopolitan given the principles of generality and universality which are at the core of every philosophical construction? Universalism and its inherent cosmopolitanism are the unexamined axiom in doing philosophy:

> the self-styled philosopher considers that philosophy is essentially universal and cosmopolitan, that national, social, idiomatic difference in general should only befall it as a provisional and non-essential accident that could be overcome. Philosophy ought not to suffer difference of idiom: it ought not to tolerate it and ought not to suffer from it. (Derrida 1992: 3)

There are nevertheless some claims to a 'national' dimension in philosophy, as examined by Derrida (1992), who refers to the untranslatability of 'philosophical idioms' and to the 'philosophical nationalism' of German authors, from Herder and Fichte to Heidegger, who claimed that the German philosophical idiom is untranslatable and thus uniquely adequate to express the universal. This tendency to express only in a certain language what ought to transcend any given language as something universal and essential, not dependent upon empirical particularities or regional idiosyncrasies, may subvert, says Derrida, the inherent cosmopolitanism of philosophy, or, at least, create aporias of 'philosophical translation'. However, the question of translatability should not encourage the affirming of a 'philosophical nationality'.[1] Leaving the untranslatability of philosophical idioms aside, we should note in Derrida's affirmation above – 'the self-styled philosopher considers that philosophy is essentially universal and cosmopolitan' – two apparently equivalent statements: 'philosophy is universal' and 'philosophy is cosmopolitan'. But are these two statements equivalent? My cosmopolitan 'application' of different philosophies suggests that for philosophy, being universal and being cosmopolitan is not necessarily the same thing, but cosmopolitanism can be 'detected' even where there is no exact affirmation of it because philosophy is essentially universal.

HOW TO DETECT COSMOPOLITANISM WHERE IT IS NOT

The first exercise in detecting a 'hidden' cosmopolitanism in the work of an anti-cosmopolitan political theorist was performed on Chantal Mouffe's agonistic theory (Caraus 2016c). I argued that Mouffe's account of pluralism cannot be consigned to 'the people' and to the Western tradition. Mouffe's presumed 'conversion' from enemy into adversary refers to a subject undergoing transformation, who is endowed with moral and rational abilities and commits himself to a way of action that is more acceptable to others, and this transformation can qualify as a 'conversion' to cosmopolitanism. As well, Mouffe's notions such as 'shared symbolic space', 'conflictual consensus' and the 'common bond of adversaries' are adequate for a cosmopolitanism that could avoid a global consensus, but it will be based nevertheless on a minimal commonality of all human beings. Thus, contestation, viewed by Mouffe as conflict in the 'tamed' mode, is a cosmopolitan possibility to contest whatever hegemony, wherever it is manifested in the world. Concomitantly, I found Lacau's theory of populism relevant in explaining how a 'we' of global protest movements is created, exploring convergences and divergences of cosmopolitanism and populism (Caraus 2016d).

The exercise of 'detecting' cosmopolitanism continued with the political philosophy of Claude Lefort. So, in different contexts, I argued that cosmopolitanism in the global condition has features of a symbolic mutation, similar to the change that emerges in the relationship between the symbolic order of the ancient regime and modern democracy, as described by Lefort (1988). Cosmopolitanism as a mutation at the symbolic level affects the way society's unity is staged or its *mise en scène*, which is not nation-state, but the world as a whole. Cosmopolitanism also affects the way society is formed, which Lefort calls its *mise en forme*, and the ways in which society is given meaning or its *mise en sens*, which reflects the ways of making the world intelligible to us in the condition of globalisation. Further, Lefort's famous argument that democracy emerges after the 'dissolution of the markers of certainty', which happened in the West, appears as inherently cosmopolitan (Lefort 1988: 9–20). Because in modern democracy the division of power does not refer to an outside that can be assigned to the Gods, the power is an 'empty place', it belongs to no one and those who exercise power do not possess or embody it. Lefort's account of democracy offers the tools for theorising about democracy beyond the borders of the nation-state without the risk of projecting a global Leviathan, since at the global level there will also be an 'empty place' of power. Concomitantly, Lefort's account of human rights has to be seen as a cosmopolitan practice. Not grounded in a metaphysical principle and not being an extra or pre-political precondition for politics, human rights are the product of past struggles and the object of the present ones. Human rights are the generative principle of politics, and the 'essence' of human rights is in the political activity of claiming them (Lefort 1986: 239–72). Political movements arise to win new rights or to expand the existing ones, and this has deep effects on the political imagination and practice: they create a new 'awareness of rights' as a radical and democratic politics of universalisation and a practice of cosmopolitanisation.

Similarly, in my reading, Jacques Rancière's approach on politics and disagreement turned out to be a matrix for a cosmopolitan politics. All his notions of police, wrong, equality and dissensus cannot be staged adequately otherwise than globally and cosmopolitically. If the Rancièrian situation of politics is staged only at the level of the nation-state, only half of the wrongs could be addressed. The world in the condition of globalisation functions as a global police, and social movements from recent decades have perceived wrongs as being global and the protests have been against global wrongs done by the global police, be it the International Monetary Fund or the World Trade Organization. Only on the world stage can politics, by counting the uncounted and making visible the invisible, adequately count those who have 'no part'. Politics, for Rancière, is either egalitarian or it is not politics, but if it is to be truly egalitarian, politics cannot be otherwise than cosmopolitics. In another context, I could not resist the temptation to unconceal the cosmopolitan light of Badiou's philosophy of Being and Event 'confirmed' by Saint Paul. Thus, Badiou's way of thinking about the universal as subtraction from existing differences appears the only way of conceiving the cosmopolitanism of a true universal, rather than as a particularity with a universal vocation or to a universal intensification of a particular.

Until I stopped to 'detect' cosmopolitanism in the work of different authors, the exercise continued with Foucault (Caraus 2021) and Agamben (Caraus forthcoming). And I was not the only one doing this exercise. Other scholars with whom I collaborated, and many others, drew resources from different non- or a-cosmopolitan authors, such as Spinoza, Hegel, Heidegger, Wittgenstein, Foucault, Butler, Bourdieu, Adorno and so on, in order to advance their cosmopolitan arguments.[2] I could go on doing this type of exercise but I stopped, realising that there was something wrong with this pattern of 'detection', but also that there was something relevant in it for understanding what it means to think about cosmopolitanism.

All these exercises seemed an 'application' of an argument elaborated with the instruments of philosophy, and therefore with principles that are supposed to be general and universal. But if the principles of generality and universality are already there, in theory, why is the theory not always cosmopolitan? What is the difference between universal and cosmopolitan? Is cosmopolitan something less than universal if it can be 'just an application' of a theory? Or it is something more than universal, since not all theories built with universal principles can be applied cosmopolitically? When Derrida envisages philosophy as 'essentially universal and cosmopolitan', this 'and' suggests a non-overlapping of the terms, but also that 'universal' precedes – or is a precondition for – 'cosmopolitan'. If this is so, then at which point does the universal start becoming the cosmopolitan, and what exactly determines this 'coming out' of the cosmopolitan from the universal? And if the detection of cosmopolitanism in a non-cosmopolitan but universal theory is possible, then what exactly is its mode of existence there, in the alleged universality of theory?

The example of Rawls's *A Theory of Justice* that was 'applied' to the world as a whole may be helpful in clarifying these questions. Elaborating a hypothetical situation called 'original position' and assuming that participants are under a 'veil of ignorance', Rawls famously endorsed two principles that should govern liberal societies: the principle of equality, protecting the equal basic liberties of all, and the difference principle, permitting social and economic inequalities when and only when these are to the greatest benefit of the least advantaged and attached to positions that are open to all under conditions of fair equality of opportunity. Some of its most attentive readers (Beitz 1979; Pogge 1989) argued that these two principles should apply globally, because the same kind of reasoning that led to their endorsement at the domestic level should apply to the global case. If the veil of ignorance excludes factors that are morally arbitrary, the fact where one happens to have been born is completely arbitrary from the moral point of view and should make it irrelevant. Thus, the theory of justice was considered valid at the global level, with a global original position which will endorse a globalised difference principle: inequalities of income and wealth should be allowed only if these inequalities work to the greatest benefit of the world's worst-off individuals. The just global society was portrayed as a fair system of cooperation among global citizens, free and equal. Through this global extension of Rawls's theory of justice, the global justice approach was born within normative political theory, its most cosmopolitan core for the time being. Rawls did not comment on the extension to his theory, which had almost become a theory of justice for the whole world. It was a big disappointment when Rawls, some twenty-eight years later, argued that the two principles of justice should apply only within liberal societies, but not across them. For the world, he proposed an outdated 'law of the people' as a 'realistic utopia', because it takes people as they are, and acknowledges the diversity existing in the world, since not all peoples of the world endorse liberal principles. The numerous criticisms of *The Law of Peoples* (Rawls 1999) showed that it was not sufficiently realistic because it does not consider the interdependence of the world and domination of powerful states, and that it is not utopian because the proposed ideals justify the status quo, offering nothing more than a modus vivendi with oppressor states.[3]

The main explanation of why Rawls retracted from the global application of his theory is that he did not want to impose Western ideas on the non-Western world, to which a certain sensibility of the postmodern ideals rejecting a 'new grand narrative' – and which was dominant in those twenty-eight years between publishing *A Theory of Justice* and *The Law of Peoples* – could be added. But this is not a complete or a compelling justification. As a philosopher, he could question 'humanity's division into mutually distinct and culturally cohesive peoples', but he did not. He took the division as a given, reflecting a moral valuation of empirical facts (Pogge 2006: 206–25). Thus, where was cosmopolitanism 'hiding' in this concrete political philosophy? In *A Theory of Justice* cosmopolitanism existed as though waiting for some reading to activate it. The activation was done mainly through one statement: nationality was declared a contingent and arbitrary feature to be eliminated by the veil of ignorance, together with all other arbitrary features. No reading can activate a cosmopolitanism in *The Law of Peoples*, since it betrays universalism by taking the division of the world in different nation-states, with their particularities, as theoretically unquestionable. Thus, cosmopolitanism appears to depend on a theory built on the principles of universality and generality, and – equally crucial – on the gesture of activating it, as did the readings of *A Theory of Justice* that inaugurated the global justice approach. And here the question of where cosmopolitanism 'hides' in a political philosophy receives clarification. It is concomitantly in two things or, to put it in other words, it has two modes of existence: a kind of 'dormant' state in a universal theory, and an act or a gesture of activating it, since, as it turns out, cosmopolitanism cannot be involuntary by virtue of the universalism inherent in theory. And these two modes of existence have to be examined separately.

THE 'EXCESS' OF THEORY

The state of cosmopolitanism being 'dormant' into a theory built on and with principles of universality and generality is difficult to delineate, since this existence depends on the very act of 'awakening' it. Although cosmopolitanism exists as a potential of a theory, it cannot pass into actuality – or into a theory of cosmopolitanism – 'by itself'. Cosmopolitanism requires an activating gesture, be it a declaration that the theory as it is already configured has to be applied to the world as a whole, as some readings did with *A Theory of Justice*, or it can be a gesture of suturing some elements in a different way in order to activate cosmopolitanism, such as in the case of my approach to Mouffe's agonistic pluralism (Caraus 2016c).

A way of delineating the 'dormant' state of cosmopolitanism in a political theory is to identify it in the 'ontological set' of a theory, since every political theory 'secretes' an ontology (see Chapter 2). Looking at the ontological set and templates of political theories of cosmopolitanism, its ontology was identified in the 'haunting' of the current polis by the ideal cosmos. As Plutarch remarked when writing about Zeno's *Republic*, 'This Zeno wrote, giving shape to a dream or, as it were, shadowy picture of a well-ordered and philosophic commonwealth' (Plutarch quoted in Heater 1996: 13). The 'shape of the dream' that Plutarch has seen as Zeno's legacy is the very state of cosmopolitanism being 'dormant' in political theories built on and with universal principles.

If ontologically the mode of existence of 'dormant' cosmopolitanism is the existence of a spectre or of a 'shape of a dream', then what is its epistemological status? Or how do we know that 'dormant' cosmopolitanism is there when reading a theory? Although the 'indicators' that a shadow of cosmopolitanism is there could differ, according to the context, usually the indicators point to an element excluded from theory. For example, Hegel affirms the universality of the human, but rejects cosmopolitanism expressly:

> *A human being counts as such because he is a human being*, not because he is a Jew, Catholic, Protestant, German, Italian, etc. This consciousness,

which is the aim of *thought*, is of infinite importance, and it is inadequate only if it adopts a fixed position – for example, as *cosmopolitanism* – in opposition to the concrete life of the state. (Hegel 1991: 240, § 209, emphasis in original)

Crucially, Hegel admits that cosmopolitanism is a work of thinking, the 'aim of the thought', although he sees it happening when thinking 'fixes' the movement of universality through particulars. Cosmopolitanism is for Hegel a side effect of thinking, an unwanted excrescence of the 'fixed' humanity that thinking might ratify. Thus, it is posited outside the theory, so that Hegel's philosophical system could be coherent and let the particularity move freely towards the universal and back. However, even Hegel's philosophy is not immune to cosmopolitan 'application', be it in the form of a cosmopolitan recognition of actors participating in a global shared community, or in the form of an argument for a world state (see Wendt 2003). At least, epistemologically speaking, with Hegel we are not ignorant of what cosmopolitanism is – it is a 'fixed position' of the thought that has to be avoided and which is pushed outside theory by Hegel himself.

By being pushed outside the theory, or by exclusion operated by the political theorist himself, cosmopolitanism enters the 'dormant' mode. Here Rawls's theory of justice is illustrative once again. In order to make his theory for a liberal state only, Rawls left outside the 'original position' one feature: the arbitrariness of nationality, which once included in the 'original position' and eliminated by the 'veil of ignorance', as with all other contingent features for an individual, instantly expands the theory to the whole world. The reading of *A Theory of Justice* from a cosmopolitan perspective was possible precisely by introducing into the theoretical reasoning the excluded feature. Epistemologically speaking, the cosmopolitanism of *A Theory of Justice* was in its readers' awareness and knowledge that one arbitrary feature for an individual was omitted. This omission and exclusion operated by Rawls is characteristic of most liberal political theories which have a 'structure of exclusion' (Cole 2000). The liberal political theory postulates a polity made up of free and equal citizens, without mentioning the existence of outsiders who are excluded from the theory on grounds which liberal theory itself would condemn as arbitrary:

Liberal political philosophy maintains the appearance of coherence at the level of theory through the strategy of concealment. The vast majority of works in liberal theory do not address the question of national belonging and political membership, and only remain plausible on the assumption that the question has been answered in a way that satisfies liberal principles; but this assumption remains highly questionable. If the question of membership is made explicit, it becomes clear that there is an irresolvable contradiction between liberal theory's apparent universalism and its concealed particularism. (Cole 2000: 2)

This excluded element will 'haunt' the theory. Cosmopolitanism stands 'dormant' exactly in the excluded part. Although excluded, or mainly because of it, it *becomes excess to the theory*. This delineation of cosmopolitanism as excess to the theory presupposes the entire post-structuralist legacy of thinking according to which no system can form itself as a totality unless it poses an exception to itself or a surplus. Thus, 'cosmopolitan excess' of political philosophy is created by excess left outside the theory in order to have a coherent fully fledged and well-rounded theory for the 'real' world. The readings that detect cosmopolitanism in a theory that does not present itself as a theory of cosmopolitanism engage with this excess, usually reintroducing it into the theory. This 'cosmopolitan excess' of a political theory constructed with the principles of universality and generality is not perceived only by some readers who are endowed with special 'sensors' to detect it, but even by those who advance theories and decide to leave the excess outside, as Hegel and Rawls did. Several ways of relating to this excess can be distinguished, such as *ignoring*, *rejecting*, *taming* and *affirming*, each with a separate 'flavour'.

Clarifying these ways of dealing with 'cosmopolitan excess' may require some lists of political philosophers who ignore it, who reject it, who tame it and who affirm it, but it is not the aim of this section to create 'blacklists', although some examples have to be mentioned. Thus, the tactic of *ignoring* is the 'original' default position in the Western canonical political philosophy and in the more recent one (and this list has to be a long list!), since political philosophy keeps silent about 'grasping the world as a whole' and lets the theory speak as though it is a universal theory. Since cosmopolitanism is not stated directly, the theory itself can serve as a ground for a cosmopolitan reading but also as a ground for an anti-cosmopolitan argument.

Different from ignoring is the *rejection* of 'cosmopolitan excess' by political theorists who affirm instead a local or a national 'supplement' to their theory, and the list includes, among others, Herder, Burke, Fichte, liberal nationalists (Walzer 1996; Miller 2016), and perhaps those who laugh at cosmopolitans, as did Rousseau, Hegel and Arendt, could be included here.

Taming the cosmopolitan excess of a political philosophy is paradoxically the work of most of the cosmopolitan theories advanced in the last three decades. The renaissance of cosmopolitanism in the

1990s, as a response to the challenges of globalisation, was happening on the waves of the Stoics' concentric circles of allegiances, as allegedly awaken by Nussbaum (see Chapter 2) and by the celebration of 200 years of Kant's *Perpetual Peace* (see Bohman and Lutz-Bachmann 1997). In these three decades, different attempts to reconcile the local with the global resulted in an avalanche of adjectival cosmopolitanisms, such as 'rooted', 'situated', 'embedded' and 'statist' cosmopolitanisms, and many others.[4] All these oxymoronic cosmopolitanisms postulate two sets of values and practices: enlightened, universalist, elitist, modernist and Western ones, and local, parochial, rooted values and practices. The local set of values and practices is considered the most authentic mode of implementing cosmopolitanism. While attempting to reconcile local attachments and global obligations, these approaches are self-congratulatory in displaying an implicit virtue of moderation, an epistemic and motivational realism, plus the benefit of bringing cosmopolitanism closer to the everyday life of individuals. As already argued in the previous chapters, the rooted cosmopolitanisms preserve the status quo and methodological nationalism in a theory which presents itself as cosmopolitan. Further, by subscribing to the status quo, these cosmopolitanisms cannot avoid making people 'illegal'. The oxymoronic cosmopolitanisms end up supporting practices that reproduce world inequalities, while vehiculating respect for multicultural differences. Treating others with respect and some curiosity is simple, while imagining a more just way of living in the world for everyone requires more substantial approaches. In this context, it is legitimate to ask what is better: to ignore 'cosmopolitan excess' and thus perpetuate the impression that each theory has a powerful cosmopolitan potential, or to tame it, as these oxymoronic approaches do, and thus minimise its potential and power?

The *fin de siècle* renaissance of cosmopolitanism included some approaches *affirming* the 'cosmopolitan excess', such as global justice and global democracy. However, even these approaches subscribe with one hand only to the cosmopolitan excess of the existing theories of justice and democracy, while another hand is still doing the work of taming, mainly to prevent the 'cosmopolitan excess' taking the theoretical form of a World Republic. As Chapter 5 showed, the most wholehearted affirmations of a full cosmopolitan stance including the idea of a World Republic were expressed not by political theorists or philosophers, but by scientists, writers, activists, artists and ordinary citizens. There are also more nuanced affirmations of 'cosmopolitan excess' and the previous chapters engaged with these approaches. However, the dominant mode of affirming it is with one hand only, since another one is doing the work of taming the excess, which is the work of the entire political theory as it currently exists.

Therefore, the mode of existence of cosmopolitanism in a theory built with universal principles is an exclusion operated by the theory itself. The philosophical reasoning can produce and ratify, as Hegel notes, a configuration of cosmopolitanism as an answer to the question of how to live together in the world as a whole. But philosophers stop the thought from going beyond the 'fences that hedge in', as Arendt defended the nation-state against a world state (Arendt 1968: 82). Thus, Rawls could have said 'Yes' to an extension of his theory of justice to the world as a whole, and this 'Yes' could have been the cornerstone of advancing further political philosophies for the world as a whole, an impetus and an encouragement for others to think further. Rawls did not embrace the cosmopolitan 'excess' of his own theory; he stopped it to prevent an alleged Evil, albeit only a theoretical one of imposing a totalising theory on the whole world. Rawls's two theories are the interrupted flight of a possible fully fledged cosmopolitan theory. It was a rebuff that diminished its own amplitude, and the amplitude of thinking about political philosophy in general. It is very improbable that a full global theory of justice would have been implemented – a theory of justice is not implemented yet in the Western liberal states for which, as it turns out, it was elaborated. However, imperialism and different forms of affirming and assuming Western superiority all over the world since 1971, the year when *A Theory of Justice* was published, continued, especially because during those decades neoliberal globalisation took over the world. The damage of withdrawing the 'application' of *A Theory of Justice* to the world as a whole was done only to political philosophy. The real world in the name of which it was withdrawn had nothing to gain from this withdrawal.

Why is the affirmation of a full cosmopolitan position in a political theory so rare? What is so difficult in affirming it? What exactly are the obstacles? Another look at the first cosmopolitan stance of the Cynics might provide a glimpse into the nature of these obstacles. The previous chapter examined the Cynic *philanthropia* which reveals that cosmopolitanism was born through a radical love of humanity that has the logic of the impossible command, 'Love your neighbour as yourself' – impossible since it displays the evil both in the neighbour and in us. Everyone desires Evil, my neighbour and I, but no one admits this, attributing evil only to the other, as in a primordial 'Cold War', but trying to keep the situation in the confines of a reciprocal good. Love of the neighbour presupposes recognition of the evil/inhuman both in the neighbour and in us, going beyond reciprocity, into an excessive and incommensurable mode of relating to the neighbours. The Cynic *mise en scène* of the dog-life experiment instantiates the impossible love by the neighbour for you in all its radicality (see Chapter 7), and the affective bond created in this way constitutes the Cynic *philanthropia*. In its incapacity to affirm its own 'cosmopolitan excess', political theory seems to express the 'horror' of loving the neighbour. The current political theory is still under the auspices of the Hobbesian insistence that the 'first political question' has always to be that of avoiding evil and of 'securing of order, protection, safety, trust, and the conditions of cooperation' (Williams 2008: 179). Looking how to achieve reciprocal good and cooperation and how to secure order, protection, safety and trust, political theory places the excluded unlovable neighbour in its own 'cosmopolitan excess'. Loving the neighbour as yourself requires going beyond order, protection, safety and reciprocal cooperation, all of which keep the neighbour at a distance and keep ourselves at a distance from the 'neighbour in us', or from the 'evil in us', and when political theory affirms cosmopolitanism, it displays (a certain degree of) incommensurability and excess. At a certain point in my research, I was confronted by the arresting questions: do theorists of cosmopolitanism 'love humanity', and why is this affection attributed to them more often than to others? Now it could be said that affirming cosmopolitanism in theory requires an act similar to loving the 'unlovable' neighbour, which is instantiated in the Cynic *philanthropia*. Political philosophy expresses the love of the neighbour by acknowledging the exclusion it produces, or the 'evil in us', and by including the 'cosmopolitan excess' left out. Political philosophy as currently exists is a philosophy of exclusion, as Cole (2000) demonstrated: it excludes the foreigner and the migrant through a strategy of concealment as though they do not exist, and borders do not exist. The theory 'cannot address the membership question without addressing itself and cannot answer it without radically transforming itself' (Cole 2000: 202), that is, the theory cannot address the exclusion otherwise than identifying the 'evil in us', or in itself, and thinking about itself in a new way. A difficult, but not impossible task.

THINKING IN A NEW WAY

Faced with the threat of the atomic bomb, the Russell-Einstein Manifesto (Russell and Einstein 1955) called citizens of all nations to suspend their particular interests and to think of themselves simply as human beings and, more crucially, to learn to think in a new way: 'consider yourselves only as members of a biological species which has had a remarkable history, and whose disappearance none of us can desire. We have to learn to think in a new way' (Russell and Einstein 1955). Karl

Jaspers heard the call to think in a new way and reiterated it as a call to 'conversion' in his book *The Future of Mankind* (1961), where he analysed philosophically the 'paradigm' of the atomic bomb and presented a solution to the nuclear problem in terms a choice: 'either all mankind will physically perish or there will be a change in the moral-political condition of man' (Jaspers 1961: 4). Writing about Jaspers' book in 1964, Maurice Blanchot points to a contradiction between what Jaspers' text declares and the text itself. The theme is that we must change radically, writes Blanchot, but in regard to Jaspers, nothing has changed – neither in the language, nor in the thinking, nor in political formulations. A prophet could say 'We must change' and remain the same, admits Blanchot, but not a man of reflection who assumes he has the authority to alert us to a threat so great that it must shatter our existence and, what is more crucial, our thinking, while 'he persists, without contestation or modification (Blanchot 1997: 102), in the same speculative framework in which he was before becoming conscious of this immanent possibility of universal catastrophe:

> Why does a question so serious, a question such that to answer it would suppose a radically new thinking, why does it not renew the language that conveys it, and why does it only give rise to remarks that are either biased, and in any case, partial, when they are of political order, or moving and urgent, when they are of spiritual order, but identical to those that we have heard in vain for two thousand years? (Blanchot 1997: 103)

It is not an *ad hominem* attack, emphasises Blanchot, but an attempt to understand where this difficulty comes from, and why a call for a total renewal is formulated in terms that we have heard in vain for two thousand years: is the question too grave, so that even thinking it is a call for help? Or because it is far from being as important as it seems to be? Or is it because the question only serves as an alibi for bringing us to spiritual or political conclusions that were formulated long ago and independently of it? The call sounds like an alibi, since the main preoccupation here is not only or not mainly the end of humanity, but also the advent of communism. The main question becomes 'Should we say "no" to the Bomb if this "no" runs the risk of weakening the defence of the "free world"?' (Blanchot 1997: 103) and the dilemma ultimately is to save oneself from total extermination or to save oneself from total domination:

> However, where the liberal philosopher – and with him a good number of men – speaks of totalitarianism without examination or critique, others – and with them a large number of men – speak of liberation and

the achievement of the community as a whole. Once again the dialogue
has stopped. The event, the pivot of history, does not change the options
or the fundamental oppositions in the least. Reflection on the atomic terror is but a pretense; what one is looking for is not a new way of thinking but a way to consolidate old predicaments. And with this 'choice' it
becomes clear that humanity will continue to turn around old values, be
it for all eternity. (Blanchot 1997: 104)

The call is to think in a new way, but thinking continues in the old ways
because

it wants to risk nothing of itself in the presence of an ambiguous event
about which it is not able to decide what it means, with its horrible face,
with its appearance as absolute – an event of enormous size but enor-
mously empty, about which it can say nothing save this banality: that it
would be better to prevent it. (Blanchot 1997: 104)

Thus, thinking continues in the old ways because the man of reflection
does not look for a new way of thinking but only to consolidate old
predicaments.

The Russell-Einstein Manifesto (Russell and Einstein 1955) acknowledged that the world is full of conflicts, minor ones as well as the 'titanic
struggle between Communism and anti-Communism', and almost everybody who is politically conscious has strong feelings and a position about
one or more of these issues. The manifesto asks 'human beings, members
of the species Man' to set aside such feelings, and to 'remember your
humanity, and forget the rest'. What is required from human being, fails
in the case of the 'men of reflection' who cannot give up their creeds and
positions, and again this is not *ad hominem* objection, but an objection
that has to be formulated in the face of the entire political philosophy
that cannot think of the world as a whole, and when confronted with
its own 'cosmopolitan excess', retract into 'realistic utopias'. The call,
'to think in a new way', prompted by the atomic bomb, sounded a call
to alter the currency of all positionings, both of ordinary men and of
'men of reflection'. The Cynics' fundamental principle, 'Alter the currency!', is reiterated in the context of the threat posed by the atomic
bomb, since reiteration cannot be avoided in any context which tries to
point to *another life* and *another world*.

The perspective of the atomic bomb and universal catastrophe introduces a turmoil in the old way of thinking: 'one still does not know what
to say about it' (Blanchot 1997: 107). This turmoil is brought about
by the idea of totality and humanity, which appear in a negative way,
that is, humanity appears as a totality only now when it is at risk of
disappearing: 'humanity risks being awakened to the idea of the whole

and pressed, as it were, to become conscious of it by giving the whole form, that is by organizing and uniting itself' (Blanchot 1997: 107). What Blanchot presents here as a 'risk' is exactly the effect sought by the Russell-Einstein Manifesto (Russell and Einstein 1955). The enigmatic appeal, 'remember your humanity', which you never really perceived is similar to the awakening to the idea of itself as a whole. The call to think in a new way is not simply 'let's do everything in our power to prevent it before it's too late', but as Zupančič observes, 'let's first built this totality (unity, community, freedom) that we are about to lose through the Bomb' (Zupančič 2018: 21). There is a choice here, which political philosophers do not want to acknowledge:

> The true choice is not between tolerating the Bomb (and hence running the risk of losing everything) on the one hand, and preventing the looming destruction of the world (but thereby running the risk of losing our liberal freedoms) on the other hand; the true choice is between "losing it all" and creating what we are about to lose (even if we lose it all in the process): only this could eventually save us, in a profound sense. (Zupančič 2018: 21)

The turmoil is fuelled further by another prospect. Once humanity is organised and united, it will have to acknowledge its power of destruction which

> for the moment we are just as incapable of mastering it as we are of wanting it, and for an obvious reason: we are not in control of ourselves because this humanity, capable of being totally destroyed, does not yet exist as a whole. On the one hand, a power that cannot be, and on the other, an existence – the human community – that can be wiped out but not affirmed, or that could be affirmed, in some sense, only after its disappearance and by the void, impossible to grasp, of this disappearance; consequently something that cannot even be destroyed, because it does not exist. (Blanchot 1997: 105–6)

Once humanity acknowledges its power of destruction it will have to decide whether or not it wants to destroy itself:

> It is very probable that humanity would have no fear of this power of the end if it could recognize in it a decision that belonged exclusively to it, on condition thus too of being truly the subject and not simply the object of it, and without having to trust to the hazardous initiative of some head of state. (Blanchot 1997: 106)

So, if humanity has this power of destruction, it has to be affirmed by humanity as a whole, not by an arbitrary head of state. There is no call here for humanity self-destruction, obviously, but a call for a totality or a whole that does not disavow its own antagonisms, or in other words, it is a call for a humanity which has to acknowledge its power of destruction or the 'evil in us'.

What happens here, in this call to think in a new way starting from the threat of the bomb and in the failure to follow it, is an 'instantiation' of political philosophy's failure to think about cosmopolitanism, that is, to think about the totality with its inherent antagonisms, to make the world One World. The spectre of humanity not yet or not fully constituted, emerges negatively and full of antagonisms, and introduces a turmoil in the old ways of thinking. The man of reflection, 'does not know what to say about it' and falls back into the old way of thinking. The call to think in a new way is made periodically, and to the threat of the atomic bomb some other threats have been added as very plausible reasons to issue the call, such as climate change, migration and development of technology. In each case, even though not acknowledged with such astute insight as in Blanchot's text, it is a call to create firstly that something which risks being destroyed but does not properly exist yet, and a call to affirm humanity with all the antagonisms and exclusions that it produces, or eventually to deactivate the very mechanism of producing the exclusions.[5]

To think in a new way in all these calls means thinking of the world as One World – a totality that will not disavow its own antagonisms. Here the 'groundless grounding' that made possible my affirmation of cosmopolitanism again becomes visible: affirming humanity means permanent questioning, a life in problematicity and shaken solidarity. The thinking in a new way implicit in each activation of the 'cosmopolitan excess' does not require a final answer but a permanent questioning that alters the currency of all current political positionings. Only a life in problematicity can acknowledge antagonisms of humanity. Political theorists will need the courage to admit that they – and, thus, we all – do not have a 'solution' to the global problems and a ready-made account of humanity, but that this is not an impediment to continuing to try to think about the world as One World.

Thinking in a new way is thinking of humanity with all its antagonisms, without excluding the dimension that does not fit our theoretical construction, shaped by 'strong feelings' and creeds which men of reflection, as all other men, cannot avoid. Political philosophy tries to be 'realistic'; however, the 'reality' that political philosophers take as the starting point of their theoretical constructions is bearable and tolerated only because an unreal and impossible dimension accompanies all realisms. People bear the 'realities' of the current configuration of the world only because an impossible possibility to reconfigure it otherwise, in a more just and equal way, is resurrected again and again in their hope and thoughts. Although the call to think in a new way is not only addressed to political philosophers, as everyone is invited to 'remember humanity and forget the rest', for the political philosopher the call goes directly to his or her very reason for being, generating some hard questions: if you do not attempt to think about the world in a new way, then what is political philosophy for? If you are a political philosopher, why are you not cosmopolitan? Or if you are a political philosopher, why do you not think about a world where No One Is Illegal?

NOTES

1. Derrida's examination of the aporia of philosophical untranslatability generated less aporetic reclamations of a 'philosophical nationalism' (see Hollander 2009).
2. For example, Ingram (2013) attempts to solve the problem of cosmopolitan democracy's self-foundation by exploring some authors and theoretical resources that until recently have been ignored by theorists of cosmopolitanism: Hannah Arendt, Claude Lefort, Sheldon Wolin, Miguel Abensour, Jacques Rancière, Étienne Balibar and other thinkers of radical democracy.
3. For critique and responses see Martin and Reidy (2006).
4. See Introduction, the section entitled 'Cosmopolitics'.
5. In 1993, Giorgio Agamben called to 'build our political philosophy anew starting from the one and only figure of the refugee' (2000: 15) and to review all the categories of thinking about politics. He addressed the call to himself as well, so in his works he identifies the originary place of Western politics in an *ex-ceptio*, an inclusive exclusion of human life in the form of bare life, and this inclusive exclusion is the foundation that defines Western ontology and metaphysics. Thus, his *Homo Sacer* series argued that it is not possible to think about another dimension of life and politics if we have not first managed to deactivate the metaphysical and ontological *dispositif* producing the exclusion or bare life, also embodied in the refugee. See Caraus (forthcoming).

CONCLUSION
'ALTER ALL CURRENCIES!':
TOWARDS A MILITANT COSMOPOLITICS

Looking back at the beginning of my odyssey of studying cosmopolitanism, an apparently paradoxical aspect may be noticed: I was afraid of grand narratives, but I have elaborated a new grand narrative which includes everything – dissent, protests, ontology, migration, a World Republic, laughter, fear, 'conversion', sex, love and thinking. However, there is no contradiction in this trajectory, since the totality presupposed by this grand narrative is a totality of critique or of 'altering the value of all currencies'. I was looking for an approach to cosmopolitanism that would resist criticisms and the discovery is that such an approach does not need moderation but radicalisation through altering the values of *all* currencies. Through this radicalisation, the thinking about cosmopolitanism reclaims the legacy of the Ancient Cynics in its radical and militant core. In addition, two more questions persist and have to be addressed: is this new grand narrative called 'totality of critique' free from a colonising intent? Is not the militant cosmopolitics a dangerous avant-garde of the few militating in the name of the whole world?

My research on cosmopolitanism started only when I overcame the fear of a grand narrative and only when I found the resources to advance a cosmopolitanism that will resist criticism such as 'a dangerous illusion of a world hegemony of one dominant power' (Mouffe 2005: 107); 'oppressiveness of abstracted universalism' (Harvey 2009: 80); 'an ideology' (Cavallar 2011: 1), a 'cosmopolitan crusade' (Hayden 2013: 195); 'another threatening modernist ideology of human betterment – a new political religion of immutable truth' (Hayden 2013: 196); and numerous criticisms of a cosmopolitanism with a colonial intent expressed by the repeated question, 'Whose cosmopolitanism?' (Latour 2004), as in an edited book where half the chapters have the title, 'Whose cosmopolitanism?' (Glick Schiller and Irving 2014). So, how does the grand narrative of the totality of critique avoid criticisms, and in particular how does it avoid a new grand narrative with a colonial intent? The answer is that the totality of critique or of 'altering the value of all currencies' not only does not have a colonial intent but, on the contrary, it inscribes itself into a continuation of decolonisation struggles.

The literature on decolonisation starts with the works of Gandhi, Franz Fanon and C. L. R. James, to which literature on post-colonialism and decoloniality were added. Post-colonialism emerged from the work of diasporic scholars from the Middle East and South Asia, refers back to those locations and their imperial interlocutors (Europe and the West), and consolidated as an intellectual movement developing around the ideas of Edward W. Said, Homi K. Bhabha, Gayatri C. Spivak and others (Bhambra 2014: 115). The decoloniality school emerged mainly from the work of the sociologists Anibal Quijano and Walter D. Mignolo and from world-systems theory. Geographically, decoloniality emerged from the work of diasporic scholars from South America and refers back to locations in South America and their imperial interlocutors which started with the European incursions upon the land known as the Americas from the fifteenth century onwards (Bhambra 2014: 115). Post-colonial and decolonial studies aim at interrogating, problematising, destabilising and ultimately transforming the colonial macro-narratives; however, they admit the need of their own grand narratives to expose the coloniality of power and to reinscribe the colonial difference: 'Events and political processes that attempt to counter the control of the state or of the global forces are in need of macronarratives from the perspective of coloniality' (Mignolo 2000b: 9). After some decades of avoiding grand narratives, it is time to acknowledge that grand narratives did not necessarily disappear, and that there is a 'pervasiveness of hegemonic macronarratives even at times when we are questioning, problematizing, and dislodging them' (Ortega 2017: 511). The radical and militant cosmopolitics advanced here admits its own grand narrative; however, it alters both the content and form of a grand narrative – it is a totality of critique, of altering the values of all currencies. It does not propose a new content, as a final new absolute meaning, since the content – that is, the permanent questioning – is also an instrument. Thus, this grand narrative as a totality of critique, both as content and form, provides the very consubstantiality of decolonisation and radical cosmopolitics.

The post-colonial movements led by Gandhi and Mandela have been examined as instances of cosmopolitanism of dissent, while the Zapatistas' struggles and the World Social Forum – considered the most representative decolonial movements – have been cornerstone case studies in mapping cosmopolitanism from below. However, unlike these movements which have been 'intensifiers'[1] of a cosmopolitical thought, the approaches of cosmopolitanism generated within the literature on decolonisation, both in the post-colonial and the decolonial versions, fall in the trap of oxymoronic cosmopolitanisms.[2] Criticising the humanist and Kantian versions of cosmopolitanism, different post-colonial and decolonial authors advanced their own versions, intended as non-imperial cosmopolitanisms, free from Eurocentrism, through such notions as 'hybridity', 'syncretism', 'ambiguity', 'vernacular', 'indigenous' and so on, claiming that, unlike theoretical constructions, these are 'living' or 'really existing' cosmopolitanisms. As argued in different chapters of this book, the 'living' or 'really existing' cosmopolitanisms, be it in Asia or among natives in South America, risk legitimatising whatever situation as cosmopolitan and leave the status quo unchanged. Cosmopolitanism should not be regarded only as 'lived' – be it by an indigenous group or by the first-class frequent flyers – it has to be thought, imagined and put into a theory of living in one world where everyone will have the same entitlements and duties. Living equally in the world was the aim of the decolonisation struggles from their inception, thus, through the proposed approach, this book inscribes itself into an ongoing decolonisation.

It is incontestable that colonisation affected both the colonisers and the colonised, and the condition of coloniality is common to all countries and nations, irrespective of whether they are former colonies or empires. So not only do the colonised have to break the chains of the coloniality but also the colonisers themselves (Mills 2015). In the last 500 years, the whole globe has been shaped by the West through industrialisation, modernity, enlightenment, reason and progress, with certain achievements but also producing bads and threats (Beck 2015). Thus, we are all post-colonial or decolonial – we are all living after colonisation, and its legacies have to be assumed by the colonised and by the colonisers. Radical cosmopolitics should be the joint attempt by both the colonised and the colonisers to accomplish global decoloniality or post-coloniality. Post-coloniality or decoloniality cannot be achieved through vernacular or living cosmopolitanisms. Post-colonial and decolonial theory should not only retract into the 'spirit of the mountains' or into 'shaman cosmopolitanism' (Assy and Rolo 2021: 131–57) that, without doubt, has a more cosmic view than current cosmopolitan political theories, but ought to ask why the 'cosmopolitan shaman' will be illegal in different parts of the world. While recovering the intellectual wealth in native knowledge and praxis of living that in the name of reason and Western civilisation were demonised as superstition, barbarism or reduced to folklore, is crucial for epistemological justice and resistance, to map a cosmopolitanism in these practices means also to subscribe to the status quo. As Spivak remarks, for all the wonderful cultural approaches to make sense, a cosmopolitan institutional framework is required: 'In order for a corrective vernacular cosmopolitanism to work, there must be a world governmentalized evenly' (Spivak 2012: 111). This call from within post-colonial and decolonial approaches to think about a 'world governmentalized evenly' remained without an echo within these fields.

Radical and militant cosmopolitics is a proposal to think beyond nation-state, empire, or the West, through the only reliable cosmopolitical 'instruments': alter the values of all currencies, permanent questioning and a life in problematicity. These instruments cannot be 'from above', male, Western, white or European, since these are the very instruments used by the post-colonial and decolonial authors in their theoretical constructions and positionings. The radical and militant cosmopolitics does not attribute to the other the capacity of critique through a colonising intent. It just assesses what is common to all post-colonial and decolonial approaches, and to all other adjectival cosmopolitanisms – critique and contestation. Critique is not always realised with the instrument of theories, it is realised through disruption that Bartelby, Deleuze's idiot, the shaman or the 'spirit of the place' brings to a situation. The capacity for disruption, even by silence or by 'preferring not to' is, as Stengers observes, an operator of 'putting into equality' (Stengers 2005: 1003). Radical and militant cosmopolitics does not attribute 'from above' the capacity of critique and disruption; it invites criticism and disruption of all imperial, Western, white, European, male and elitist perspectives in this world. This is what the Cynics did when they ignored the traditional barriers that made female inferior to male, slave to master, foreigner to Greek, by this acknowledging everyone's capacity to alter the value of the currency, to bark and bite with the discerning precision of a dog. As with the Cynics, radical and militant cosmopolitics, in its permanent questioning, postulates that everyone has to be made a citizen of the world by virtue of this capacity for disruption, if only through simple presence. We should imagine a world where everyone will be entitled to be equally disruptive and this disruption will be equally acknowledged by the others.

Therefore, the critique of the West and of the nation-state should be one gesture. It is time to acknowledge that the post-colonial system of nation-states is not capable of realising liberation for the former colonised subject (Sharma 2020: 154). The nation and the state do not aim to achieve liberation or decolonisation; these are just forms of regulating capitalism and managing populations through borders which became instruments of control and exploitation of labour. The pandemic has shown how illusory is the attempt to move to a decolonised world only through cultural and epistemological reinterpretations. The divide between the Global North and the Global South re-emerged as 'vaccine nationalism': countries in the Global North have used their wealth to purchased many more vaccines than the size of their populations, while in the Global South even those most at risk were unable to access vaccines. In a post-pandemic world, post-colonial and decolonial approaches should take a bold step and argue for world citizenship for all, as the only meaningful way of achieving decoloniality. And this is not an argument for a return to empires, but once again an argument pointing to the consubstantiality of decolonisation and cosmopolitics: 'Only after the death of the national liberation project can we renew our commitment to decolonization' (Sharma 2020: 276).

Thus, the grand narrative of a totality of critique advanced in this book not only does not have a colonising intent, but it is also consubstantial with the decolonisation struggle. The post-colonial and decolonial theories, as well as radical cosmopolitics, in theoretical terms still should formulate the declaration of the Zapatistas to 'Brothers and Sisters of Asia, Africa, Oceania, Europe and America', made on 27 July 1996, at the First Intercontinental Meeting For Humanity and Against Neoliberalism: 'We can build a new path . . . It is necessary because on it depends the future of humanity' (EZLN 1996). The 'totality of critique' is not only a critique, but also a work of imagination of how to live together in One World. In this orientation towards living differently, the totality of critique 'grounds' a militant cosmopolitics. And here the second challenging question of these concluding remarks has to be tackled: is not militant cosmopolitics a dangerous avant-garde of the few militating in the name of the whole world? This question encapsulates two challenges in one: a danger and a vanguard of the few – could it be worse than that?

Derived from the fifteenth-century Latin word *militare*, meaning 'to serve as a soldier', in current usage the word 'militant' as an adjective is defined, in different dictionaries, as showing a fighting disposition, aggressive, engaged in war, belligerent, war-ridden, obtrusively energetic in pursuing particular goals and bold self-confidence in expression of opinions. As a noun, a militant is someone engaged in a war, fighting or ready to fight, or who acts aggressively for their cause, and only rarely is it also defined as a reformer or activist. The contemporary discourse of counterterrorism associates figures of militancy with groups named 'terrorist', so it appears as dangerous terminology pointing to a far from universally applicable strategy or tactic. So, if militancy is dangerous, why associate cosmopolitanism, which is the target of various criticisms, with a dangerous word, thus making it a target of a new criticism?

Apart from being associated with dangerous ways of acting, historically militancy has often been associated with Marxist–Leninist and Maoist vanguardism and the ways these ideologies have informed revolutionary class struggles. Militancy was later expressed in different movements throughout the twentieth century, up to the beginning of the twenty-first century. Historical militancy is seen as a group 'setting out the party line', more aware than 'the masses', and who would usher in the revolution through a correct interpretation of theory and the unfolding of history.[3] This tendency points to 'a central paradox of militancy' which means that once a militant group constitutes itself as a unified body 'it tends to become closed to the outside, to the non-militant, those who would be the basis of any mass movement' (Thoburn 2010: 134). Thus, by advancing a militant cosmopolitics,[4] how do I avoid attributing cosmopolitanism to a restricted group, although this time not an elite 'from above', but a group of radicals 'from below'?

Militant cosmopolitics is neither dangerous, nor a privilege for the few. Cosmopolitanism was born militant in the Cynic milieu, and it could not be otherwise. The Cynic dog barks, bites and attacks. As Foucault argued, the Cynic gave himself with a mission which 'takes the form of a battle. It has a polemical, bellicose character' (Foucault 2011: 279). The Cynics compare themselves to soldiers in an army who have to confront enemies and engage in combat against vices which 'afflict humankind as a whole, the vices of men which take shape, rely upon, or are at the root of their customs, ways of doing things, laws, political organizations, or social conventions' (2011: 279). The Cynic is an aggressive benefactor fighting with his own life by inversing 'the theme of the sovereign life (tranquil and beneficial: tranquil for oneself, enjoyment of self, and beneficial for others)' and by 'dramatizing it in the form of what could be called the militant life, the life of battle and struggle against and for self, against and for others' (2011: 283). Thus, to the idea of the Cynic as a guard dog which accosts enemies and bites them, the theme of the combatant, soldier or athlete, who fights against the evils of the world, is added. Foucault acknowledges that employing the term 'militant' is an anachronism, but argues that a number of notions, images and terms employed by the Cynics will later become the theme of the militant life in Western ethics. However, there is a crucial difference between Cynic militancy and all other militancy, be it philosophical militancy from antiquity or modern revolutionary militancy. Thus, the philosophical schools of antiquity operated within a closed world, in the form of the sect, with a small number of privileged members, but practiced proselytism to gain new adherents. The Cynic militancy was singular and distinct from all the others because it was 'a militancy in the open' addressed to everyone:

> a militancy addressed to absolutely everyone, which precisely does not require an education (a *paideia*), but which resorts to harsh and drastic means, not so much in order to train people and teach them, as to shake them up and convert them, abruptly. It is a militancy in the open in the sense that it claims to attack not just this or that vice or fault or opinion that this or that individual may have, but also the conventions, laws, and institutions which rest on the vices, faults, weaknesses, opinions shared by humankind in general. It is therefore a militancy which aspires to change the world. (Foucault 2011: 284–5)

Although 'Cynicism forms the matrix' (2011: 286) for a long series of historical figures in Christian asceticism who fight their own temptations and also struggle for humanity to free it from its evils and vices, and for the revolutionary militantism of the nineteenth century, a definitory feature of the Cynics is lost in these forms of militancy, and Foucault does not mention this: the militancy under the principle 'Alter the Currency!', that is, a militancy which continuously alters the value of all currencies, with no 'party line'.

As critical approaches of the modern revolutionary militancy have pointed out, the 'party line' widens the gap between the group and those outside. The historical revolutionary militancy displays fidelity to the 'party line' or, as Badiou famously argued, fidelity to the Event. Event, the fundamental term for Badiou's philosophy, is a moment of rupture and disorder but necessarily the moment of truth: it is Truth-Event. If there has been an Event, then truth consists in declaring it and then in being faithful to this declaration. 'Truth is entirely subjective' (Badiou 2003: 15), and nothing pre-existing can support it. Thus 'Fidelity to the declaration is crucial, for truth is a process, and not an illumination' (2003: 15). Militants are those marked out by fidelity to the universal status of a singular Event (Badiou 2001: 42). What Badiou describes as fidelity to the Truth-Event in the ontological dimension of being, in the historical form of militancy it was fidelity embodied in the following the 'party line'. Paradoxically, the Cynic militancy attacks the currency of fidelity, to say so. Referring to an episode about Diogenes, Foucault shows how the very notion of fidelity is challenged. So, the story goes, Diogenes praises Heracles in a discourse which aroused the enthusiasm of those listening. Everyone is ready to follow him. But in the midst of this enthusiasm, Diogenes squats on the ground and performs an indecent act by displaying animality. Seeing this, the crowd became angry and claimed he was mad. Instead of having followers, he became the target of derision and ridicule. Thus, the militant life of the Cynics is unlike any other form of militancy because the Cynics do not command authority; they do not stand above the lives of others as a vanguard organisation (Hardt 2011: 33). On the contrary, they invite scorn and ridicule. There is no authority and there is no 'party line' in the Cynic militancy; however, it remains 'an aggressive, constant and endless battle to change the world' (Foucault 2011: 286).

A cosmopolitan stance could not have been possible without this particular form of militancy: 'an overt, universal, aggressive militancy; militancy in the world and against the world' (2011: 285), and whose instrument is the continuous alteration of the values of all currencies. The 'Alter the currency!' principle makes the Cynic militant life a life in problematicity and the fidelity that it generates cannot be otherwise than permanent questioning and solidarity of the shaken which takes place on the battlefront (Patočka 1998: 136). It is a solidarity in saying 'No' to mobilisation for an ultimate meaning. It is an open militancy that does not reveal the ultimate meaning but invites a perpetual quest for meaning and abandoning the meanings which brought us to the battlefront: a post-battlefront cosmopolitical militancy, neither from above, nor from below, but of everyone, since militant cosmopolitics is for everyone.

Militant cosmopolitics is for everyone, as is the Cynic militancy – 'a militancy addressed to absolutely everyone, which precisely does not require an education (a *paideia*)' (Foucault 2011: 284). The idea of the citizen of the world, or the instant appeal of 'No Borders No Nations' and 'No One Is Illegal', is immediately understandable, acceptable and thinkable by everyone, yet the very fact of saying it sounds unacceptable, invites scorn and ridicule, and those who say it are declared naive and dangerous in their naivety. By this paradox, the idea of the citizen of the world confirms once more its Cynic origins. The Cynics do not have to undertake any study to acquire the Cynic philosophy. The Cynic is reproached for his ignorance and lack of culture, they have a 'limited, meager, and elementary theoretical framework' (Foucault 2011: 202), but on the one hand, the Cynics had a broad presence in society. Cobblers, joiners, fullers and wool carders, if they decided to become philosophers, could join the Cynics school. The theoretical poverty of the Cynic doctrine, its thinness and the banality of its doctrinal teachings, made it easy to recruit people to Cynicism. However, although Cynic philosophy made it easy to recruit people and it is banal in its doctrinal elements, it was constantly accompanied by scandal, and met with mockery. The Cynics' ideas are for everyone and at the same time scandalous. Similarly, the idea of citizen of the world is what everyone would like to have or to be entitled to, yet the idea is ridiculed, be it advanced by ordinary citizens or by some political theorists 'risking their careers'.

Militant cosmopolitics is for everyone. The call to think like a citizen of the world is addressed periodically to everyone. The Russell-Einstein Manifesto (1955) addressed everyone 'not as members of this or that nation, continent, or creed, but as human beings', inviting everyone 'to learn to think in a new way'. The call to think in a new way is present more or less directly in all accounts of cosmopolitanism, including those which try to provoke thinking or just a reaction to the pictures of the suffering distant others. It is not a superior way of thinking, requiring some kind of 'advanced thinking skills', but a thinking that is within the capacity of reflection of everyone. The slogan 'act locally, think globally' is another example of the invitation addressed to everyone to think like a citizen of the world. To 'act locally' and to 'think globally' does not require advanced specialised skills of thinking about the world and our place in it. The political philosophers have these alleged advanced skills – who else if not them? – but too many political philosophers think locally and act globally. The reluctance of political philosophers to think about the idea of citizen of the world induces a paradoxical presupposition: they avoid thinking about it as though, once thought, it will start functioning, as though the old distinction between thinking and acting will be erased, a world state will be created instantly, and it will turn into a global Leviathan. What if this fear and reluctance reveal that thinking about cosmopolitanism is immediately accessible to everyone and by this very fact it is a radical way of thinking? What if the radicality of cosmopolitics is hidden in the very fact that it is thinkable and desirable by everyone?

Militant cosmopolitics is for everyone, as is the Cynic militancy, yet it presupposes another paradox. The Cynic had a broad presence in society; cobblers, joiners, wool carders and so on could join the Cynics school, although one qualifies as a Cynic only after a long series of tests of endurance. To become a true Cynic, one has to pass through the practice of askesis, endurance, poverty and destitution, of wandering without ties to land or a family, to learn to live without clothes and shelter, to accept the insults and so on. For the Cynics, the alteration of the value of the currency was not an easy action – it is made possible through askesis, endurance, poverty, destitution and exile, that is through a radical change in their life. This Cynics' paradox is confirmed once again in the case of cosmopolitanism. Obviously, to become cosmopolitan one does not need to practice askesis, poverty and destitution, or to renounce shelter, clothes or family ties, but the stance does not become easier. The idea of a citizen of the world is immediately understandable, acceptable and thinkable by everyone, yet it is possible to have a cosmopolitan stance only after a 'forced' choice: it requires a self-transformation or even a 'conversion' (see Chapter 5). The call to think in a new way is addressed to everyone, but thinking continues in the old ways because 'it wants to risk nothing of itself' (Blanchot 1997: 104), but one has to risk in order to think in a new way, and to fight with his or her own life. The appeal of the 'No Borders No Nations' and 'No One Is Illegal' declarations is immediately acceptable and thinkable by everyone, yet it requires a struggle with oneself and with the world in order to think about and affirm these visions further.

Thus, militant cosmopolitics displays two paradoxes: the idea of the citizen of the world is appealing to everyone, yet it is scandalous and provokes mockery, and the idea of the citizen of the world is appealing to everyone, yet it requires a radical change in one's life in order to affirm it further. The paradoxes are interrelated and converge in the very structure of the militant cosmopolitics: cosmopolitics is for everyone, yet one has to struggle and fight for it. And the weapons of the fight are simple but the most powerful: permanent questioning and the 'alteration of the values of all currencies' that makes one's life a militant life in problematicity. The cosmopolitical militant lives a life in problematicity, he does not allow solidification of meaning and does not allow the seeing of evil only in others. Thus the cosmopolitical militant keeps us from going to the battlefront where the fight is with traditional deadly weapons. The cosmopolitical militant shakes the given grounds and finds meaning only in a quest for meaning.

Militant cosmopolitics is an open militancy which aspires to change the world. All those who have seized the appeal of the idea of a citizen of the world together can alter the values of the currency, change their life and change the world. Everyone can be a militant for another, more just and equal, world. All of us can lead a life aiming at the horizon of another world whose glimpse and promise have been put in simple words addressed to everyone: Another World Is Possible and in which No One Is Illegal, a world which has to be thought about and imagined not by postulating a final meaning for everyone, but through questioning all meanings.

NOTES

1. This is a paraphrase of an expression by Foucault, 'Use political practice as an intensifier of thought' (Foucault 1983: xiv).
2. See Introduction, the section entitled 'Cosmopolitics'.
3. These ideals of militancy have been challenged, especially by Black, Indigenous, feminist, anarchist, queer and other groups that have connected

direct action and struggle to the liberation of desire, foregrounding the importance of creativity and experimentation, trying to bring joy and militancy together, with the aim of thinking through the connections between fierceness and love, resistance and care, combativeness and nurturance (see Bergman and Montgomery 2017).

4. It has to be specified that the militant cosmopolitics advanced in this book does not claim to be militant research as it was defined and carried out in the last decade, mainly inspired by the Colectivo Situaciones manifesto. The figure of the researcher–militant is distinct from both the academic researcher and the political militant, and 'carries out theoretical and practical work oriented to co-produce the knowledges and modes of an alternative sociability, beginning with the power (*potencia*) of those subaltern knowledges' (Colectivo Situaciones 2003). Research militancy is about 'working in immanence', while immanence, as 'a constitutive co-belonging', refers to 'a modality of inhabiting the situation and operates from composition – love or friendship – in order to bring about new possible materials of such a situation' (Colectivo Situaciones 2003). The research conducted for this book was done with academic tools. Although it is based on several sets of case studies – Eastern European dissidence and dissent all around the world, global protests, the migrants and refugees' protest movements – the research was not in immanence, since the decision to look at these protests from a cosmopolitan perspective came after the events.

BIBLIOGRAPHY

Agamben, G. (2000) *Means without Ends*, Minneapolis: University of Minnesota Press.

Allen, A. (2020) *Cynicism*, Cambridge, MA: The MIT Press.

Alonso, F. L. (2013) 'Cosmopolitanism and Natural Law in Cicero', in Contreras F. (eds), *The Threads of Natural Law. Ius Gentium: Comparative Perspectives on Law and Justice*, vol 22, Dordrecht: Springer.

Amoore, L. (ed.) (2005) *The Global Resistance Reader*, New York: Routledge.

Anderson, B. (1991) *Imagined Communities: Reflections on Origins and Spread of Nationalism*, London: Verso.

Appiah, K. A. (1997) 'Cosmopolitan Patriots', *Critical Inquiry*, 23: 616–39.

Apter, E. (2020) 'Cosmopolitics' in Stoler, A. L. et al. (eds), *Thinking with Balibar. A Lexicon of Conceptual Practice*, New York: Fordham University Press.

Archibugi, D. (ed.) (2003) *Debating Cosmopolitics*, London: Verso.

Archibugi, D. and Held, D. (2011) 'Cosmopolitan Democracy: Paths and Agents', *Ethics & International Affairs*, 25(1): 433–61.

Arendt, H. (1968) *Men in Dark Times*, New York: A Harvest Book.

Arendt, H. (1973) *The Origins of Totalitarianism*, New York: A Harvest Book.

Arrighi, G., Hopkins, T. K., Wallerstein, I. (1989) *Antisystemic Movements*, London: Verso.

Assy, B. and Rolo, R. (2021) 'Shaman Cosmopolitanism: Amerindian Resistance and Perspectivism', in C. Foroni Consani, J. T. Klein and S. Nour Sckell (eds), *Cosmopolitanism. From the Kantian Legacy to Contemporary Approaches* (Berlin: Duncker & Humblot).

Ataç, I., Rygiel, K. and Stierl, M. (2016) 'The Contentious Politics of Refugee and Migrant Protest and Solidarity Movements', *Citizenship Studies*, 20(5): 527–44.

Atkins, E. M. (1990) '"Domina Et Regina Virtutum": Justice and Societas in *De Officiis*', *Phronesis*, 35(1): 258–89.

Atkins, J. W. (2013) *Cicero on Politics and the Limits of Reason: The Republic and Laws*, Cambridge: Cambridge University Press.

Badiou, A. (2001) *Ethics: An Essay on the Understanding of Evil*, London: Verso.

Badiou, A. (2003) *Saint Paul: The Foundation of Universalism*, Stanford: Stanford University Press.

Baker, G. (2018) 'Cynical Cosmopolitanism', *Theory & Event*, 21(3): 607–26.

Baldry, H. C. (1965) *The Unity of Mankind in Greek Thought*, Cambridge: Cambridge University Press.

Balibar, E. (2018) 'Philosophies of the Transindividual: Spinoza, Marx, Freud', *Australasian Philosophical Review* 2(1): 5–25.

Bataille, G. (1997) *The Bataille Reader*, Botting, F. and Wilson, S. (eds), Oxford: Blackwell.

Baynes, K. (2007) 'The Hermeneutics of Situated Cosmopolitanism', *Philosophy and Social Criticism*, 33(9): 301–8.

Beauchamp, G. (1989) 'All's Well That Ends Wells': The Anti-Wellsian Satire of Brave New World', *Utopian Studies* 2: 12–16.

Beck, U. (2004) 'Cosmopolitical Realism: On the Distinction between Cosmopolitanism in Philosophy and the Social Sciences', *Global Networks*, 4(2): 131–56.

Beck, U. (2011) 'Cosmopolitanism as Imagined Communities of Global Risk', *American Behavioral Scientist*, 55(10): 1346–61.

Beck, U. (2015) 'Emancipatory Catastrophism', *Current Sociology*, 63(1): 75–88.

Beck, U. (2016) *The Metamorphosis of the World*, Cambridge: Polity Press.

Beck, U. and Szneider, N. (2006) 'Unpacking Cosmopolitanism for the Social Sciences: A Research Agenda', *The British Journal of Sociology*, 57(1): 1–23.

Beck, U. et al. (2013) 'Cosmopolitan Communities of Climate Risk', *Global Networks*, 13(1): 1–21.

Bedau, H. A. (ed.) (1991) *Civil Disobedience in Focus*, New York: Routledge.

Beitz, C. (1979) *Political Theory and International Relations*, Princeton: Princeton University Press.

Beja, J. P. et al. (eds) (2012). *Liu Xiaobo, Charter 08 and the Challenges of Political Reform in China*, Hong Kong: Hong Kong University Press.

Beltrán, C. (2009) 'Going Public: Hannah Arendt, Immigrant Action, and the Space of Appearance', *Political Theory*, 37(5): 595–622.

Benda, V. (1991) 'The Parallel Polis' in Skilling, H. G. and Wilson, P. (eds), *Civic Freedom in Central Europe. Voices from Czechoslovakia*, Basingstoke: Palgrave.

Benda. V. et al. (1988) 'Parallel Polis, or an Independent Society in Central and Eastern Europe: An Inquiry', *Social Research*, 55(1/2): 211–46.

Benhabib, S. (2006) *Another Cosmopolitanism*, Oxford: Oxford University Press.

Bergman, C. and Montgomery, N. (2017) *Joyful Militancy. Building Thriving Resistance in Toxic Times*, Chico, CA: AK Press/IAS.

Berlant, L. and Freeman, E. (1993) 'Queer Nationality', in M. Warner (ed.), *Fear of a Queer Planet: Queer Politics and Social Theory*, Minneapolis: University of Minnesota Press.

Berlant, L. and Edelman, L. (2014). *Sex, or the Unbearable*, Durham, NC: Duke University Press.

Bersani, L. (1987) 'Is the Rectum a Grave?', *October* 43: 197–222.

Bhabha, H. K. (1996) 'Unsatisfied: Notes on Vernacular Cosmopolitanism', in Garcia-Morena, L. and Pfeifer, P. C. (eds), *Text and Nation*, London: Camden House.

Bhambra, G. K. (2014) 'Postcolonial and Decolonial Dialogues', *Postcolonial Studies*, 17(2): 115–21.

Blanchot, M. (1997) 'The Apocalypse is Disappointing', Rottenberg, E. (trans.), in *Friendship*, Stanford: Stanford University Press.

Blaser, M. (2016) 'Is Another Cosmopolitics Possible?', *Cultural Anthropology*, 31(4): 545–70.

Bohman, J. and Lutz-Bachmann, M. (eds) (1997) *Perpetual Peace: Essays on Kant's Cosmopolitan Ideal*, Cambridge, MA: The MIT Press.

Boltanski, L. (2011) *On Critique: A Sociology of Emancipation*, Cambridge: Polity Press.

Boltanski, L. and Chiapello, E. (2005) *The New Spirit of Capitalism*, London: Verso.

Bosman, P. R. (2007) 'Citizenship of the World – the Cynic Way', *Phronimon*, 8: 25–38.

Branham, R. B. (1994) 'Defacing the Currency: Diogenes' Rhetoric and the Invention of Cynicism', *Arethusa* 27: 329–59.

Branham, R. B. and M.-O. Goulet-Cazé (eds) (1996) *The Cynics: The Cynic Movement in Antiquity and Its Legacy*, Berkeley: University of California Press.

Bratton, B. H. (2016) *The Stack. On Software and Sovereignty*, Cambridge, MA: The MIT Press.

Breines, W. (1989) *Community and Organization in the New Left, 1962–1968: The Great Refusal*, New Brunswick: Rutgers University Press.

Brennan, T. (1997) *At Home in the World: Cosmopolitanism Now*, Cambridge, MA: Harvard University Press.

Burns, K. (2012) 'Cosmopolitan Sexual Citizenship and the Project of Queer World-making at the Sydney 2002 Gay Games', *Sexualities* 5(3–4): 314–35.

Burns, K. and Davies, C. (2009) 'Producing Cosmopolitan Sexual Citizens on The L Word', *Journal of Lesbian Studies* 13(2): 174–88.

Butler, J. (2015) *Notes Toward a Performative Theory of Assembly*, Cambridge, MA: Harvard University Press.

Cabrera, L. (2004) *Political Theory of Global Justice: A Cosmopolitan Case for the World State*, New York: Routledge.

Cabrera, L. (2008) *The Practice of Global Citizenship*, Cambridge: Cambridge University Press.

Cabrera. L. (ed.) (2018) *Institutional Cosmopolitanism*, Oxford: Oxford University Press.

Cabrera, L. (2020) *The Humble Cosmopolitan: Rights, Diversity, and Trans-State Democracy*, Oxford: Oxford University Press.

Caraus, T. (2003) *Ethical Perspectives on the Postmodern Rewriting*. Bucharest: Paralela 45.

Caraus, T. (2011) *Traps of Identity*, Chisinau: Cartier.

Caraus, T. (2013) 'Cosmopolitanism and the Legacies of Eastern European Dissidence', in Lettevall, R. and Petrov, K. (eds), *Critique of Cosmopolitan Reason: Timing and Spacing the Concept of World Citizenship*, Oxford: Peter Lang.

Caraus, T. (2014a) 'Cosmopolitanism of Dissent', in Caraus, T. and Parvu, C. (eds), *Cosmopolitanism and the Legacies of Dissent*, New York: Routledge.

Caraus, T. (2014b) 'Aung San Suu Kyi and Cosmopolitanism as the Revolution of Spirit', in Caraus, T. and Parvu, C. (eds), *Cosmopolitanism and the Legacies of Dissent*, New York: Routledge.

Caraus, T. (2015a) 'Dissent as "Foundation" of Cosmopolitanism', in Caraus, T. and Lazea, D. (eds), *Cosmopolitanism Without Foundations?*, Chisinau: Zeta Books.

Caraus, T. (2015b) 'Cosmopolitanism without Foundations or Cosmopolitanism with Plurality of Grounds?, in Caraus, T. and Lazea, D. (eds), *Cosmopolitanism without Foundations?*, Chisinau: Zeta Books.

Caraus, T. (2016a) 'Re-grounding Cosmopolitanism', in Caraus, T. and Paris, E. (eds), *Re-Grounding Cosmopolitanism: Towards a Post-foundational Cosmopolitanism*, New York: Routledge.

Caraus, T. (2016b) 'Cosmopolitan Ontology or the Cosmo-Political', in Caraus, T. and Paris, E. (eds), *Re-Grounding Cosmopolitanism: Towards a Post-foundational Cosmopolitanism*, New York: Routledge.

Caraus, T. (2016c) 'Towards an Agonistic Cosmopolitanism: Exploring the Cosmopolitan Potential of Chantal Mouffe's Agonism', *Critical Horizons*, 17(1): 94–109.

Caraus, T. (2016d) 'Cosmopolitanism and Populism: From Incompatibility to Convergence, and Back', *Annals of the University of Bucharest*, 18(1): 83–102.

Caraus, T. (2016e) 'Patocka's Radical and Agonistic Politics', in Tava, F. and Meacham, D. (eds), *Thinking after Europe: Jan Patočka and Politics*, Lanham: Rowman & Littlefield International.

Caraus, T. (2017) 'Cosmopolitanism beyond Mottos: Cosmopolitan Representation in Global Protests', *Globalisations*, 14(5): 730–46.

Caraus, T. (2018a) 'Migrant Protests as Radical Cosmopolitics', in Caraus, T. and Paris, E. (eds), *Migration, Protest Movements and the Politics of Resistance: A Radical Political Philosophy of Cosmopolitanism*, New York: Routledge.

Caraus, T. (2018b) 'Becoming In/Visible – A Strategy of Migrant Resistance', in Caraus, T. and Paris, E. (eds), *Migration, Protest Movements and the Politics of Resistance: A Radical Political Philosophy of Cosmopolitanism*, New York: Routledge.

Caraus, T. (2018c) 'Migrant Protests as Acts of Cosmopolitan Citizenship', *Citizenship Studies*, 22(8): 791–809.

Caraus, T. (2021) 'The Horizon of Another World: Foucault's Cynics and the Birth of Radical Cosmopolitics', *Philosophy & Social Criticism*. https://doi.org/10.1177/0191453720987867

Caraus, T. (forthcoming) 'Thinking Political Philosophy Anew: Arendt, Agamben and the Avant-garde of the Refugee', *Constellations*.

Caraus, T. and Paris, E. (eds) (2016) *Re-Grounding Cosmopolitanism: Towards a Post-Foundational Cosmopolitanism*, New York: Routledge.

Caraus, T. and Paris, E. (2018) (eds) *Migration, Protest Movements and the Politics of Resistance: A Radical Political Philosophy of Cosmopolitanism*. New York: Routledge.

Caraus, T. and Parvu, C. (eds) (2014) *Cosmopolitanism and the Legacies*, New York: Routledge.

Caraus, T. and Parvu, C. A. (2017a) 'Cosmopolitanism and Global Protests', *Globalisations*, 14(5): 659–67.

Caraus, T. and Parvu, C. A. (eds) (2017b) 'Cosmopolitanism and Global Protests', Special Issue of *Globalisations* 14(5).

Caraus, T. and Parvu, C. A. (2018) 'Cosmopolitanism and Migrant Protests', in Delanty, G. (ed.), *Handbook of Cosmopolitan Studies*, New York: Routledge.

Carens, J. H. (2013) *The Ethics of Immigration*, Oxford: Oxford University Press.

Castoriadis, C. (1987) *The Imaginary Institution of Society*, Cambridge: Polity

Cavallar, G. (2011) *Imperfect Cosmopolis: Studies in the History of International Legal Theory and Cosmopolitan Ideas*, Cardiff: University of Wales Press.

Charter 08 (2008) <https://rsf.org/sites/default/files/Charter08.pdf> (last accessed 10 January 2022).

Charta 77 (1977) 'Declaration of Charter '77', <https://www.files.ethz.ch/isn/125521/8003_Charter_77.pdf> (last accessed 30 November 2021).

Cheah, Ph. (1998) 'Introduction Part II. The Cosmopolitical – Today', in Cheah, Ph. and Robbins, B. (eds), *Cosmopolitics: Thinking and Feeling beyond the Nation*, Minneapolis: University of Minnesota Press.

Chin, C. (2013) *Cosmopolitan Sex Workers. Women and Migration in a Global City*, Oxford: Oxford University Press.

Cicero (1913) *De Officiis*. Loeb Classical Library, vol. XXI, Cambridge, MA: Harvard University Press.

Cicero (1971) *On Friendship*, Copley, F. O. (trans.), Ann Arbor: University of Michigan Press.

Clifford, J. (1992) 'Traveling Cultures', in Grossberg, L., Nelson, C. and Treichler, P. (eds), *Cultural Studies*, New York: Routledge.

Clootz, A. (1792) *La république universelle ou adresse aux tyrannicides*, Paris: Chez les Marchands de nouveautes

Clootz, A. (1793) *Bases constitutionnelles de la république du genre humain*, Paris: De l'imprimerie nationale.

Cohen, G. A. (2000) 'If You're an Egalitarian, How Come You're So Rich?', *The Journal of Ethics*, 4(1/2): 1–26.

Cohen, M. (1992) 'Rooted Cosmopolitanism', *Dissent* (Fall): 478–83.

Cole, P. (2000) *Philosophies of Exclusion: Liberal Political Theory and Immigration*, Edinburgh: Edinburgh University Press.

Cole, P. (2014) 'Beyond Reason: The Philosophy and Politics of Immigration', *CRISPP*, 17(5): 503–20.

Cole. P. (2016) 'Global Displacement and the Topography of Theory', *Journal of Global Ethics*, 12(3): 260–68.

Colectivo Situaciones (2003) 'On the Researcher-Militant', <http://transform.eipcp.net/transversal/0406/colectivosituaciones/en.html> (last accessed 30 November 2021).

Conner, Ch. T. and Okamura, D. (eds) (2021) *The Gayborhood: From Sexual Liberation to Cosmopolitan Spectacle*, Lanham: Rowman & Littlefield.

Dallmayr, F. (2003) 'Cosmopolitanism: Moral and Political', *Political Theory*, 31(3): 421–42.

Daly, K. (1998) 'Worlds beyond England: Don Juan and the Legacy of Enlightenment Cosmopolitanism', *Romanticism* 4(2): 189–201.

Dante (Alighieri) (1995) *De Monarchia*, Shaw, P. (trans. and ed.), Cambridge: Cambridge University Press.

Dauvergne, C. (2008) *Making People Illegal. What Globalization Means for Migration and Law*, Cambridge: Cambridge University Press.

De Boer, K. and Sonderegger, R. (eds) (2012) 'Introduction', in *Conceptions of Critique in Modern and Contemporary Philosophy*, Basingstoke: Palgrave Macmillan.

De Genova, N. (2013) 'Spectacles of Migrant "Illegality": The Scene of Exclusion, the Obscene of Inclusion', *Ethnic and Racial Studies*, 36(7): 180–98.

De la Cadena, M. (2010) 'Indigenous Cosmopolitics in the Andes', *Cultural Anthropology*, 25 (2): 334–70.

De Sade, Marquis (1990a) *120 Days of Sodom*, compiled and translated by A. Wainhouse and R. Seaver, London: Arrow Books.

De Sade, Marquis (1990b) *Justine, Philosophy in the Bedroom, and Other Writings*, compiled and translated by R. Seaver and A. Wainhouse, New York: Grove Weidenfeld.

De Sousa Santos, B. (2005) 'The Future of the World Social Forum: The Work of Translation', *Development*, 48(2): 15–22.

De Sousa Santos, B. (2018) *The End of The Cognitive Empire*, Durham, NC: Duke University Press.

Delanty, G. (2009) *The Cosmopolitan Imagination: The Renewal of Critical Social Theory*, Cambridge: Cambridge University Press.

Delanty, G. (2012) 'The Idea of Critical Cosmopolitanism', in Delanty, G. (ed.), *Handbook of Cosmopolitan Studies*, New York: Routledge.

Delanty, G. (2014) 'The prospects of cosmopolitanism and the possibility of global justice', *Journal of Sociology*, 50(2): 213–28.

Derrida, J. (1981) *Positions*, Chicago: The University of Chicago Press.

Derrida, J. (1992) 'Onto-theology of National-humanism (Prolegomena to a Hypothesis)', *Oxford Literary Review*, 14 (1/2): 3–23.

Derrida, J. (1994) *Specters of Marx: The State of the Debt, the Work of Mourning and the New International*, London and New York: Routledge.

Derrida, J. (2001) *On Cosmopolitanism and Forgiveness*, London: Routledge.

Desmond. W. (2008) *Cynics*, Stocksfield: Acumen.

Dio Chrysostom (2012) 'Oration 6', in Dobbin, R. (ed. and trans.), *The Cynic Philosophers from Diogenes to Julian*, London: Penguin Classics, pp. 122–5.

Dobbin, R. (ed. and trans.) (2012) *The Cynic Philosophers from Diogenes to Julian*, London: Penguin Classics.

Dudley, D. R. (1937) *A History of Cynicism from Diogenes to the Sixth Century A.D.*, London: Methuen & Co.

DuFord. R. (2017) 'Must a World Government Violate the Right to Exit?', *Ethics & Global Politics*, 10(1): 19–36.

Edelman, L. (2004) *No Future: Queer Theory and the Death Drive*, Durham: Duke University Press.

Einstein, A. (1947) 'Atomic War or Peace', *The Atlantic*, <https://www.the-atlantic.com/magazine/archive/1947/11/atomic-war-or-peace/305443/> (last accessed 10 January 2022).

Enlace Zapatista (2005) 'Sixth Declaration of the Selva Lacandona', <http://enlacezapatista.ezln.org.mx/sdsl-en/> (last accessed 5 December 2021).

Erskine, T. (2008) *Embedded Cosmopolitanism*, Oxford: Oxford University Press.

EZLN (1996) 'Remarks of the General Command of the EZLN in the opening ceremony of the First Intercontinental Meeting For Humanity and

Against Neoliberalism', <https://archive.org/stream/fp_Zapatista_Inter-national_Encuentro/Zapatista_International_Encuentro_djvu.txt> (last accessed 30 November 2021).

Falk, B. (2003) *The Dilemmas of Dissidence in East-Central Europe*, Budapest: Central European University Press.

Falk, R. and Strauss, A. (2001) 'Toward Global Parliament', *Foreign Affairs*, 80: 212–20.

Fine. S. and Ypi, L. (eds) (2016) *Migration in Political Theory. The Ethics of Movement and Membership*, Oxford: Oxford University Press.

Foucault, M. (1983) 'Preface', in Deleuze, G. and Guattari, F. *Anti-Oedipus: Capitalism and Schizophrenia*, Minneapolis: University of Minnesota Press.

Foucault, M. (2005) 'Method', in Amoore, L (ed.), *The Global Resistance Reader*, New York: Routledge.

Foucault, M. (2011) *The Courage of the Truth: The Government of Self and Others II*, Burchell, G. (trans.), Basingstoke: Palgrave-Macmillan.

Fraser, A. (2005) 'From the Critique of Institutions to an Institution of Critique', *Artforum*, 44(1): 278–83.

Freeden, M. (1996) *Ideologies and Political Theory: A Conceptual Approach*, Oxford: Clarendon Press.

Freud, S. (1953–74) *Three Essays on the Theory of Sexuality, The Standard Edition of the Complete Psychological Works of Sigmund Freud*, vol. 7, London: Hogarth Press.

Freud, S. (1961) *Civilization and its Discontents*, Strachey, J. (trans.), *The Standard Edition of the Complete Psychological Works of Sigmund Freud* XXI, London: The Hogarth Press.

Fumerton, R. and Hasan, A. (2010) 'Foundationalist Theories of Epistemic Justification', *The Stanford Encyclopedia of Philosophy*, <http://plato.stanford.edu/archives/sum2010/entries/justep-foundational/> (last accessed 1 December 2021).

Gebh, S. (2013) 'Shameless Cosmopolitanism', *History of Political Thought*, 2(1): 65–81.

Gellner, E. (1983) *Nations and Nationalism*, Oxford: Basil Blackwell.

Getachew, A. (2018) *Worldmaking after Empire*, Princeton: Princeton University Press.

Gilroy, P. (2005) *Postcolonial Melancholia*, New York: Columbia University Press.

Glick Schiller, N. and Irving, N. A. (eds) (2014) *Whose Cosmopolitanism? Critical Perspectives, Relationalities and Discontents*, New York and Oxford: Bergham Books.

Graeber, D. (2015) *The Utopia of Rules: On Technology, Stupidity, and the Secret Joys of Bureaucracy*, London: Melville House Publishing.

Gündogdu, A. (2015) *Rightlessness in an Age of Rights. Hannah Arendt and the Contemporary Struggles of Migrants*, Oxford: Oxford University Press.

Gurley Brown, H. (1962) *Sex and the Single Girl*, New York: Bernard Geis Associates.

Habermas, J. (2001) *The Postnational Constellation*, Cambridge, MA: The MIT Press.

Hardt, M. (2011) 'The Militancy of Theory', *South Atlantic Quarterly*, 110(1): 19–35.

Hardt, M. and Negri, A. (2017) *Assembly*, Oxford: Oxford University Press.

Harvey, D. (2009) *Cosmopolitanism and Geographies of Freedom*, New York: Columbia University Press.

Haslanger, A. (2015) 'The Cynic as Cosmopolitan Animal', in Nagai, K. et al. (eds), *Cosmopolitan Animals*, Basingstoke: Palgrave Macmillan

Havel, V. (1978) 'The Power of the Powerless', <https://www.nonviolent-conflict.org/wp-content/uploads/1979/01/the-power-of-the-powerless.pdf> (last accessed 30 November 2021).

Hayden, P. (2013) 'Albert Camus and Rebellious Cosmopolitanism in a Divided World', *Journal of International Political Theory*, 9: 194–219.

Heater, D. (1996) *World Citizenship and Government: Cosmopolitan Ideas in the History of Western Political Thought*, Basingstoke: Macmillan.

Heclo, H. (2011) *On Thinking Institutionally*, Oxford: Oxford University Press.

Hegel, G. (1991) *Elements of the Philosophy of Right*, Nisbet, H. B. (trans.), Cambridge: Cambridge University Press.

Hennessey, R. (2000) *Profit and Pleasure: Sexual Identities in Late Capitalism*, New York: Routledge.

Hobbes, Th. [1651] (1996) *Leviathan*, Oxford: Oxford University Press.

Hobbs, J. (2020) 'Cosmopolitan Anger and Shame', *Journal of Global Ethics*, 16(1): 58–76.

Holland, S. P. (2012) *The Erotic Life of Racism*, Durham, NC: Duke University Press.

Hollander, D. (2009) *Exemplarity and Chosenness. Rosenzweig and Derrida on the Nation of Philosophy*, Stanford: Stanford University Press.

Honig, B. (2001) *Democracy and the Foreigner*, Princeton: Princeton University Press.

Howard. P. N. (2015) *Pax Technica*, New Haven: Yale University Press.

Husserl, E. (1970) *The Crisis of European Sciences and Transcendental Phenomenology: An Introduction to Phenomenological Philosophy*, Carr, D (trans.), Evanston: Northwestern University Press.

Huxley, A. (2006) *Brave New World*, London: Harper's Perennial.

Ingram. J. D. (2013) *Radical Cosmopolitics. The Ethics and Politics of Democratic Universalism*, New York: Columbia University Press.

Isin, E. F. and Neilsen, G. M. (eds) (2008) *Acts of Citizenship*, London: Zed Books.

Jaeggi, R. (2018) *Critique of Forms of Life*, Cambridge MA: Harvard University Press.

Jaspers, K. (1961) *The Future of Mankind*, Chicago: The University of Chicago Press.

Kant, I. (1991) *Political Writings*, Nisbet, H. B. (trans.), Cambridge: Cambridge University Press.

Karatani, K. (2003) *Transcritique*, Cambridge, MA: The MIT Press.

Karatani, K. (2014) *The Structure of World History: From Modes of Production To Modes of Exchange*, Durham, NC: Duke University Press.

Kedourie, E. (ed.) (1970) *Nationalism in Asia and Africa*, London: Weidenfeld & Nicolson.

King, M. L. (1991) *Testament of Hope: The Essential Writings and Speeches of Martin Luther King, Jr.*, San Francisco: HarperCollins.

Kleingeld, P. (2004) 'Approaching Perpetual Peace: Kant's Defence of a League of States and His Ideal of a World Federation', *European Journal of Philosophy*, 12(3): 304–25.

Kleingeld, P. and Brown, E. (2019). 'Cosmopolitanism', *The Stanford Encyclopedia of Philosophy*, <https://plato.stanford.edu/archives/win2019/entries/cosmopolitanism/> (last accessed 30 November 2021).

Kristeva, J. (1991) *Strangers to Ourselves*, New York: Columbia University Press.

Kyaw, Y. H. (2007) 'Aung San Suu Kyi of Myanmar: A Review of the Lady's Biographies', *Contemporary Southeast Asia*, 29(2): 359–76.

Lacan. J. (1992) *The Seminar of Jacques Lacan*, Book VII: *The Ethics of Psychoanalysis*, 1959–1960, Porter, D. (trans.), New York: Norton & Company.

Lacan, J. (2009) 'L'étourdit', *The Letter* 41: 31–80, translated by C. Gallagher.

Laertius, Diogenes (1925) *Lives of Eminent Philosophers*. Volume II, Hicks, R. D (trans.), Loeb Classic Library, Cambridge, MA: Harvard University Press.

Lambert, A. (2019) 'Intimacy, Cosmopolitanism, and Digital Media: A Research Manifesto', *Qualitative Inquiry* 25(3): 300–11.

Lampedusa Charter (2014) <https://euroalter.com/%C2%93the-charter-of-lampedusa%C2%94-and-the-quest-for-alternative-citizenship-and-migration-policies/> (last accessed 10 January 2022).

Latour, B. (1991) *We Have Never Been Modern*, Cambridge MA: Harvard University Press

Latour, B. (2004) 'Why Has Critique Run Out of Steam?', *Critical Inquiry*, 30(2): 225–48.

Lefort, C. (1986) *The Political Forms of Modern Society: Bureaucracy, Democracy, Totalitarianism*, Cambridge, MA: The MIT Press.

Lefort, C. (1988) *Democracy and Political Theory*, Minneapolis: University of Minnesota Press.

Leinen, J. and Bummel, A. (2018) *A World Parliament: Governance and Democracy in the 21st Century*, Berlin: Democracy Without Borders.

Lichtenberg, J. (2014) *Distant Strangers: Ethics, Psychology, and Global Poverty*, Cambridge: Cambridge University Press.

Long, A. A. (1995) 'Cicero's Politics in *De officiis*', in Laks, A. and Schofield, M. (eds), *Justice and Generosity: Studies in Hellenistic Social and Political Philosophy*, Cambridge: Cambridge University Press.

Lu, C. (2021) 'World Government', *The Stanford Encyclopedia of Philosophy*, <https://plato.stanford.edu/archives/spr2021/entries/world-government/> (last accessed 5 December 2021).

Lyotard, J. F. (1984) *The Post-modern Condition: A Report on Knowledge*, Minneapolis: University of Minnesota Press.

McGowan, T. (2016) *Capitalism and Desire: The Psychic Cost of Free Markets*, New York: Columbia University Press.

McLaughlin, P. (2012) *Radicalism. A Philosophical Study*, Basingstoke: Palgrave Macmillan.

McNevin, A. (2007) 'Irregular Migrants, Neoliberal Geographies and Spatial Frontiers of "the political"', *Review of International Studies*, 33(4): 655–74.

McNevin, A. (2013) 'Ambivalence and Citizenship: Theorising the Political Claims of Irregular Migrants', *Millennium*, 41(2): 182–200.

Maggin, P. and Steinmetz, C. (eds) (2015) *(Sub)Urban Sexscapes: Geographies and Regulation of the Sex Industry*, New York: Routledge.

Marchart, O. (2007) *Post-foundational Political Thought: Political Difference in Nancy, Badiou, Lefort and Laclau*, Edinburgh: Edinburg University Press.

Marchart, O. (2016) 'The Political, the Ethical, the Global: Towards a Post-foundational Theory of Cosmopolitan Democracy', in Caraus, T. and Paris, E. (eds), *Re-grounding Cosmopolitanism: Towards a Post-foundational Cosmopolitanism*, New York and London: Routledge.

Marciniak, K. and Tyler, I. (2013) 'Immigrant Protest: An Introduction', *Citizenship Studies*, 17(2): 143–56.

Martin, R. and Reidy, D. A. (eds) (2006) *Rawls's Law of Peoples: A Realistic Utopia?* New York: Wiley-Blackwell.

Marx, K. (1975) 'Economic and Philosophic Manuscripts of 1844', in *Marx/Engels Collected Works*, vol. 3, New York: International Publishers.

Marx, K. (1976) 'A Contribution to the Critique of Political Economy', in *Marx/Engels Collected Works*, vol. 29, New York: International Publishers.

Marx, K. and Engles, F. (1974) *German Ideology*, Arthur, C. J. (ed.), London: Lawrence & Wishart.

Marx, K. and Engles, F. (1978) 'The Communist Manifesto', in Tucker, R. C. (ed.), *The Marx-Engels Reader*, New York: Norton & Company.

Masters, D. and Way, K. (eds) (1946) *A Report to the Public on the Full Meaning of the Atomic Bomb: One World or None*, New York: The New Press.

Mensch, J. (2011) 'Patočka's Conception of the Subject of Human Rights', *Idealistic Studies*, 41(1–2): 1–10.

Merleau-Ponty, M. (1970) *Themes from the Lectures at the Collège De France*, 1952–1960. Evanston: Northwestern University Press.

Mezzadra, S. (2004) 'The Right to Escape', *Ephemera*, 4(3): 267–75.

Mezzadra, S. and Neilson, B. (2013) *Border as Method, or the Multiplication of Labor*, Durham, NC: Duke University Press.

Mignolo, W. (2000a) 'The Many Faces of Cosmo-polis: Border Thinking and Critical Cosmopolitanism', *Public Culture*, 12(3): 721–48.

Mignolo, W. (2000b) 'Local Histories and Global Designs: An Interview with Walter Mignolo', *Discourse*, 22(3): 7–33.

Miller, D. (2002) 'Cosmopolitanism: A Critique', *Critical Review of International Social and Political Philosophy*, 5: 80–5.

Miller, D. (2016) *Strangers in Our Midst: The Political Philosophy of Immigration*, Cambridge, MA: Harvard University Press.

Mills, Ch. (2015) 'Decolonizing Western Political Philosophy', *New Political Science*, 37(1):1–24.

Mittelman, J. H. (2000) *The Globalization Syndrome: Transformation and Resistance*, Princeton: Princeton University Press.

Moles, J. L. (1995) 'The Cynics and Politics', in Laks, A. and Schofield, M. (eds), *Justice and Generosity: Studies in Hellenistic Social and Political Philosophy*, Cambridge: Cambridge University Press.

Moles, J. L. (1996) 'Cynic Cosmopolitanism', in Branham, R. B. and Goulet-Cazé, M. O. (eds), *The Cynics: The Cynic Movement in Antiquity and Its Legacy*, Oakland: University of California Press.

Molière [1665] (1966) 'Don Juan or The Statue at the Feast', in *The Miser and Other Plays*, London: Penguin.

Monbiot, G. (2003) *The Age of Consent: A Manifesto for a New World Order*, London: Harper-Perennial.

Morreall, J. (2020) 'Philosophy of Humour', *The Stanford Encyclopedia of Philosophy* <https://plato.stanford.edu/archives/fall2020/entries/humor/> (last accessed 9 December 2021).

Mouffe, Ch. (2005) *On the Political*, New York: Routledge.

Muñoz, J. E. (2009) *Cruising Utopia: The Then and There of Queer Futurity*, New York: New York University Press.

Nagel, Th. (2005) 'The Problem of Global Justice', *Philosophy and Public Affairs*, 33(2): 113–47.

Nail, T. (2015) *The Figure of the Migrant*, Stanford: Stanford University Press.

Navia, L. E. (1996) *Classical Cynicism: A Critical Study*, Westport, CT: Greenwood.

Nederman, C. J. (2020a) *The Bonds of Humanity: Cicero's Legacies in European Social and Political Thought*, University Park: Pennsylvania State University Press.

Nederman, C. J. (2020b) 'Cicero between Cosmopolis and Republic', in Ward, L. (ed.), *Cosmopolitanism and Its Discontents. Rethinking Politics in the Age of Brexit and Trump*, Lanham: Lexington Books.

Nicgorski, W. (2016) *Cicero's Skepticism and His Recovery of Political Philosophy*, London: Palgrave Macmillan.

Nili, S. (2015) 'Who's Afraid of a World State? A Global Sovereign and the Statist-cosmopolitan Debate', *CRISPP*, 18(3): 241–63.

Nkrumah, K. (1965) *Neo-colonialism: The Last Stage of Imperialism*, New York: International Publishers.

No Border (2002) Manifesto, <http://noborder.org/index.php.html> (last accessed 30 November 2021).

No One Is Illegal (2003) Manifesto, <http://www.tacticalmediafiles.net/articles/3238/No-One-is-Illegal_-Manifesto;jsessionid=7BF90D89B801E0BE84C525FEA7FAEF7F> (last accessed 30 November 2021).

Nussbaum, M. (1997) 'Kant and Stoic Cosmopolitanism', *The Journal of Political Philosophy*, 5(1): 1–25.

Nussbaum, M. (2006) *Frontiers of Justice*, Cambridge, MA: Harvard University Press.

Nussbaum, M. (2019) *The Cosmopolitan Tradition: A Noble but Flawed Ideal*, Cambridge, MA: Harvard University Press.

Nyers, P. (2003) 'Abject Cosmopolitanism: The Politics of Protection in the Anti-deportation Movement', *Third World Quarterly*, 24(6): 1069–93.

Nyers, P. and Rygiel, K. (eds) (2012) *Citizenship, Migrant Activism, and the Politics of Movement*, New York: Routledge.

O'Neill, O. (2000) *Bounds of Justice*, Cambridge: Cambridge University Press.

Ong, J. C. (2017) 'Queer Cosmopolitanism in the Disaster Zone: "My Grindr became the United Nations"', *The International Communication Gazette* 79(6–7): 656–73.

Ortega, M. (2017) 'Decolonial Woes and Practices of Un-knowing', *The Journal of Speculative Philosophy*, 31(3), 504–16.

Orwell, G. (1941) 'Wells, Hitler and the World State', *Horizon*, August.

Pagden, A. (2000) 'Stoicism, Cosmopolitanism, and the Legacy of European Imperialism', *Constellation*, 7(1): 3–22.

Pangle, Th. L. (1998) 'Socratic Cosmopolitanism: Cicero's Critique and Transformation of the Stoic Ideal', *Canadian Journal of Political Science*, 31(2): 235–62.

Paone, C. (2018) 'Diogenes the Cynic on Law and World Citizenship', *Polis: The Journal for Ancient Greek Political Thought*, 35: 478–98.

Papadopoulos, D. and Tsianos, V. S. (2013) 'After Citizenship: Autonomy of Migration, Organisational Ontology and Mobile Commons', *Citizenship Studies*, 17(2): 178–96.

Partington, J. S. (2003) 'H.G. Wells and the World State: A Liberal Cosmopolitan in a Totalitarian Age', *International Relations*, 17(2): 233–46.

Patočka, J. [1952] (1989a) 'Negative Platonism', Kohák, E. (trans.), in *Jan Patočka: Philosophy and Selected Writings*, Chicago: The University of Chicago Press.

Patočka, J. (1989b) 'Two Charta 77 texts', Kohák, E. (trans.), in *Jan Patočka: Philosophy and Selected Writings*, Chicago: The University of Chicago Press.

Patočka, J. (1996) *Heretical Essays in the Philosophy of History*, Kohák, E. (trans.), Chicago and La Salle, IL: Open Court.

Patočka, J. (1998) *Body, Community, Language, World*, Kohák, E. (trans.), Chicago: Open Court.

Patočka, J. (2007) *Living in Problematicity*, Prague: Oikoymenh.

Patočka, J. (2016) 'Intellectuals and Opposition', Tava, F. and Leufer, D. (trans.), in Meacham, D. and Tava, F. (eds), *Thinking after Europe: Jan Patočka and Politics*, Lanham: Rowman & Littlefield.

Patomäki, H. and Teivainen, T. (2004) 'The World Social Forum An Open Space or a Movement of Movements?.*Theory, Culture & Society*, 21(6): 145–54.

Pérez, H. (2015) *A Taste for Brown Bodies. Gay Modernity and Cosmopolitan Desire*, New York: New York University Press.

Plummer, K. (2015) *Cosmopolitan Sexualities: Hope and the Humanist Imagination*, Cambridge: Polity.

Plutarch (1957) 'On the Fortune or Virtue of Alexander', Babbitt, F. C. (trans.), in *Moralia* vol. IV, London: Heinemann.

Pogge, Th. (1989) *Realizing Rawls*, Ithaca: Cornell University Press.

Pogge, Th. (1992) 'Cosmopolitanism and Sovereignty', *Ethics*, 103(1): 48–75.

Pogge, Th. (2006) 'Do Rawls's Two Theories of Justice Fit Together?', in Martin, R. and Reidy, D. A. (eds), *Rawls's Law of Peoples: A Realistic Utopia?*, Oxford: Wiley-Blackwell.

Prozorov, S. (2017) 'Foucault's Affirmative Biopolitics: Cynic Parrhesia and the Biopower of the Powerless', *Political Theory*, 45(6): 801–23.

Puar, J. (2007) *Terrorist Assemblages: Homonationalism in Queer Times*, Durham, NC: Duke University Press.

Puar, J. (2013) 'Rethinking Homonationalism', *International Journal of Middle East Studies*, 45(2): 336–9.

Rancière, J. (1999) *Disagreement*, Minneapolis: University of Minnesota Press.

Rapport, N. (2012) *Anyone. The Cosmopolitan Subject of Anthropology*, Oxford: Berghahn.

Rawls, J. (1971) *A Theory of Justice*, Cambridge, MA: Harvard University Press.

Rawls, J. (1999) *The Law of Peoples with 'The Idea of Public Reason Revisited'*, Cambridge, MA: Harvard University Press.

Reinhard, K. (1997) 'Freud, My Neighbour', *American Imago* 54(2): 165–95.

Reves, E. (1945) *The Anatomy of Peace*, New York: Harper and Brothers.

Risse, M. (2012) *Global Political Philosophy*, Basingstoke: Palgrave Macmillan.

Robbins, B. (1998) 'Introduction Part I: Actually Existing Cosmopolitanism', in Cheah Ph. and Robbins, B. (eds), *Cosmopolitics: Thinking and Feeling beyond the Nation*, Minneapolis: University of Minnesota Press.

Robbins, B. and Cheah, Ph. (eds) (1998) *Cosmopolitics: Thinking and Feeling Beyond the Nation*, Minneapolis: University of Minnesota Press.

Russell, B. and Einstein, A. (1955) 'Statement: The Russell-Einstein Manifesto', <https://pugwash.org/1955/07/09/statement-manifesto/> (last accessed 30 November 2021).

Sager, A. (2018) *Toward a Cosmopolitan Ethics of Mobility: The Migrant's-eye View of the World*, New York: Springer.

Sayad, A. (2004) *The Suffering of the Immigrant*, Cambridge: Polity Press.

Scheffler, S. (1999) 'Conceptions of Cosmopolitanism', *Utilitas*, 11: 255–76.

Scheuerman, W. E. (2014) 'Cosmopolitanism and the World State', *Review of International Studies*, 40(3): 419–41.

Schlereth, Th. (1977) *The Cosmopolitan Ideal in Enlightenment Thought: Its Form and Function in the Ideas of Franklin, Hume, and Voltaire, 1694–1790*, Notre Dame: University of Notre Dame Press.

Schmitt, C. (2007) *The Concept of the Political*, Chicago: The University of Chicago Press.

Schofield, M (2021) *Cicero: Political Philosophy*, Oxford: Oxford University Press.

Scott, D. (2004) *Conscripts of Modernity: The Tragedy of Colonial Enlightenment*, Durham, NC: Duke University Press.

Scott, J. C. (1985) *Weapons of the Weak: Everyday Forms of Peasant Resistance*, New Haven: Yale University Press.

Scott, J. C. (1998) *Seeing Like a State: How Certain Schemes to Improve the Human Condition Have Failed*, New Haven: Yale University Press.

Searle, J. (1995) *The Construction of Social Reality*, New York: Free Press.

Searle, J. (2005) 'What is an Institution?', *Journal of Institutional Economics*, 1(1): 1–22.

Sellars, J. (2007) 'Stoic Cosmopolitanism and Zeno's Republic', *History of Political Thought*, 28 (1): 1–29

Sharma, N. (2020) *Home Rule: National Sovereignty and the Separation of Natives and Migrants*, Durham, NC: Duke University Press.

Shea, L. (2010) *The Cynic Enlightenment: Diogenes in the Salon*, Baltimore: Johns Hopkins University Press.

Shklar, J. (1989) 'Liberalism of Fear', in Rosenblum, N. L. (ed.), *Liberalism and the Moral Life*, Cambridge: Harvard University Press.

Singer, P. (1972) 'Famine, Affluence, and Morality', *Philosophy & Public Affairs* 1(3): 229–43.

Siskind, M. (2014) *Cosmopolitan Desires: Global Modernity and World Literature in Latin America*, Evanston, IL: Northwestern University Press.

Sloterdijk, P. (1987) *Critique of Cynical Reason*, Minneapolis: University of Minesota Press.

Smith, A. D. (1999) *Myths and Memories of the Nation*, Oxford: Oxford University Press.

Smith, G. B. (2018) *Political Philosophy and the Republican Future: Reconsidering Cicero*, Notre Dame: University of Notre Dame Press.

Spivak, G. (2012) 'Cosmopolitanisms and the Cosmopolitical', *Cultural Dynamics*, 24(2–3): 107–14.

Srinivasan, A. (2021) *The Right to Sex. Feminism in the Twenty-first Century*, London and New York: Bloomsbury.

Steel, C. (ed.) (2013) *The Cambridge Companion to Cicero*, Cambridge: Cambridge University Press.

Stengers, I. (2005) 'The Cosmopolitical Proposal', in Latour, B. and Weibel, P. (eds), *Making Things Public: Atmospheres of Democracy*, Cambridge, MA: The MIT Press.

Stengers, I. (2010) *Cosmopolitics I*, Minneapolis: University of Minnesota Press.

Stengers, I. (2011) *Cosmopolitics II*, Minneapolis: University of Minnesota Press.

Stengers, I. (2018) *Another Science is Possible: A Manifesto for Slow Science*, Cambridge: Polity.

Steyerl, H. (2009) 'The Institution of Critique', in Raunig, G. and Ray, G. (eds), *Art and Contemporary Critical Practice: Reinventing Institutional Critique*, London: MayFlyBooks.

Suu Kyi, A. S. (1991) *Freedom from Fear and Other Writings*, London: Penguin Books.

Suu Kyu, A. S. (2008) *The Voice of Hope*, London: Random House.

Szakolczai, A. (1994) 'Thinking beyond the East-West Divide: Foucault, Patocka, and the Care of the Self', *Social Research*, 61(2): 297–334.

Sznaider, N. (2007) 'Hannah Arendt's Jewish Cosmopolitanism: Between the Universal and the Particular', *European Journal of Social Theory* 10(1): 112–22.

Sznaider, N. (2015) 'Hannah Arendt: Jew and Cosmopolitan', *Socio* 4: 197–221.

Tännsjö, T. (2008) *Global Democracy: The Case for a World Government*, Edinburgh: Edinburgh University Press.

Thoburn, N. (2010) 'Weatherman, the Militant Diagram, and the Problem of Political Passion', *New Formations*, 68(1): 125–42.

Thorburn, E. D. (2012) 'A Common Assembly: Multitude, Assemblies, and a New Politics of the Common', *Interface*, 4(2): 254–79.

Torpey, J. (2000) *The Invention of the Passport: Surveillance, Citizenship and the State*, Cambridge: Cambridge University Press.

Tucker, A. (2000). *The Philosophy and Politics of Czech Dissidence from Patočka to Havel*, Pittsburgh: University of Pittsburgh Press.

Ulaş, L. (2017) 'Transforming (But Not Transcending) the State System? On Statist Cosmopolitanism', *CRISPP*, 20(6): 657–76.

Usborne, H. C. (1947) 'Crusade for World Government', *Bulletin of the Atomic Scientists*, 3(12): 359–60.

Virno, P. (2009) 'Anthropology and Theory of Institutions', in Raunig, G. and Ray. G. (eds), *Art and Contemporary Critical Practice: Reinventing Institutional Critique*, London: MayFlyBooks London.

Walker, B. (1997) 'Social Movements as Nationalisms, or, On the Very Idea of a Queer Nation', *Canadian Journal of Philosophy* 26(1): 505–47.

Wallerstein, I. (2004) 'The Dilemmas of Open Space: The Future of the WSF', *International Social Science Journal*, 56: 629–37.

Walters, G. J. (1988) 'Karl Jaspers on the Role of "Conversion" in the Nuclear Age', *Journal of the American Academy of Religion*, 56(2): 229–56.

Waltz, K. (2010) *Theory of International Politics*, Long Grove, IL: Waveland Press.

Walzer, M. (1996) 'Spheres of Affection', in Nussbaum, M. et al., *For Love of Country?* Boston: Beacon Press.

Walzer, M. (2004) *Arguing About War*, New Haven: Yale University Press.

Weiss, T. (2009) 'What Happened to the Idea of World Government', *International Studies Quarterly*, 53: 253–71.

Wells, H. G. (1901) *Anticipations of the Reaction of Mechanical and Scientific Progress upon Human Life and Thought*, London: Chapman & Hall.

Wells, H. G. (1905) *A Modern Utopia*, London: Chapman & Hall.

Wells, H. G. (1923) *Men Like Gods*, London: Macmillan.

Wells, H. G. (1928) *The Open Conspiracy*, London: Gollancz.

Wells, H. G. (1933) *The Shape of Things To Come*, London: Macmillan.

Wenar, L. (2006) 'Why Rawls is Not a Cosmopolitan Egalitarian', in Martin, R. and Reidy, D. (eds), *Rawls' Law of Peoples: A Realistic Utopia?*, Oxford: Blackwell.

Wendt, A. (2003) 'Why a World State is Inevitable', *European Journal of International Relations*. 9(4): 491–542.

White, S. K. (2000) *Sustaining Affirmation. The Strength of Weak Ontology in Political Theory*, Princeton: Princeton University Press.

Williams, B. (2008) *Philosophy as a Humanistic Discipline*, Princeton: Princeton University Press.

Wimmer, A. and Glick Schiller, N. (2002) 'Methodological Nationalism and beyond: Nation–State Building, Migration and the Social Sciences', *Global Networks*, 2(4): 301–34.

Wohlgemut, E. (2009) 'Pilgrim, Exile, Vagabond: Byron and the Citizen of the World', in *Romantic Cosmopolitanism*, London: Palgrave Macmillan.

Woods. K. (2012) 'Whither Sentiment? Compassion, Solidarity, and Disgust in Cosmopolitan Thought', *Journal of Social Philosophy*, 43(1): 33–49.

Worth, O. and Buckley, K. (2009) 'The World Social Forum: Postmodern Prince or Court Jester?'. *Third World Quarterly*, 30(4): 649–61.

WSF (2001) 'Charter of Principles', <https://transformadora.org/en/about/principles> (last accessed 30 November 2021).

WSF (2002) 'The Call of Social Movements of the Second World Social Forum', *Antipode*, 34(4): 625–32.

Xiaobo, L. (2012) *No Enemies, No Hatred. Selected Essays and Poems*, Cambridge, MA: Belknap.

Young-Bruehl, E. (2010) 'Sexual Diversity in Cosmopolitan Perspective', *Studies in Gender and Sexuality* 11(1): 1–9.

Ypi, L. (2012) *Global Justice and Avant-Garde Political Agency*, Oxford: Oxford University Press.

Žižek, S. (1992) *Enjoy Your Symptom!: Jacques Lacan in Hollywood and Out*, New York: Routledge.

Žižek, S. (2005) 'Neighbours and Other Monsters: A Plea for Ethical Violence', in *The Neighbour: Three Inquiries in Political Theology*, Chicago: The University of Chicago Press.

Žižek, S. (2007) *The Universal Exception*, London: Bloomsbury.

Žižek, S. (2012) *Less Than Nothing*, London: Verso.

Žižek, S. (2019) *Sex and the Failed Absolute*, London: Bloomsbury.

Žižek, S., Santer, E. and Reinhard, K. (2005) *The Neighbour. Three Inquiries in Political Theology*, Chicago and London: The University of Chicago Press.

Zupančič, A. (2000) *Ethics of Real*, London: Verso.

Zupančič, A. (2017) *What Is Sex?*, Cambridge, MA: The MIT Press.

Zupančič, A. (2018) 'The Apocalypse is (Still) Disappointing', *Journal of the Circle for Lacanian Ideology Critique*, 10–11: 16–30.

Zupančič, A. (2019) 'Love Thy Neighbour as Thyself?!', *Problemi International*, 3(3): 89–108.

INDEX

EU representative:
Easy Access System Europe
Mustamäe tee 50, 10621 Tallinn, Estonia
Gpsr.requests@easproject.com

www.ingramcontent.com/pod-product-compliance
Lightning Source LLC
Chambersburg PA
CBHW070325270326
41926CB00017B/3763